NATION AND RELIGION

NATION AND RELIGION

PERSPECTIVES ON EUROPE AND ASIA

Edited by
Peter van der Veer and Hartmut Lehmann

PRINCETON UNIVERSITY PRESS   PRINCETON, NEW JERSEY

Library of Congress Cataloging-in-Publication Data

Nation and religion: perspectives on Europe and Asia / edited by Peter
van der Veer and Hartmut Lehmann.
p. cm.
ISBN 0-691-01233-4 (cl: alk. paper). — ISBN 0-691-01232-6 (pb: alk.
paper)
1. Religion and state—Comparative studies. 2. Nationalism—Religious aspects—Comparative studies. I. Veer, Peter van der. II. Lehmann, Hartmut.
BL65.S8N36   1999
322'.1'09—dc21   98-40357 CIP

This book has been composed in Sabon

The paper used in this publication meets the minimum requirements
of ANSI/NISO Z39.48-1992 (R1997) (*Permanence of Paper*)

http://pup.princeton.edu

Printed in the United States of America

10 9 8 7 6 5 4 3 2 1

10 9 8 7 6 5 4 3 2
(Pbk.)

Contents

Acknowledgments

THIS BOOK is the product of a conference on Religion and Nationalism in Europe and Asia, organized by the Research Centre for Religion and Society, Amsterdam, and the Max-Planck-Institut für Geschichte, Göttingen, which was held at the University of Amsterdam, 27–29 November 1995. It received financial support from the Max-Planck-Institut für Geschichte, the International Institute for Asian Studies, the Royal Dutch Academy of Sciences, and The Netherlands Foundation for Scientific Research, for which we are truly grateful. We want to express our thanks to our colleagues Alf Lüdtke and Peter van Rooden for their organizational and intellectual contributions to the shaping of this conference. We also thank Ingrid van der Broek and Jasper Klapwijk for their attention to the preparation of the manuscript. Finally, we owe special thanks to Mary Murrell and the staff of Princeton University Press for their strong support of this project.

Harmut Lehmann
Peter van der Veer

NATION AND RELIGION

1

Introduction

PETER VAN DER VEER AND
HARTMUT LEHMANN

THANKS TO Benedict Anderson's influential book on the topic, it has become almost a cliché to suggest that the nation is an imagined community.[1] To argue that a religious community is an imagined construct will not surprise anyone either. Yet to analyze nation and religious community as cultural constructs, as products of the social imagination, does not detract from their efficacy in everyday life. In fact, it is hard to miss the social force of both religion and nationalism in many contemporary movements all over the world. When dealing with religion and nationalism, it is necessary to offer an analysis of their social force that cuts across conventional dichotomies. Social theory as well as Western common sense have often been content to assume an ideological a priori distinction between the nationalist and the religious imagination. As the argument goes, nationalism belongs to the realm of legitimate modern politics. Nationalism is assumed to be "secular," since it is thought to develop in a process of secularization and modernization. Religion, in this view, assumes political significance only in the underdeveloped parts of the world—much as it did in the past of the West. When religion manifests itself politically in the contemporary world, it is conceptualized as *fundamentalism*. This term, derived from early-twentieth-century American evangelicalism, is now taken by scholars and media as an analytical term to describe collective political action by religious movements.[2] It is almost always interpreted as a negative social force directed against science, rationality, secularism—in short, against modernity.[3]

The dichotomy between religion and nationalism is an ideological element in the Western discourse of modernity.[4] It functions not only in the Western perception of the Non-West, but also in the way the West understands itself. The most influential philosophical exposition of that self-understanding appears in Hegel's *Vorlesungen über die Philosophie der Geschichte*.[5] Based partly on this philosophical notion of the rationality of the West is the current but much less sophisticated idea that Western Europe and the United States have had a unique historical experience of secularization, whereas Asia (and South Asia in particular) has had a history of dangerous politicization of religious difference. This impression is plainly wrong, since it perpetuates the old, mistaken view of the great divide between the modern West and the backward Rest. The present collection of essays on both the Western European (that is, British and Dutch) and the Asian (that is, Indian and Japanese) historical experience problematizes the understanding of Western modernity and its function as a model for the rest of the world.

It is important to realize that both "nation" and "religion" are conceptualized as universal categories in Western modernity and that their universality is located precisely in the history of Western expansion. The modernity of the concept of the nation needs little discussion beyond mentioning the relationship between the ideas of "nation" and "ethnicity" as raised by the reference to "birth" in the very word *nation*.[6] The modernity of the concept of religion, as applied in the modern era to Hinduism, Shintoism, Islam, but also Christianity, is much less an accepted truism in the social sciences.

In a recent critical reflection on Clifford Geertz's celebrated ahistorical and universal definition of religion, Talal Asad argues that it ignores the genealogy of the modern Western understanding of religion.[7] In his view universalization of the concept of religion is closely related to the dawning of modernity in Europe and the expansion of that modernity over the world. The modern understanding of religion, which Geertz's essay exemplifies, is very different from what medieval Christians would have regarded as such, and this is still more the case for Muslims, Hindus, and other non-Christians. This discrepancy raises the broad, historical question of the ways in which Western modernity has assumed universal importance and, more specifically, how a modern Western category such as religion has come to be applied as a universal concept.[8] The project of modernization that is crucial to the spread of colonial power over the world has provided new forms of language through which subjects understand themselves and their actions. It is therefore almost impossible to escape from categories, originating in Western modernity, such as "public" and "private," "religion," or "history" when writing the history of other societies.[9]

This situation does not have to force us into an "epistemological hypochondria," to use the Comaroffs' phrase. It asks for a social and comparative history of religion with an emphasis on the social conditions of particular discourses and practices. Only through historical analysis can one deconstruct the commonplace dichotomy of a supposedly secular and modern West and a religious and backward Rest. The location of religion in the modern world should, in our view, be addressed in relation to the historical emergence of the modern idea of the nation and its spread over the world.

Let us briefly recapitulate the accepted social science view of nationalism and its relation to religion. The emergence of the European nation-state is commonly seen to depend on three connected processes of centralization: "the emergence of supra-local identities and cultures (the 'nation'); the rise of powerful and authoritative institutions within the public domain (the 'state'), and the development of particular ways of organizing production and consumption (the 'economy')."[10] In an influential book, Ernest Gellner connects these three processes in a characteristically sweeping manner.[11] He argues that modern industrial society depends on economic and cognitive growth, which in its turn requires a homogeneous culture. A crucial factor in his scheme is the centralization of resources by the state to run an educational system that imparts a standardized, literacy-based high culture. Industrial division of labor requires a shared culture; that shared culture is nationalism; and nationalism holds together an anonymous, impersonal society with mutually substitutable atomized individuals.[12] Such a culture of nationalism is by definition secular, since economic and cognitive growth are possible only when the absolutist cognitive claims of the literate high cultures of the agrarian (preindustrial) age are replaced by open scientific inquiry.[13] Nationalism comes thus in a package with individualism and secularism, as required by the industrial transformation of an agrarian world.

It is plausible, of course, that there are significant relations between the emergence of an industrial economy and the gradual homogenization of culture through a state-controlled education system, but Gellner exaggerates the universal success of homogenization and simplifies its nature. His argument subsumes a variety of local histories under the mechanical laws of a universal history, and it is doomed to analytical defeat in the face of any nationalism that is religious rather than secular. The history told by Gellner unfolds itself independent of human agency. It is the story of the victory of a fetishized historical force, capitalism, which celebrates objective imperatives and ignores meaningful and innovative action by individuals and groups who make history in everyday practices. Gellner pays little attention to the contradictions of homogenization as well as the forms of resistance that it meets. The basic flaw in the modernization theory he espouses, as well as in many Marxist analyses of the expansion of capitalism, is the assumption that a common, shared culture (or ideology) is necessary to integrate the social system. While it can be seen that the social constraints of the division of labor as well as the physical constraints of political force produce to some extent what we can call "social order," there is no need to assume (and plentiful evidence against) the assumption that social order depends on common culture and moral consensus.[14]

One reason for the influence of texts that universalize the modernization of Western Europe—and those by Anderson and Hobsbawm are not
different from Gellner's in this respect—is that they stylize a picture of
nationalism typical not only for social theory but for an entire commonsensical way of thinking.[15] Crucial is the way in which *the* nation-state
is presented as *the* sign of modernity. The discussion of nationalism
concludes, predictably, with its own axiomatic dichotomy between "traditional" and "modern." Tradition is what societies have before they are
touched by the great transformation of capitalism, and what seems
to characterize traditional societies most is that they are under the sway
of religion.

Much of the writing on modernity and modernization in the social sciences has been inspired by Max Weber, who in the first two decades of
this century published his famous treatises on the role of religious and
political as well as social and economic factors in the processes of modernization. Nationalism, however, was not one of the forces he discussed.
This omission was not unusual, but indeed a position taken by many
other scholars, by Weber's contemporaries, and by the generation that
followed. With few exceptions and for many years, the debates about the
relationship of modern nationalism and the modern state have ignored
the role of religion.[16] Recently, this has begun to change, and attempts
have been made to show how the notion of chosenness by God, which
had first been experienced by the Israelites and formulated in the texts of
the Old Testament, has been adopted by modern nationalist movements.[17]
On one hand are studies that examine the ways in which the idea of chosenness served to underscore and justify imperialistic political aims and
actions; on the other hand, the same notion has been used to explain
suffering and to provide a stimulus for political emancipation and national liberation. In both variations chosenness can be blended with ideas
of racial purity and uniqueness: the men who believed that they carried a
special burden in late-nineteenth-century British colonial affairs were very
consciously both Christian and white, and so were their counterparts in
countries like the Netherlands, Germany, or the United States.

Three related concepts developed by nineteenth-century thinkers deserve special attention in understanding the interaction of religious elements, nationalism and the notion of race or special racial qualities. First
is this idea of the chosenness of a certain people, which involves and incor-
porates political and social, as well as religious, ingredients. Second is the
theme of the revival or rebirth of a whole nation. Pietists and Methodists
had introduced the metaphor of an awakening—a kind of collective
regeneration—into eighteenth-century Protestantism. Nineteenth-century
Christian nationalists then used the notion of revival in order to explain
and advance the idea of a Christian nation, "a nation under God," as it

was called in the United States. Among those who advocated national renewal in nineteenth-century Europe, Protestants were very typically in the forefront, and even more typical is the fact that, in the German case, they believed in the idea of a symbiosis of Christian and Germanic (or Teutonic) elements. Through this combination, they argued, a new stage of development in the history of the world—as well as a new stage in the history of the salvation of God's true children—could be attained.

The third idea was closely connected with these two assumptions. In context with the notions of chosenness and national revival we can also find the belief in a new messiah, that is, the belief in a savior who is supposedly called by God and who comes in order to resurrect a whole people. Sometimes this new leader is portrayed like Moses, leading his people from servitude to the promised land; sometimes he resembles Jesus (the Jesus of the Second Coming, who inaugurates the Last Judgment). In this context religious elements such as divine election, ordeals as a means of reaching inner strength, and martyrdom are being projected into the lives and careers of politicians in order to outfit them with the aura of a national savior. In examining the sources it is sometimes hard to tell which of these attributes are simply metaphors and which carry a deeper spiritual meaning. Perhaps people in the mid- to late-nineteenth century did not know themselves. In any case, before 1914 even Europeans who had received a secular education were so well acquainted with biblical stories that they were able to imagine political leadership in biblical terms and with the spiritual qualifications explained in the Old and New Testaments.

The belief in chosenness, the belief in rebirth or revival, and the hope for a savior are important for understanding the relationship between the notions of religion, nation, and race in the European, Christian case. Some of these ideas are also salient in the Hindu, Muslim, and Shinto cases, but within entirely different symbolic configurations. The general point we want to make here is that it is essential to follow the transformation of religious notions when they are transferred from a purely religious context to the sphere of national politics.[18] Nationalism feeds on a symbolic repertoire that is already available but also transforms it in significant ways. In the South Asian context this is noticeable in the transformation of specific religious notions of martyrdom and sacrifice but also in broader conceptions of death and the afterlife. A good example of a transformation of conceptions of spirits and demons as well as of the role of spirit possession under the influence of an emergent Sinhalese Buddhist nationalism is given in Obeyesekere's work on the Sri Lankan shrine of Kataragama.[19] Similarly, in the Shinto case, discussed by Harry Harootunian in this volume, there is a sharp transition from folk practices centering around guardian spirits to the nationalist practices of the Yasukuni Shrine focusing on the spirits of the war dead.

When Max Weber began to study non-Christian religion at the beginning of this century, he was guided in his analyses by three convictions: he believed, first, that scholars had to explore the causes of the fact that modern capitalism had risen in the West and nowhere else. He believed, second, that the predominant feature in the course of modernization was disenchantment (*Entzauberung*); and he believed, third, that with his studies on the Protestant ethic he had found the one and only viable answer to these questions.[20] Weber's studies deserve much credit because they demonstrate how important it is to look beyond Europe in order to understand the specific role, impact, and variations of religion within Europe. However, Weber used an ideal-typical comparative approach. One of the problems of that approach is that it compares civilizations as unified wholes. It thus tends to neglect the interaction between societies in the capitalist world system, and more specifically, it tends to ignore the colonial process.

The present collection of essays also adopts a comparative approach, but one that is based on the idea that a combination of metropolitan and colonial perspectives should lead to very different kinds of conversations and insights than have previously been possible among scholars who tend to work along the divide of colonizing and colonized nations.[21] It also suggests that, at least in some cases, comparative work on these issues at both sides of the divide might show that what seemed entirely separate is, in fact, related. This is, at least, the outcome of recent work on literary education in India and Britain.[22] In this way the book hopes to revitalize discussion of religion's place in modern society, which theories of secularization have brought to a dead end. It focuses on 1850 to the present, which is the period of both high colonialism and high nationalism as well as their aftermath.

The essays discuss the historical development of religion and nationalism in India, Japan, Britain, and the Netherlands. They do not take the relation between religion and nationalism for granted but explore religion's place in relation to ideas of language, race, and history in the formation of nationalism. They also examine the specific qualities of religious discourse and practice that can be used for nationalist purposes. For example, if the nation is something to die for, religion offers ways to understand sacrifice and to remember and celebrate those who have died for the nation. On the other hand, there are also limits to the nationalization of religion, which are discussed in several case studies.

This volume explores three general themes. First, it examines the nationalization of religion in the modern era. Second, it discusses the relation between secular and religious nationalisms. Third, it explores the ways in which religious views of death and the afterlife are inflected in the commemoration of the violent past of nation and religious community.

The first theme is explored in the contributions by van der Veer, McLeod, Bayly, van Rooden, and Metcalf. They ask to what degree traditional religion persisted within modern nationalism. On one hand, the part played by clergy, Shinto priests, and by churches and shrines seems to suggest such persistence. On the other hand, it seems obvious that the strongest religious energies were discharged by entirely new, voluntary organizations, often headed by laypersons. This indicates that organized religion itself was being transformed and modernized in the course of the nineteenth and twentieth centuries. While McLeod and van Rooden discuss this process in Western Christianity, Metcalf shows a comparable development in twentieth-century Indian Islam. In fact, the way religion influenced other spheres of life resembled to a certain degree the means by which modern nationalism shaped politics. Modernizing religion and emerging nationalism formed a kind of vibrant symbiosis that produced and provided political values and moral guidelines and that was able, as van der Veer and Bayly show, to adopt and also to incorporate the racial elements within nationalism.

If one argues that modern nationalism itself is a kind of religion, traditional religion is reduced to the role of an example from which proponents of nationalism can borrow certain elements but which retains an autonomous area in theological and spiritual terms. Much depends, furthermore, on how one defines religion and how one describes the constitutive elements of religion. Which of these elements do we find in modern nationalism? To be sure, nationalism defines the past of a people, their future, or salvation, and the sacrifices necessary in order to claim salvation and win the future. Are these ingredients enough to qualify nationalism not as a substitute for religion (a quasi-religion, or *Ersatzreligion*) but as religion authentic and proper? If so, racial elements within nationalism, and in particular the idea of racial purity, would be part of the quest for national salvation. This is true both for the case of British Christian nationalism, as Bayly demonstrates and for the Aryan definition of Hindu India, discussed by van der Veer. It is an open question whether the definition of nationalism as religion should be seen as a part of the process of secularization or whether we should think in terms of a redefinition of religion and speak of a sacralization of the idea of the nation.

The second theme in the volume is a central, comparative one, that of "secularity." Western nation-states are invariably seen as secular, whereas Asian nation-states are seen as either religious or hybrid, that is, in between religious and secular.[23] In this volume we look at Britain and the Netherlands as examples of modern nation-states in Western Europe. As we have seen in our discussion of Gellner, understanding nationalism in the social sciences depends largely on a conceptualization of historical developments in Europe and should therefore fit these two exemplary cases.

It is a fundamental assumption of the discourse of modernity that religion in modern societies loses its social creativity and is forced to choose between a sterile conservation of its premodern characteristics and a self-effacing assimilation to the secularized world. Contrary to this assumption, new and highly original religious organizations proliferated in Britain and the Netherlands in the nineteenth century, as we have argued already. Ideological pluralization, resulting in ecclesiastical and theological strife, only served to reinforce these mobilizations. Similarly, we find throughout the colonized world from the late nineteenth and continuing throughout the twentieth century a revitalization of religious forms of activism in the public sphere. These religious organizations across the colonial divide are crucial for understanding the development of nationalism in the contemporary world.

The assumed secularism of modern British and Dutch societies makes sense only as a colonial theory. One of the strongest legitimations for colonial rule in India was that the British were an enlightened and rational race of rulers who had to lead and develop the Indian people, who were steeped in ancient prejudices and communal violence. An important dialectical element of this argument, as van der Veer shows, was that the British were a secular yet Christian nation who could thus take a rational interest in establishing a utilitarian morality. Hindu society, on the contrary, was completely under the authority of priests and given to endless, absurd rituals.[24] The Muslims of India were at the same time "backward" and "bigoted," prone to zealous revolutionary activism.[25] The emergence of religious forms of nationalism and the partition of India and Pakistan appear to confirm the colonial view. As Chatterjee shows in this volume, however, the Indian nationalist imagination could produce a rhetoric of Hindu-Muslim brotherhood as easily as one of Hindu resistance against Muslim tyranny. While the historical process seems utterly contingent in this respect, the historical narrative inscribes it in the teleology of religious antagonism. Metcalf clarifies the difficulties one encounters when describing religious movements that do not fit the accepted historical narrative. The spatial imaginations of the pietist Muslim Tablighi Jama'at movement go against the grain of the territorial imaginations of the secular and religious nationalisms of the period.

It is instructive in the context of this comparative volume to consider secularization in an Asian state that has not been colonized. The case of Japan, discussed by Harootunian, makes it abundantly clear that religion's organization, its place in society, and patterns of recruitment are so different in Japan that not only a simple form of the secularization theory itself but also many of the empirical and theoretical problems derived from it in the context of Western Christianity become meaningless. Extremely important for our comparative purposes is the extent to which the modernization of the state in Japan was instrumental not to the secularization of society but to its sacralization.

The third theme in the volume, that of mourning and commemoration, is discussed by Harootunian and Groot. Given the importance of theological and ecclesiastical strife and conflict, the mechanisms developed to pacify tensions between religious groups in modern Europe merit further study. For instance, since the eighteenth century British and Dutch nationalism were imbued with a generalized Protestantism, which transcended the differences between the various Protestant churches.[26] Catholics were the significant Other. Both in the Netherlands and in Britain the formal reestablishment of a Roman-Catholic hierarchy in the 1850s called into question this traditional identification of national identity with an undenominational Protestantism. In the second half of the nineteenth century this religious nationalism came under attack from different directions. Right-wing Protestant movements rejected its enlightened base. Catholics strove to prove their own adherence to the nation. New forms of political discourse endeavored to found the nation on race or history. The Protestant-Catholic divide and mutual antagonism were gradually pacified in the later nineteenth century in both Britain and the Netherlands. A similar pacification has not occurred between Hindus, Sikhs, and Muslims on the Indian subcontinent. On the contrary, this antagonism was a major factor in the partition between India and Pakistan and continues to be a crucial element in the various expressions of religious antagonism on the subcontinent.

Pacification of religious antagonism depends crucially on the management of memory and mourning. Groot and Harootunian explore several ways in which the memory of violence is negotiated. Religion gives meaning both to violence and to the suffering incurred by it. Remembering can put things to rest, but it can also reactivate antagonisms by opening old wounds.[27] In the Dutch case, analyzed by Groot, the commemoration of past violence has immediate consequences for communal relations in the present. In the case of the Yasukuni Shrine in Japan, discussion about the war dead also implies an externalization of war guilt and thus a political stance of great consequence in the present. Striking in the analysis of mourning and memory in this volume is the extent to which the boundaries between private suffering, public acts of national remembering, and religious rituals are blurred.[28] Death and the afterlife form the stuff of which both religion and nationalism are made. This volume explores some of the ways in which these two modern ideological formations feed on each other in dealing with violence and its pacification.

In lieu of a general conclusion, the volume ends with two reflective essays by Asad and Anderson. Asad examines the secularization thesis and its alternatives by showing the ways in which the secular and the religious presuppose each other in post-Enlightenment modernity. He emphasizes that nationalism requires the space of the secular to make sense. Anderson reflects upon the dead and the yet unborn, collectivities with which the national imagination is much preoccupied. The responsibility the living have toward their ancestors and their progeny constitutes the morality of the nation. This kind of imagination borrows in a number of ways from the religious one, but it is also strikingly different in Anderson's view. These two essays form a fitting epilogue to a volume that does not seek to propose an alternative to the secularization thesis but opens up the question of the multiple relations of secularity and religiosity in nationalism across the colonial divide. There is an obvious danger in scholarly work on both nationalism and religion to reproduce the seamless narratives of the ideologies under study while neglecting the contradictions and tensions inherent in the historical processes that produce the religious morality of the nation-state. This volume attempts to avoid the dangers of a grand synthesis by mapping out the problem areas in this neglected but highly significant field of inquiry.

Notes

1. Benedict R. Anderson, *Imagined Communities: Reflections on the Origin and Spread of Nationalism,* 2d ed. (London: Verso, 1991).

2. George M. Marsden, *Fundamentalism and American Culture: The Shaping of Twentieth-Century Evangelicalism, 1870–1925* (Oxford: University Press, 1980); Martin E. Marty and R. Scott Appleby, eds., *The Fundamentalism Project,* 5 vols. (Chicago: University of Chicago Press, 1991–95).

3. Bruce Lawrence, *Defenders of God: The Fundamentalist Revolt against the Modern Age* (San Francisco: Harper and Row, 1989).

4. Peter van der Veer, *Religious Nationalism: Hindus and Muslims in India* (Berkeley: University of California Press, 1994).

5. See Prasanjit Duara's discussion of the influence of Hegel's text on nationalist thought in his *Rescuing History from the Nation: Questioning Narratives of Modern China* (Chicago: University of Chicago Press, 1995).

6. Cf. John Hall, "Nationalisms: Classified and Explained," *Daedalus* 122 (1993): 1–29, esp. 2–3; on ethnicity and "birth," see A. D. Smith, *The Ethnic Origins of Nations* (Oxford: Blackwell, 1986); Marc Shell, *Children of the Earth: Literature, Politics, and Nationhood* (New York: Oxford University Press, 1993).

7. Clifford Geertz, "Religion as a Cultural System," in *The Interpretation of Cultures: Selected Essays* (New York: Basic Books, 1973), 87–125; Talal Asad, *Genealogies of Religion: Discipline and Reasons of Power in Christianity and Islam* (Baltimore, Md.: Johns Hopkins University Press, 1993), 27–54.

8. See also S. N. Balagangadhara, *"The Heathen in His Blindness": Asia, the West, and the Dynamic of Religion* (Leiden: Brill, 1994).

9. Dipesh Chakrabarty, "Postcoloniality and the Artifice of History: Who Speaks for 'India's' Pasts," *Representations* 37 (1992): 1–26.

10. Ralph D. Grillo, ed., *"Nation" and "State" in Europe: Anthropological Perspectives* (London: Academic Press, 1980), 1.

11. Ernest Gellner, *Nations and Nationalism* (Oxford: Blackwell, 1983).

12. Ibid., 57.

13. Ibid., 77, 142.

14. Nicholas Abercrombie and Bryan S. Turner, "The Dominant Ideology Thesis," *British Journal of Sociology* 29 (1978): 149–70.

15. Eric J. Hobsbawm, *Nations and Nationalism since 1780: Programme, Myth, Reality* (Cambridge: Cambridge University Press, 1990).

16. See, for example, Koppel S. Pinson, *Pietism as a Factor in the Rise of German Nationalism* (New York: Columbia University Press, 1934), and Gerhard Kaiser, *Pietismus und Patriotismus im literarischen Deutschland: Ein Beitrag Zum Problem der Säkularisation* (Wiesbaden: Steiner, 1961).

17. William R. Hutchison and Hartmut Lehmann, eds. *Many Are Chosen: Divine Election and Western Nationalism* (Minneapolis, Minn.: Fortress Press, 1994).

18. For attempts to clarify these transformations in the case of German nationalism, see Hartmut Lehmann, "Friedrich von Bodelschwingh und das Sedanfest," "Pietism and Nationalism: The Relationship between Protestant Revivalism and National Renewal in Nineteenth-Century Germany," and "The Germans as a Chosen People: Old Testament Themes in German Nationalism," in *Religion und Religiosität in der Neuzeit: Historische Beiträge* (Göttingen: Vandenhoeck und Ruprecht, 1996), 205–59.

19. Gananath Obeyesekere, *Medusa's Hair: An Essay on Personal Symbols and Religious Experience* (Chicago: University of Chicago Press, 1981).

20. Max Weber, "Die Wirtschaftsethik der Weltreligionen" and "Die protestantische Ethik und der Geist des Kapitalismus," in *Gesammelte Aufsätze zur Religionssoziologie*, 3 vols. (Tübingen: Mohr, 1920–21). Of the many works on Max Weber, we would like to mention Hartmut Lehmann and Günther Roth, eds., *Weber's "Protestant Ethic": Origins, Evidence, Contexts* (New York: Cambridge University Press, 1994).

21. See Ann Stoler "Rethinking Colonial Categories: European Communities and the Boundaries of Rule," *Comparative Studies in Society and History* 31 (1989): 134–61.

22. Gauri Viswanathan, *Masks of Conquest: Literary Study and British Rule in India* (New York: Columbia University Press, 1989).

23. E.g., Louis Dumont, *Homo Hierarchicus: Essai sur le système des castes*, 3d ed. (Paris: Gallimard, 1979), 376–95.

24. See, e.g., the discussion of James Mill's *History of British India* (1858) by L. Ronald Inden, *Imagining India* (Oxford: Blackwell, 1990), 90–93.

25. The classic text is W. W. Hunter, *The Indian Musalmans* (London, 1876). See also Gyanendra Pandey, "The Bigoted Julaha," in *The Construction of Communalism in Colonial North India* (Delhi: Oxford University Press, 1990), 66–108.

26. Linda Colley, *Britons: Forging the Nation, 1707–1837* (New Haven, Conn.: Yale University Press, 1992).

27. Cf. Peter van der Veer, "Writing Violence," in David Ludden, ed., *Contesting the Nation* (Philadelphia: University of Pennsylvania Press, 1996), 250–70.

28. See also Don Handelman *Models and Mirrors: Towards an Anthropology of Public Events* (Cambridge: Cambridge University Press, 1990).

2

The Moral State: Religion, Nation, and Empire in Victorian Britain and British India

PETER VAN DER VEER

IN 1988, when British Muslims petitioned their government to ban Salman Rushdie's *Satanic Verses*, they discovered that the existing blasphemy law did not prohibit insults to the prophet Muhammad. It applied only to Christianity, and accordingly, the government rejected the petition. The home minister for race relations, John Patten, subsequently wrote a document lecturing the Muslims and the general public "on being British." Talal Asad has brilliantly analyzed the political implications of the liberal views expressed in this text. One of its crucial aims was to delineate "a common national culture." According to Patten, this commonality was to be found in "our democracy and our laws, the English language, and the history that has shaped modern Britain."[1] In this essay I address two things that are erased in Patten's discussion of "being British": Christianity and empire. It is, of course, quite understandable that a politician would not mention Christianity as a major component of British culture at the height of the Rushdie affair. Nevertheless, the laws to which Patten referred included a blasphemy law that protected only Christian sentiments. Moreover, no one doubts that Christianity is a crucial element in the history that shaped Britain.

Similarly, there is a silent assumption in Patten's document that being British has nothing to do with empire. In other words, the problem of conflicting values, as it emerged in the Rushdie case, was a new problem, brought to Britain by immigration; it had to do with empire only insofar as the immigrants came from the former empire, another instance of "the empire strikes back." Nevertheless, it could well be argued that Patten's arguments, calling for acceptance of a common national culture, as well as those of Muslim leaders, calling for the religious neutrality of the state, as shown by the political protection of the beliefs of all religious communities, are rooted in the same history of empire but as experienced on opposite sides of the colonizing process. It is sometimes said that the British are unaware of their history, because it took place elsewhere. My own readings in British history suggest, that the imperial connection is indeed too seldom consciously reflected upon by historians of Britain, let alone British politicians. Historians of India are much more aware of the imperial connection, but tend to ignore the developments in the metropolis, afraid of making the history of the colony into a footnote of European history. In this essay I attempt to show some structural similarities and differences between the development of religion and nationalism in Britain and India.

That Patten could get away with not mentioning Christianity as a component of Britain's national culture is due to the fact that organized Christianity has been gradually marginalized in British society over the course of the twentieth century. Britain is now a so-called secular society, in which Christianity, allegedly, has become a private matter for individuals, with no political relevance in the public sphere. Without denying significant changes in the location of religion in British society in this century I am wary of the assumptions inherent in the concept of secularity. One major element in that concept is the separation of church and state. However, as we know, this element is not found in Britain. The Church of England is the National Church of England. The queen is still head of that state church and the bishops, appointed by the Crown on the recommendation of the prime minister, are present in the House of Lords. Even in 1980 a leading article in the *Times* argued that it would be undesirable for the prince of Wales to marry a Roman Catholic.[2] In the meantime a number of undesirable things appear to have happened in the British royal house and one wonders whether this particular opinion would be expressed today. Nevertheless, this quite recent opinion from a leading newspaper in a so-called secular society is quite remarkable in its insistence on the Protestant nature of the state.

Another way of looking at secularity is developed in the secularization thesis, about which I have some general doubts. The boredom that takes hold of almost any audience when one speaks about contemporary religion is perhaps the most striking effect of the thesis, which basically expresses that we already know everything there is to be known about religion—namely, that it declines. The success of industrialization, science, and technology has made religion in the modern world obsolete. In sociological theories of modernity the transition from the premodern, rural community to the modern, industrial, and urbanized society is said to be marked by the decline of religion as an expression of the moral unity of society.

In the European discussion of secularization decline of church attendance and numbers of churches are good indicators of change. Starting with the last decades of the nineteenth century, there seems to be such a decline in England, although there is considerable debate about periodization and interpretation of that decline. Catholicism, for instance, continued to grow substantially until World War II. In the Netherlands—to take another European example—decline began only in the 1950s. In the United States it all looks somewhat different. American churches have always been very creative in recruiting church members, as witnessed over the last decades by televangelism. For Christianity, church membership and church attendance are good indicators and from them we can only conclude that the historical picture is rather different from one Western society to another, so that a generalized secularization story will not do. This is true not only for the facts and figures of church attendance and membership but also for the causal explanations of industrialization and rationalization offered by secularization theory. For example, there is more evidence for religious expansion during the Industrial Revolution in England than for secularization. Similarly, there is currently a consensus among historians that the impact of scientific discoveries, such as those of Darwin, on the decline of religion has previously been much exaggerated.

If the secularization thesis does not account for the history of Western Christianity, it is even less applicable to the history of Islam, Hinduism, Buddhism, and most other religions. In the latter cases the question about church attendance and membership cannot even be raised, since there are no churches. The organization of religion, the place of religion in society, and the patterns of recruitment are so different that not only secularization theory itself but also the empirical and theoretical problems derived from it in the context of Western Christianity become meaningless. This has not prevented social scientists from universalizing the ill-founded story about the West to include the rest. Since all societies modernize and secularization is an intrinsic part of modernization, all societies secularize. So the rhetoric, dressed up as argument, goes.

In recent years much doubt has been thrown on the secularization of India and the ultimate triumph of secularism. The anthropologist T. N. Madan has, for instance, argued that "secularism as a widely shared worldview has failed to make headway in India."[3] Since Indians are Hindus, Muslims, Buddhists, or Sikhs, they are not Protestant Christians. They cannot and will not privatize their religion.[4] Madan points out that in sociological theory, especially that of Max Weber, there is an essential linkage between Protestantism, individualism, and secularization.[5] He argues, accordingly, that secularism is a "gift of Christianity to mankind" and that it is part of Europe's unique history.[6] Madan expresses what appears to be a general consensus among both social scientists and the general public that the modern West is uniquely secular and the East uniquely religious. The problem is that this reduces complex and diverse histories to the binary opposition of secularity and religiosity. We have already seen that the history of secularity in Western societies is varied and complex; the same can be said about the development of religious institutions in India. Nevertheless, the appeal of these essentializations cannot be dismissed by providing ever more complicated narratives of social change. It is in fact hard to go beyond theories of modernization and secularization, however much one tries to get away from them. One is forced to address the conceptual complexities and contradictions involved in them.

In my view the crucial relationship to be analyzed is that of state, nation, and religion. The modern state is a nation-state; the hyphen indicates that the modern state requires a nation and vice versa. Although Britain and India are now both nation-states, in the colonial period only Britain was a nation-state, whereas India was a colony. This, at least, seems to indicate a time lag, in which colonizing Britain was an established nation-state and colonized India became one—perhaps as a result of colonization. However, one has to remember that the nation is a nineteenth-century historical formation, so that the time lag is relatively minor. Another way of putting this is to say that while Britain was colonizing India, England was colonizing Great Britain, trying to unify what was not yet (and would only partially be) the united kingdom. We can see the historical outcome of the latter process even today in Northern Ireland and Scotland. I do not want to make too much of this but simply want to point out that a notion of time lag, in which blueprints of a finished nation-state are exported to less evolved societies via colonialism, may lead us to miss the gradual and differential nature of nation-state formation—and to miss that this process involved Britain and India simultaneously, within the same historical period.

Often the question is raised, what comes first in this hyphenated phenomenon, nation or state? Does the state produce the people or the people the state? I agree with Marcel Mauss, who in his unfinished work on "the nation" argues that the idea of the nation combines in the collective spirit the idea of the fatherland (*patrie*) and the idea of the citizen:

> [T]hese two notions of fatherland and citizen are ultimately nothing but a single institution, one and the same rule of practical and ideal morals and, in reality, one and the same central fact which gives the modern republic all its originality, all its novelty and its incomparable moral dignity. . . . The individual— every individual—is born in political life. . . . A society in its entirety has to some extent become the State, the sovereign political body; it is the totality of citizens."[7]

In his provocative and profound way Mauss does away with any sharp distinction between state and society. Where Renan had suggested that the nation was a daily plebiscite, a deliberate choice, Mauss argued that it was a collective belief in homogeneity, as if the nation were a primitive clan, supposedly composed of equal citizens, symbolized by its flag (its totem), having a cult of the fatherland, just as the primitive clan has its ancestor cults.[8] In Mauss's view the modern nation believes in its race ("it is because the nation creates race that one believes that the race creates the nation"), its language, its civilization, its national character. This collective belief is recent, modern, and to a very considerable extent the result of public, obligatory education. The idea of national character is intimately tied to the idea of progress.[9]

What we find in Mauss is a rejection of the common distinction between civil ties and primordial bonds, between citizenship and ideas of ethnicity, race, language, and religion. In his view they all go together in a complex transformation of society into the nation-state. For Mauss one of the most interesting aspects of this process is that it produces the individual and the nation simultaneously. In Foucault's terms, the state is totalizing and individualizing at the same time. The boundaries of the state are notoriously difficult to define. The state appears to be a sovereign authority above and outside society, but Foucault has pointed out that the modern state works internally through disciplinary power, not by constraining individuals and their actions but by producing them. The individual, civil political subject is produced in churches, schools, and factories. Timothy Mitchell has recently argued that it is the peculiarity of the modern state phenomenon that "at the same time as power relations become internal in this way, and by the same methods, they now appear to take the novel form of external structures."[10] The state is thus to be analyzed as a structural effect.

Where does this leave religion? In Mauss (as in Durkheim) there are constant allusions to the idea that nationalism is the religion of modern society, just as clan totemism is the religion of primitive society. If that is the case, could one then say that Christianity (or Hinduism, Islam, Buddhism) is the religion of the ancien régime and nationalism the secular religion of modern society? Our previous argument about the secularization thesis has already shown that this is a much too simple idea of one thing replacing another. An implication of Mauss's argument appears to be that what happened to race and language in the age of nationalism also happened to religion. It becomes a defining feature of the nation and for that purpose it is transformed in a certain direction. Religion is nationalized, so to speak. It becomes one of the fields of disciplinary practice in which the modern civil subject is produced. Not the only one, obviously, since language, literature, race, and civilization are all other fields producing what Mauss called "the national character."

That religion is important in producing the modern subject should not sound too strange for those familiar with Weber's discussion of the Protestant ethic. That it also is important in producing the modern public is perhaps more startling, especially if one stresses that in the nineteenth century not only Protestantism is nationalized but also Catholicism and many other religions, such as Islam and Hinduism in India. One can hear the immediate objection that Protestantism became the national religion of England and the Low Countries by the sixteenth century. However, I would suggest that in the early-modern period there were Protestant state churches in these countries, but since they were not yet nation-states there was no national religion. In other words, in the eighteenth and nineteenth centuries there were major changes in religion underway that affected its organization, its impact, its reach. These changes had to do with the rise of that hyphenated phenomenon, the nation-state.

Implicit in my argument thus far is that the modern subject is produced together with the modern public. Consequently, religion is important not only in the shaping of individual conscience and civilized conduct, but also in the creation of the public sphere. This may come as a surprise to those who accept Jürgen Habermas's understanding of the rise of "the public sphere." In his *Strukturwandlung der Oeffentlichkeit* Habermas argued that private individuals assembled into a public body began to discuss the exercise of political power by the state critically in the eighteenth century. These citizens had free access to information and expressed their opinion in a rational and domination-free (*herrschaftsfreie*) manner. In my view Habermas's analysis of the Enlightenment tradition very much belongs, at the theoretical level, to a discourse of modern, European self-representation. A striking element in this self-representation is the neglect of religious, public opinion that cannot be regarded as "rational" and "critical."[11]

In Habermas's model we have a picture of European development in which secularity is one of the distinguishing features of modernity. This picture is simply false. Enlightenment did not kill religion in Europe. On the contrary, in the eighteenth century there was a direct connection between natural science and natural religion. As Margaret Jacob has recently argued: "Habermas's individuals are far too secularized."[12] Jacob focuses on the new religiosity of the enlightened few, such as the Deists in England.[13] I would, however, like to draw attention to the organizational activities that developed out of eighteenth century evangelism. While early evangelism—for example, Methodism—was already developing new communication networks, this development received a very strong impetus at the turn of the century. I am thinking here of antislavery societies, Bible societies, and missionary societies around 1900 that—at least in Britain (the prime subject of Habermas's analysis)—were instrumental in creating a modern public sphere on which the nation-state could be built. I would therefore suggest that the notions of publicity, the public, and public opinion, captured by Habermas's concept of the public sphere are important and can be used for comparative purposes if we are not going to be constrained by Habermas's Enlightenment perspective.

In the remainder of this essay I look at the nationalization of religion in Britain and India. I hope to show that developments in the metropolis and in the colony had important features in common, but that there were also substantial differences that had to do with the way state, nation, and religion are related in these two sites of the empire.

The Moral State in Britain

In nineteenth-century Britain two major religious developments connect religion to nationalism. The first is the enormous growth and impact of evangelicalism on the entire religious culture of Britain. The second is the inclusion and enfranchisement of Catholics in the nation. Let me start with evangelicalism. Evangelical Revival starts conventionally with John Wesley in the first half of the eighteenth century, but there was an important second wave in the 1790s, which lasted into the nineteenth century.[14] The growth of evangelical movements in the first half of the nineteenth century is spectacular, but more significant than these numbers is the considerable impact evangelicalism had on religious groups and individuals of every kind. The evangelical expansion coincided largely with that of the Industrial Revolution, which has led to all kinds of more or less economistic causal explanations, ranging from those given by Élie Halévy to those offered by Edward Thompson.[15] All these explanations have subsequently been subjected to substantial criticisms, which I prefer not to explore here. Whatever the causalities involved it is important for my purpose to point out that evangelicalism aimed at inward conversion, but also at an outward activity in converting others. Itinerant preachers and later Bible and missionary societies reached far and deep. What one has here is a strong civilizing and educational effort aimed at transforming people's personal lives. There can be little doubt about evangelicalism's importance in producing modern, civil, and hard-working individuals.

At the same time evangelicalism had a very significant political impact. Obviously the term *evangelicalism*, covers a broad range of ideas and attitudes, but its campaign for the abolition of slavery in the first decades of the nineteenth century shows how evangelicalism, despite its diversity, could have a strong political message. Here we see also how evangelicalism at home was connected to the empire, as exemplified in the words of William Wilberforce, one of the leaders of the evangelical Clapham sect:

> I consider it my duty to endeavour to deliver these poor creatures from their present darkness and degradation, not merely out of a direct regard for their

well being . . . but also from a direct persuasion that both the colonists and we ourselves shall be otherwise the sufferers. The judicial and penal visitations of Providence occur commonly in the way of natural consequence and it is in that way I should expect the evils to occur.[16]

David Brion Davis suggests that the abolition of the slave trade in 1807 and of slavery in 1833 were "genuine rituals," evoking fantasies of death and rebirth, and "designed to revitalize Christianity and atone for national guilt."[17]

These attitudes toward the rest of the world were new and thoroughly modern. Until the 1790s there was hardly any interest in missionization abroad. The 1790s proved a turning point, however, perhaps best captured in the title of William Carey's book *An Enquiry into the Obligations of Christians to Use Means for the Conversion of the Heathens*.[18] A great number of missionary societies were founded, including the well-known London Missionary Society (LMS) and Church Missionary Society (CMS). All saw themselves engaged in a battle against idolatry and an endeavor to save heathen souls. Not only were these souls thought to go to hell, if not saved, but it came to be seen as a Christian duty to save them. One can only wonder about the extent to which Christian imagination in Britain was fueled by the imagery of the poor Hindus, Muslims, and others being lost for eternity. We do know that one of every two missionary speakers at provincial anniversary meetings of missionary societies between 1838 to 1873 came from India.[19] There can be little doubt that the simultaneous evangelical activities of Bible societies, missionary societies, and Sunday schools created a public awareness of a particular kind of world and of an imperial duty of British Christians in the empire.

I see evangelicalism as a very broad, religious force, active both within and outside the established church. By 1850 about one-third of Anglican clergymen, including many of the best, brightest, and could be designated evangelical and so could the vast majority of Nonconformists.[20] I take this to imply that the earlier strong divide between the established church and Nonconformism was, to some extent, bridged by evangelicalism. This divide obviously continued to exist in political debates about church-state relations, but Dissent appears to have lost its radical antiestablishment politics within evangelicalism, which basically promoted a middle-class piety with strong elements of civil and frugal behavior and national honor. Certainly, one can point at the extremist elements within the movement with their millenarian, adventist antinomianism that seem to perpetuate the earlier characteristics of eighteenth-century Dissent. These elements remained significant throughout the nineteenth century and into the twentieth century. In a number of cases their outbursts of religious fervor pushed influential men, like the Liberal leader Gladstone (1809–98), from evangelicalism toward High Church. Nevertheless, one can see in Gladstone a strong evangelical streak that informed his political views and actions.[21] Similarly, several generations later, C. F. Andrews (1871–1940), missionary and later friend of Tagore and Gandhi, left the Irvingite congregation, in which his father was a minister, for High Church, only to become a missionary and later a moralist supporter of Indian nationalism. Andrews did not feel close to the religious atmosphere in which his father, who had the powers of prophesy and healing, conducted his services. Nevertheless, he became a missionary who soon felt the constraints of High Church Anglicanism as too limiting. One can easily see the influence of evangelical moralism in C. F. Andrews's positions.[22]

In mainstream evangelicalism religious enthusiasm was channeled into public activity, spreading middle-class values over the larger population. By and large it does not seem correct to see the evangelical movement as antirational. Rather it tried to combine rational thought and religious feeling, sense and sensibility. In that and other aspects I interpret it as a typical nationalist movement that tries to combine enlightenment with romanticism. While there is constant debate between utilitarian liberals and evangelicals there is considerable evidence of the common ground between them in the way John Stuart Mill tried to distance himself from his father's hyperrationalism.[23] The evangelical project was to convert the people to a morally inspired existence, in which individual conscience of sins and atonement are catchwords, within a nation with a mission.

Gladstone is an interesting example of the combination of liberalism and evangelical moralism. Brought up in a devoutly evangelical family, he began his career under the influence of the poet-philosopher Coleridge's book *On the Constitution of the Church and State*.[24] To defend the established church in the aftermath of Catholic Emancipation, he wrote a book titled *The State in Its Relations with the Church*, in which he endowed the state with a conscience that transcends that of individuals.[25] In this treatise he not only argued for a strong tie between church and state, but endowed the state with high moral qualities:

[T]he State is properly and according to its nature, moral. . . . It means that the general action of the State is under a moral law. . . . In the government and laws of a country we find not a mere aggregation of individual acts but a composite agency. . . . This composite agency represents the personality of the nation; and, as a great distinct moral reality, demands a worship of its own, namely, the worship of the State, represented in its living and governing members, and therefore a public and joint worship. To sum up then in a few words the result of these considerations, religion is applicable to the State, because it is the office of the State in its personality to evolve the social life of man, which social life is essentially moral in the ends it contemplates, in the subject-matter on which it feeds, and in the restraints and motives it requires; and which can only be effectually moral when it is religious. Or, religion is directly necessary to the right employment of the energies of the State.[26]

Since Gladstone later in his career became a defendant of the rights of Dissenters and Catholics, it has been argued that he completely repudiated his earlier views.[27] I would, however, suggest that we see in Gladstone a shift from the early-modern view of the public church to the moral nation-state, in which not the state bureaucracy but individual and national conscience were paramount. What remains constant is the moral/ religious nature of political activity. Instead of excluding others from this moral life of the nation, he wanted to include them all. This meant a repudiation of a strictly Calvinist notion of the "few elect" to be replaced by a moral universalism that extended grace to all the inhabitants of the world. This vision of a national church or the nation as a church goes beyond the visible, institutional Church of England.

Such a fusion of church and nation-state was also crucial to the civilizing mission, as envisioned by Thomas Arnold in his *Principles of Church Reform*.[28] While Arnold was still doubtful of the desirability of including Roman Catholics (Irish barbarians) and the chance that dissenting groups would join this Christianizing and civilizing mission, these concerns were soon overtaken by new realities. The liberal doctrine of the improvement of society fits extraordinarily well with Arnold's Christian moralism. He derived his ideas from Coleridge, who also influenced Gladstone and, interestingly, John Stuart Mill, principal spokesman of liberal ideas in the nineteenth century.[29] In Gladstone, there is a liberal view of progress instead of the usual evangelical views of damnation and the end of times, but added to this is the notion that progress is the Christian improvement of society and that in such progress we see the hand of God. This mixture of liberal and evangelical ideas leads to a quite general emphasis on the moral character of the English people and their duty to lead the world.[30] These views of progress and grace for all were not confined to the British isles, but included the "white man's burden" to bring the gospel to the colonies.

The shift from an Anglican exclusivist vision of the nation to an inclusivist nationalism is reflected in the other major religious development of the period, the emancipation of the Catholics. Eighteenth-century England had been very much a Protestant state, but the creation of the British nation-state required the inclusion of the Catholic minority. There was a considerable history of anti-Catholic hostility in England, which resulted in excluding Catholics from most areas of public life. From 1800 Roman Catholicism, like evangelicalism, experienced tremendous growth. In England this was the result of both an increase of English Catholics and a great influx of Irish immigrants. In Ireland there was an expansion of Roman Catholic activity, marked by the foundation of an Irish priest-training college at Maynooth in 1795. Roman Catholicism, like evangelicalism, also had an influence outside its fold. This is most clear in the Oxford movement (also called the Tractarians), from 1833 onward a movement toward emphasizing the Catholicity of the Church of England, called Anglo-Catholicism. John Henry Newman (1801–90), one of the movement's luminaries, replaced "Anglo" with "Roman" in 1845 and rose to become a Roman Catholic cardinal in 1879.

Evangelicals saw the growth in numbers of Roman Catholics as a threat that was compounded by their understandable fear for "the enemy within" constituted by the Oxford movement. In the 1820s the political struggle was about Roman Catholics' right to sit in the united Parliament of Great Britain and Ireland, which was decided in 1829 by the emancipation. Not only Roman Catholics were now allowed to become part of the nation, but also Dissenters whose civil disabilities were revoked by the Test and Corporation Acts in 1828. One has to interpret Coleridge, Arnold, and Gladstone in the light of these events, which definitely served to transform the religious and political character of British society in significant ways.

The enfranchisement of the Catholic minority in the British isles did little, however, little to prevent the strong connection that grew between Roman Catholicism and Irish nationalism.[31] This connection emerged very clearly in the repeal agitation of 1843, in which the Roman Catholic clergy and Irish nationalists worked hand in hand to attack the legislative union between Britain and Ireland. This movement, supported by Roman Catholic organizational structures, drew huge popular support. It is not exaggerated to see Irish nationalism as the strongest example of religious nationalism in Greater Britain. The emancipation of Catholics had thus not succeeded in drawing in the Irish Catholics into the British nation, which continued to have a too strong English character. Likewise, the Scottish Presbyterians were not immediately inclined to be part of an English/British nation, which was marked by the disruption in 1843, when half of the established church's clergy left to form the Free Church of Scotland. As in England, evangelicalism worked here to promote the cause of nationalism, but this time it was Scottish nationalism. The main inspiration to form the Free Church was an evangelical urge to be close to "the people," but, as a corollary, the disruption was marked by anti-English sentiments (which remain strong until the present day) as expressed in opposition to Westminster as well as to anglicized landlords. Not nearly as strong as in Ireland, nationalism in Scotland was nevertheless also marked by religious overtones. The same may be true for the connection between Welsh linguistic nationalism and Nonconformist religion.

The Catholic Emancipation undid any illusion people like Thomas Arnold may have had about Britain as a Protestant nation. Anti-Catholic feelings among the Protestant majority did not prevent Roman-Catholics from becoming the largest single church in England in the twentieth century.[32] At the same time, building "Greater Britain," including Ireland, into a nation proved impossible in the face of the successful combination of Roman Catholicism and Irish nationalism. Anti-Catholicism was very strong in the evangelical movement, but I want to emphasize that both Catholicism and evangelicalism—in a dynamic fed by mutual rivalry—expanded substantially in the first half of the nineteenth century. Both movements were simultaneously expanding and trying to dominate an emerging public sphere, which made nationalism possible. Evangelical Awakening and Roman Catholic Revival are most profitably seen as two connected movements that derived much of their expansionist energy from their mutual rivalry.[33] In this connection it is interesting to note that evangelicalism, despite its anti-Catholicism, even influenced the nineteenth century's most famous convert to Catholicism, John Henry Newman, as he candidly admitted in his *Apologia Pro Vita Sua*.[34]

From the 1830s to the 1860s anti-Catholicism and antiritualism within the Anglican Church were major themes of what John Wolffe has called "the Protestant Crusade."[35] This implied widespread agitation and popular mobilization of both Protestants and Catholics. Again, I would suggest that we see them in their interaction. Both evangelicals and Catholics were eager to underline their nationalism. Protestants in particular liked to emphasize their link to the paramount symbol of imperial nationalism, Queen Victoria.[36] While Irish Catholics obviously emphasized their Irishness, English Catholics were trying even harder to distance themselves from allegations of antinational allegiance to the pope. My contention is that both movements helped significantly in creating an imperial and missionary nationalism, characterized by superior national qualities of a ruling race: a nation with a mission. As Mandell Creighton, Anglican bishop of London, asserted at the turn of the century, "the question of the future of the world is the existence of Anglo-Saxon civilisation on a religious basis."[37] Creighton explicitly had the Church of England in mind when speaking about the conquest of the world, but I would suggest that religious diversity was encompassed by a notion of the duties of a superior race.

The notion of racial superiority in the second half of the nineteenth century depended to an important extent on comparison. Civilization was defined by its antithesis, barbarism or savagery. The internal rivalries, animosities, and political conflicts within British Christianity faded into the background of what came to be seen as the difference between British Christian civilization and the barbarity of the colonized peoples. The biblical affirmation that humankind was one, derived from a single pair in the Garden of Eden, as well as the Enlightenment notion of universal sameness and equality were rapidly giving way to ideas of radical racial difference in the second half of the nineteenth century.[38] Philologists like Renan and Max Müller equated race and language, and Renan asserted the right of superior races to colonize inferior ones. Where Thomas Arnold had been very concerned about the relation between religion and nation, his son Matthew Arnold, the author of *Culture and Anarchy*, relocated that concern by emphasizing a racialized view of culture. That the Arnoldian view of culture continued to be religiously inspired should be clear from the following quotation from *Culture and Anarchy*:

> The aim of culture [is to set] ourselves to ascertain what perfection is and to make it prevail; but also, in determining generally, in what perfection consists, religion comes to a conclusion identical with that which culture . . . likewise reaches. Religion says: The Kingdom of God is within you; and culture, in like manner, places human perfection in an internal condition, in the growth and predominance of our humanity proper, as distinguished from our animality. . . . Not a having and a resting, but a growing and a becoming, is the character of perfection as culture conceives it; and here, too, it coincides with religion.[39]

It is important to note that Arnold was the inspector of schools and in that capacity responsible for the education of the British in the nation's new racialized mission. Modern science supported this ideological formation of national culture, in which language and race took central stage and the culture of the colonized was turned into an object of academic study, with its own university chair.[40] Gradually race came to take precedence over religion as the dominant element in British nationalism in the second part of the nineteenth century.

The Colonial Mission in India

One of the great policy debates in the East India Company in the early nineteenth century was between orientalists who argued that the company should continue its policy of supporting native religious and educational institutions, and Anglicists who argued that there was little of value in these native institutions, which should be replaced by the more civilized and advanced institutions of England. This was clearly a complex debate, more or less decisively won by the Anglicists, when Thomas Babington Macaulay's *Minute on Indian Education* of 1835 was accepted as the basis of official policy. In this battle evangelicals sided with Anglicists. Evangelicals, such as those of the Clapham sect (William Wilberforce, Zachary Macaulay, John Venn, Samuel Thornton, Charles Grant) prominent in the antislavery campaign, were indignant at the support the company had given to Hinduism and Islam in India. They concurred with the utilitarian Anglicists in their disdain for the native institutions and literatures of India. William Wilberforce told the English Parliament that the orientalists were as skeptical about Christianity as the French revolutionaries whose actions it regarded with horror.[41] Not only should the company allow missionaries to work in India (which it did after 1813), but it should stop the support of native institutions.

In the early decades of the nineteenth century the company was still giving patronage to Hindu temples and festivals, especially in the south. Under strong pressure from the evangelicals the company had to withdraw from that policy. It did so very hesitantly. Even as late as 1838 a committee had to be formed in England for the purpose of "diffusing information relative to the connection of the East India Company's Government with the superstitious idolatrous systems of the natives, and for promoting the dissolution of that connection."[42] We have to see this as a withdrawal of sorts, however, since the British became active in setting up systems and committees to manage religious endowments. These committees became important arenas for organizing the public sphere, for both Hindus and Muslims. As such, it was another instance of a new colonial politics of representation that replaced the older patronage networks, in which the company had participated to further its prime purpose; trade.

Utilitarians and evangelicals agreed that the religious institutions of India needed to be dismantled and replaced by Christian civilization. They disagreed, however, on how to bring civilization to the natives. Religious neutrality was seen as essential first for trading purposes and later to British rule in India. The company continued to resist direct support for missionary projects. The Anglican Society for the Propagation of the Gospel in Foreign Parts (est. 1701) had always been a colonial church providing clergy for the British in the colonies until it was transformed in the 1830s under evangelical influence.[43] Serious missionary activity among the natives originated only in the nineteenth century outside the company in evangelical circles, which raised money from the British public. The company's neutrality, however, did nothing to prevent attempts to reform Indian society through education, an endeavor fully supported by the utilitarian Anglicists. This, however, turned out to be a field in which missionaries were extremely active.

Whatever the debates between evangelicals and utilitarians—and they were considerable—none of them would have denied that civil society and the forms of knowledge on which it was based were ultimately part and parcel of Christian civilization. Gauri Viswanathan has argued forcefully that the teaching of secular English literature, as recommended in

Macaulay's *Minute*, amounts to a relocation of cultural value from belief and dogma to language, experience, and history.[44] This relocation can be detected in the intellectual differences that simultaneously divide and connect Matthew Arnold and his father, Thomas, as well as Thomas Babington Macaulay and his father, Zachary. Despite their differences, these people occupied the same moral universe. Their differences were not about the moral mission of the state, but about matters of policy. The developments in that universe were similar in Britain and among the British in India. For evangelicals and utilitarians the world was no longer limited to England or Greater Britain. The antislavery campaigns had made the British public aware of Britain's role in a larger world. This role had to be one of reform and uplift, friend and foe agreed.

However much the British tried to hide the Christian roots of their colonial policies behind the mask of religious neutrality, the colonized "natives" were not to be fooled. It is often observed that there were great differences between the operations of the missionary societies in India and those of the state, but these were within a shared colonizing project. It is certainly true that the officers of the company and later the colonial state looked down upon the missionaries and that, in general, there was a substantial social gap between them. Nevertheless, their concerns colluded in the crucial fields of education and reform, as they did back home in Britain. The real difference was, obviously, not between the colonial state and the missionaries, but between the colonizing British and the colonized Indians. Where in Britain the state would gradually occupy the social spaces opened up by the religious organizations, in India these spaces were occupied by rival religious organizations of native "subjects." Their ideas and actions could not be incorporated in a British nation characterized by its Christian civilization. In due course they became oppositional toward the colonial state and, by the same token, bearers of Indian nationalism.

Despite the official policy of religious neutrality, the British interfered with every aspect of Indian religion and society. Considering the nature of the colonial project there was actually no choice and the tropes of withdrawal, secularity, and neutrality only tried to hide that discursively. I have to limit myself here to a discussion of the British involvement with Hinduism and its consequences, but I want to suggest that the developments that took place in Indian Islam and Sikhism were not altogether different.[45] British policies set off a whole chain of reformist reaction in Hinduism. As in the case of the evangelical Awakening in Britain, the causalities involved are extremely complex and Reform should not be viewed merely as a reaction to the colonial project. I would like to draw attention to the creation of a public sphere by reformist organizations in a way that reminds one of the evangelical activities in Britain. I want to look briefly at the construction of Hindu spirituality in the Brahmo Samaj and the Ramakrishna mission as well as at the construction of the Aryan race in the Arya Samaj.

One of the early instances of a Hindu public responding to colonial rule is the abolition of sati (widow immolation) by the British in 1829. Sati was perhaps the most definite sign of Hindu depravity and Christian moral superiority that evangelicals could get. Consequently they focused their campaign against native institutions on the abolition of this particular practice. They succeeded in convincing governor-general William Bentinck, who later also enacted Macaulay's Anglicist proposals for Indian education. A statue for Bentinck, erected soon after his departure from India in 1835, showed a sati scene under Bentinck's stern figure, and in an inscription on the rear of its base, it was recorded that Britain was now committed to "elevat[ing] the moral and intellectual character" of the Indian subjects.[46] Beneath the evangelical moralism, however, one may well detect a sexual fantasy of "white men saving brown women from brown men."[47]

More important than the evangelical actions and the government's responses is the position taken by "enlightened" citizens of Calcutta. Rammohan Roy (1772–1833), sometimes called "the father of the Bengal Renaissance," wrote a great deal on this subject between 1818 and 1832. In January 1830 Rammohan, together with three hundred residents of Calcutta, presented a petition to Bentinck in support of the regulation prohibiting sati. Rammohan rejected the practice on the basis of his reading of Hindu scripture. He distinguished authoritative sources (such as the Vedas) from other sources. It is interesting to note that he did not refer to any authoritative interpretation of these sources by learned gurus but relied entirely on his private, rational judgment. This is certainly an important step in the laicization of Hinduism. What we also see here is that scriptural authority can be referred to by a layperson without mediation of a sacred interpreter. One of Rammohan's most important objectives was to abolish the rules of the caste-based, hereditary qualification to study the Veda.[48] Following Lata Mani, I would suggest that the colonialist insistence on the unmediated authority of written evidence for Indian traditions, enabled by the orientalist study of these texts, made possible a gradual shift in emphasis from the spoken to the written in Hinduism.[49] I would add, however, that the centrality of the text was also insisted upon by the evangelicals who railed against the sati practice. Rammohan's position participated in both the orientalist and the Protestant ways of thinking. His privileging of his own rational judgment, based on reading and discussion, enabled the rise of a public and a certain kind of public debate in Habermas's sense.

Rammohan was strongly influenced by English and American unitarianism, a Christian creed characterized by a rational and universalist theology as well as a social reformist conscience. He contributed to its theology an interesting tract, called *The Precepts of Jesus*, published in 1820. He was very interested in Christian theology and, to a certain degree, he was a unitarian, but as his involvement in the sati debate shows, he also remained a Hindu. In 1828 Rammohan founded the Brahmo Samaj. This was a small movement, propagating a deist and universalist kind of religion, based, however, on Hindu sources and especially the Upanishads and the philosophical commentaries on the Upanishads (together known as the Vedanta). It was particularly opposed to "superstitious customs" of "ignorant people," deceived by their Brahman leaders. The deception by Brahmans is a crucial point. It is, of course, tempting to see it as a straightforward adoption of British attacks on Brahmans, as, for example, in James Mill's *History of British India*, but I would suggest that it is a bit more complex. Roy himself came from a Brahman family and his attack is based on his reading of Brahmanical sources. The British attack on Brahman priests gave support to a particular argument against priesthood in a Brahmanical debate about religious authority. Christian rational religion and certain Brahmanical arguments, of long standing, fitted together quite well as the basis of a Hindu rational religion. Reason and "the dignity of human beings" became as important as for its Christian counterparts in Europe. Also interesting was its attempt to come to a universal religion, reminiscent of the Deist view that the great truths of religion were all universal and that true religion was ultimately natural religion, not bound to particular historical events of revelation that divided one religious community from another.[50]

I would like to stress the strong parallelism of the development of Indian and European "rational religion." There is, however, a crucial difference: whereas the European Christians tried to universalize their Christian tradition, Indian Hindus did the same with their Hindu tradition. This reproduced the Hindu-Christian opposition, which was also the colonized-colonizer opposition. Colonialism provides the discursive frame in which Hindu rational religion emerges. As Ranajit Guha demonstrates, this is also clear in the work of someone outside the circle of the Brahmo Samaj, the humanist thinker Bankimchandra Chattopadhyay (1838–94), who was very much influenced by August Comte.[51] Bankimchandra (again a Brahman), like many European thinkers, centers his view of "humanness" (*manusyatva*) on the notion of the perfectibility of man. In contrast to European thinkers, however, he thought it possible to give examples of *Adarsa Purush*, "ideal man," whose perfection had to be emulated. These examples were taken from Hindu religious history with, at the highest rank, the god Krishna. The most perfect man was thus a Hindu god.

The Enlightenment question about the nature of man had found in the colonial setting a particular answer in terms of religious nationalism.

The intellectual Vedantic and unitarian views of the Brahmos left them to an important extent isolated from the larger Bengali Hindu society. In this larger environment a particular Bengali brand of Vaishnava devotionalism had become important since the sixteenth century. This devotionalism focused on the god Krishna and on gurus who descended from the disciples of the great sixteenth-century guru Chaitanya. It is interesting to see that in the second half of the nineteenth century this devotional tradition had begun to exercise considerable influence on the rational religion of the Brahmos. In the 1860s Keshabchandra Sen (1838—84), one of the most influential Brahmo leaders, introduced devotional singing in the Brahmo congregational meetings.[52] He also no longer spoke English but Bengali. He moved to the rural outskirts of Calcutta and introduced an ascetic lifestyle among his followers. The next step seems to have been his encounter with the contemporary guru Ramakrishna (1836—86), a priest in a temple for the mother goddess Kali in Calcutta. In his two newspapers (one in English, one in Bengali) he introduced Ramakrishna to the wider, reading public as a true saint in the authentic Hindu tradition. In that way he authorized this illiterate Hindu ascetic as an acceptable guru for the Hindu middle classes. In a recent book on Indian nationalism Partha Chatterjee portrays the meeting of these two personalities as constituting the "middle ground" occupied by the emergent middle classes, between European rational philosophy and Hindu religious discourse. In his view this "middle ground" enables the anticolonial nationalists to divide the world into two domains—the material, outer world, which is dominated by Western science, and the spiritual, inner world of the home, which is dominated by Hindu values.[53]

The spirituality of Hindu civilization, however, is not only signified by the home, but also by reformist and political action, such as much later in Gandhi's nonviolent action (satyagraha). The theme of Hindu spirituality in opposition to Western materialism definitely becomes the principal theme in Hindu nationalist discourse from this period onward. A major step in the popularization of Hindu reformist ideas was made by linking it to emergent nationalism. Hindu spirituality had to be defended against the onslaught of colonial modernity. Perhaps the most important expounder of the doctrine of Hindu spirituality has been the founder of the Ramakrishna mission, Vivekananda (1863—1902). Vivekananda was an extremely talented student who had been thoroughly educated in contemporary Western thought. He joined the Brahmo Samaj briefly before he met Ramakrishna.

The encounter with Ramakrishna had a transformative impact on the young Narendranath Datta, who adopted the name Vivekananda when he took his ascetic vows. As Tapan Raychaudhuri emphasizes, Vivekananda was "more than anything else a mystic in quest of the Ultimate Reality within a specific Indian tradition."[54] This tradition was vividly presented to Vivekananda not by learned discourse in which he himself was a master, but by the charismatic presence of a guru, Ramakrishna, whose trances had first been treated as insanity, but later became regarded as possession by the goddess. I want to argue that the articulation of Brahmo rational religion with the religious discourse of Ramakrishna produced the specific brand of Hindu spirituality that Vivekananda came to propagate.

The typical strategy of Vivekananda was to systematize a disparate set of traditions, make it intellectually available for a Westernized audience and defensible against Western critique, and incorporate it in the notion of Hindu spirituality carried by the Hindu nation, which was superior to Western materialism, brought to India by an aggressive and arrogant British nation. His major achievement was to transform the project to ground Hindu spirituality in a systematic interpretation of the Vedanta (the Upanishads and the tradition of their interpretation). This project, started with Rammohan Roy and which had produced rational Hinduism, was now combined with disciplines to attain perfection from the ascetic traditions in what Vivekananda called "practical Vedanta." The practical side also included participation in social reform. This kind of spiritual Hinduism was later carried forward by Mahatma Gandhi and Sarvepalli Radhakrishnan, but it has also become a main inspiration for the current brand of Hindu nationalism today.

A good example of the construction of Hindu spirituality are Vivekananda's efforts to systematize disparate notions of ascetic practice in an ancient system of yoga that is now India's main export article on the spirituality market. Yoga is a Sanskrit word that can be translated as "discipline." The classical text is Patanjali's *Yoga-Sutras*, probably composed around the fifth century A.D. Vivekananda systematized this tradition in a doctrine of salvation, in which rational thought, Patanjali's ideas on meditation, social action, and religious devotion were combined. This is a new doctrine, although Vivekananda emphasized that it was "ancient wisdom." It is a remarkable step in systematizing Hindu spirituality as healthy for body and spirit. It is also noteworthy that Vivekananda's project got a major impetus when he was enthusiastically received in Europe and the United States. His visit to the World's Congress of Religions in Chicago in 1893 made him a celebrity in the United States and consequently in India also. His new status as international guru strengthened his view of India's contribution to world civilization.

A major element of Vivekananda's message was nationalist. He saw his project very much in terms of a revitalization of the Hindu nation. In 1897 he founded an ascetic order, the Ramakrishna mission, to make ascetics available for the nationalist task. National self-determination, social reform, and spiritual awakening were all linked in his perception. The Ramakrishna mission established itself throughout India and also outside India. It did not become a mass movement, but Vivekananda's rhetoric of spiritualism exerted an immense influence on the way Hindu gurus in the twentieth century came to communicate their message. Vivekananda transformed Hindu discourse on asceticism, devotion, and worship into the nationalist idiom of "service to the nation" for both men and women.

Vivekananda's construction of Hindu spirituality gave notion of self-sacrifice a new meaning that drew simultaneously from Hindu traditions of devotion (*bhakti*) and evangelical notions of female morality. In this complex mixture, femininity is the signifier of Hindu spirituality, while actual women should be self-sacrificing in accordance with both Victorian notions of domesticity and Hindu notions of total devotion to their husbands. The abolition of sati by the colonial government thus set a far-reaching series of Hindu responses in motion, which ultimately led to the formation of a modern conception of spirituality through which the Hindu nation got defined.

While gender was the dominant issue in the prohibition of sati and crucial to the definition of Hindu spirituality with its emphasis on feminine devotion and self-sacrifice,[55] race and caste formed the dominant issue in the formation of Hindu Aryanism. The mutiny of sepoys of the Bengal army and the ensuing revolt in northern India in 1857 as well as its suppression in 1858 contributed immensely to the notion of racial and religious difference between the colonizers and the colonized. In this period of great anxiety about the loss of control over India, stories about inhuman atrocities inflicted on British women and children were rapidly circulated throughout Britain and confirmed the general view of the barbarity of the Indians already established in the depiction of sati. The suppression of the revolt demonstrated once and for all to the British that they were a superior race. This feeling was most clearly (and outrageously) expressed by Charles Dickens:

> I wish I were commander in Chief in India. The first thing I would do to strike that Oriental race with amazement (not in the least regarding them as if they lived in the Strand, London, or at Camden Town) should be to proclaim to them in their language, that I considered my holding that appointment by the leave of God, to mean that I should do my utmost to exterminate the Race upon whom the stain of the late cruelties rested; and that I was . . . now proceeding, with all convenient dispatch and merciful swiftness of execution, to blot it out of humankind and raze it off the face of the earth."[56]

Evangelicals, however, argued that the British had not taken their civilizing mission as a superior race serious enough. They took the events as divine judgment upon Britain for her sins as a nation. These sins consisted largely of a neglect by the company to promote the gospel. On Sunday, 7 October 1857, a great number of churches in Britain, both Anglican and Nonconformist, participated in "a day of national humiliation," proclaimed by Queen Victoria.[57] In the sermons of that day almost every preacher agreed to the necessity of wiping out that humiliation, repressing the revolt by military means, and inflicting retribution on the Indian population. The Christian qualities of some of the British officers during the revolt were extolled at great length, just as Henry Havelock attributed his victory at Fatehpur "to the blessing of Almighty God on a most righteous cause, the cause of justice, humanity, truth, and good government in India."[58] In the longer run, however, the revolt convinced most colonial officers that conversion to Christianity was an uphill struggle and reinforced the idea that religious neutrality was essential to colonial rule. For them it became difficult to see how the Indian barbarians would ever become equal to British Christians. Lord Canning dismissed the evangelical Herbert Edwardes, commissioner of Peshawar, as "exactly what Mahomet would have been if born at Clapham instead of Mecca."[59] Racial difference between the British and the colonized, and among the colonized themselves, became the explanation and legitimation of colonial rule.

While this reinvigorated racism in India colluded with the rise of racial nationalism in the metropolis, at the level of scientific thought the notion that the higher castes of India belonged to the same Aryan race as the British was widely accepted. In India the idea of race had to be combined with that of culture or civilization to explain why the British as "younger brothers" of the Aryan family had to guide the "older brothers" to civilization. This intervening cultural element continued to be religious difference. The story of the Aryan race in India was a story of decline, caused by a variety of things, such as racial mixing or climate, but especially by the inherent barbarity of Hindu polytheism.

Ideas of race were not exclusively theoretical, but also informed recruiting patterns for the army, which included "martial" races, such as the Punjabi Sikhs, and excluded "effeminate" races, such as the Bengalis. Another important distinction was between the Aryans and the Dravidians in southern India. The missionary Robert Caldwell based his linguistic and ethnological theories about Dravidian languages and peoples on that distinction. In the second half of the nineteenth century he developed a myth of the Aryan (Brahmanical) invasion of southern India and the subsequent subjection of the Dravidian people to a Hindu caste system in which the invaders were on top. His argument was meant to support his own missionary work among the "original" Dravidian population by delegitimizing Brahman priests, but ultimately his theory of a Dravidian race was used in the south for political purposes that had nothing to do with Christian conversion.[60]

The Aryan race theory was taken up in northern India by Hinduism's most important reformist movement, the Arya Samaj. Its founder, Swami Dayananda Sarasvati (1824–83), was one of India's many gurus in the nineteenth century. He was initiated in the order of the Shivaite Dasha-namis, a prestigious Hindu ascetic order that allowed only Brahmans to take the ascetic vows. Like other ascetics of his order, Dayananda traveled through India, visiting sacred places. He became rather successful and seemed on his way to form his own, limited community of ascetic and lay followers. In 1872 Dayananda visited the Brahmo leader Debendranath Tagore in Calcutta for four months. This visit seems to have transformed his style. He abandoned his ascetic robe and exchanged his use of Sanskrit oratory for Hindi.[61]

Dayananda did already have a strong reformist sense that Hindu religion had degenerated and that it had to be revitalized. In his own representation he had been summoned by his own, blind guru of the Dashanami order to campaign for a return to a pristine Hinduism based on the Vedas. This was a command entirely within the Hindu discursive tradition, in which the Vedas are seen as the ultimate, authoritative source of knowledge. Before Dayananda appeared on the stage, it was, however, more or less an imaginary source. Knowledge of the Vedas was transmitted in Brahman families, largely orally, with some help from manuscripts. Moreover, the Vedas are lengthy, obscure texts, riddled with internal contradictions, by no means a straightforward source for authorization of human practice. In this period, however, Max Muller, the towering figure of orientalist scholarship in Britain, had provided a definitive edition and translation of the Rg-Veda, financially underwritten by the East India Company. This was one of the major gifts brought to India by the prince of Wales on his tour in 1875–76. Dayananda thus accepted the degeneration doctrine, implicit in the Aryan theory. Hinduism as it actually existed was a degeneration of a pristine Aryan religion, as laid down in the Vedas.

It is not possible to follow here in any detail the development of Dayananda's thinking and of the movement, Arya Samaj (the Society of Aryans), that he founded in Bombay in 1875. Let me just summarize the points that made Dayananda's Aryan religion (*Arya Dharm*) a radically new religious program. First of all, he proposed to get back to the basic Vedic texts, to supersede the traditional commentators of these texts. He provided his own Sanskrit commentaries to these texts, in which he sought to show that all the scientific knowledge of the West in fact was already present in the Vedic revelation. He spoke of the Vedic teachings of telecommunications, about the construction of ships and aircraft, and about gravity and gravitational attraction. The importance given to science and its appropriation is, of course, extremely significant. Vedic religion was a universal, rational religion of an Aryan people. It was the cradle of all human civilization. In this we can see the influence of the rational religion arguments in Calcutta.

Like the Brahmos, Dayananda argued that the Vedic revelation was monotheistic. A monistic argument could very well be developed from an early medieval interpretation of the Upanishads by Shankara, the founder of the Dashanamis, the order to which Dayananda belonged. Moreover, there is also a monotheistic tendency in the ascetic orders that focus their meditation on one god. Dayananda, however, wanted to obscure the reference to many gods in the Vedic hymns. He did not use the traditional Hindu argument that one particular god is higher than all the other gods (or that he encompasses all the others). He wanted to get rid of the Hindu pantheon and the practice of image worship.

In the nineteenth-century European evolutionary worldview monotheism was seen as the highest form of religion. A religion had to be monotheistic to be rational and to allow a scientific understanding of the world. In that sense Dayananda's discourse on Hindu monotheism looks derivative, but I would like to draw attention to the very specific Hindu, discursive underpinnings. The reference to the Vedas, the monism of the Vedanta, and the monotheism of the Shivaite and their depreciation of image worship are all present in Dayananda's thinking. The lay response to Dayananda's message was also very much predetermined by existing Hindu discursive frames. Dayananda's rejection of image worship limited the appeal of his message considerably. Image worship is dominant in popular Hinduism and it is inconceivable that a radical iconoclastic movement would succeed in India. The Arya Samaj did, however, have a considerable following in the Punjab, where one finds a long history of imageless worship.

Second, an important point in Dayananda's program was an attack on the caste system, which he saw as a degeneration of the original, natural ordering of Vedic society in four functional groups: priests, warriors, traders, and servants. This natural order was entirely rational and functional, if only because it was based on achievement rather than ascription. Dayananda's privileging of this ancient social hierarchy may have been related to the fact that the census operations, starting in the 1870s, tried to use it to rank actual castes (whose social relations were only salient on a regional basis) hierarchically on an all-India basis. As Bernard Cohn has powerfully argued, the census operations enhanced the importance of caste distinctions in the new arenas for competition created by the British. Dayananda's solution to take over the all-India grid of the census, explain it in functional terms, and do away with actual hereditary caste relations was original and radical. It was used much later in Gandhi's social philosophy to include the untouchables in the Hindu nation.[62]

More than anything else this meant in the Arya Samaj that everyone—regardless of caste—could become priest and officiate in the principal rite of the Arya Samaj, the Vedic sacrifice, which is commonly the strict prerogative of Brahmans. Despite his emphasis on Brahmanical scripture and Brahmanical ritual, Dayananda launched a direct attack on the ritual hegemony of Brahman priests. Dayananda continued a discourse on priesthood that, as we have seen with Rammohan Roy, has its roots both in Brahmanical debates and in colonial attacks on Brahmans. Dayananda took his attack one crucial step further by allowing non-Brahmans to perform the Vedic sacrifice. While this had a *Wahlverwantschaft* with the aspirations of a new class of English-educated Indian officials, Dayananda's program was too radical for many. Again, it had most of its appeal in the Punjab, where religions like Sikhism had done away not only with the worship of images but also with Brahman priesthood. We have to see the radical novelty of Dayananda's program: the Arya Samaj became a religious community in which all religious power gravitated toward the laity. After his death, Dayananda was not succeeded by another guru but by a committee of lay members.

A third important point of innovation was the great emphasis the Arya Samaj put on education. A large number of schools were founded in the Punjab and elsewhere that continue to attract many non-Arya Hindu students. This kind of social activity made the Arya Samaj, into a strong competitor of the Christian missions. Following the Arya Samaj a great number of religious movements, with or without a core of ascetic gurus, entered the quickly expanding fields of education, social welfare, and medical care. The Arya Samaj had discovered the larger Indian public as the target of internal missionization. Special rituals were devised to purify those who had been converted to other religions and to bring them back to the Hindu fold. The larger Indian public also came to include those who had left India as indentured laborers to work in British plantations overseas. Arya Samaji missionaries were sent to these areas and had considerable success in them.

What we see here is that the Arya Samaj became an important factor in creating a Hindu public. It brought the debate about the nature of Hinduism in a much more direct manner to the popular masses than Rammohan or Bankim had been able to do. Dayananda's message developed in the colonial context from important Hindu discursive traditions and remained close to them. Dayananda was a prolific writer and talker constantly in debate with other Hindu leaders, following again an old tradition of the public contestation of religious opinion (*shastrartha*). At the end of his life he found the revolutionary issue, the protection of Mother Cow against British and Muslim butchers, which introduced mass participation in the public sphere.

Conclusion

I hope to have conveyed that (1) religion has been crucial in the making of the modern nation-state in both Britain and India; (2) the processes of nation building in these two countries have been connected through empire; and (3) the imperial relation has affected the location of religion in Britain and India. The modern state depends in liberal theory on the formation of a civil society, consisting of free but civilized subjects, as well as on the formation of a public sphere for the conduct of rational debate. In that theory the notions of freedom and rationality are defined in terms of secularity. I have tried to show that, contrary to theory, religion is a major source of rational, moral subjects and a major organizational aspect of the public spheres they create. Antislavery societies, Bible societies, anti-Catholic agitation, antisati petitions, Ramakrishna missions, cow-protection movements—what they all have in common is the creation of public spheres of political interaction central to the formation of national identities. The moral tenor of these movements is essential to understanding the mission of empire as well as the mission of anticolonial nationalism.

I hope also to have demonstrated that the supposition that the British polity is secular and the Indian religious is false. I have suggested that a sharp, structural distinction between nation and state cannot be made. In the modern period the nation-state is produced as a hyphenated entity, that is to say that they go together. There is, of course, a liberal notion that the state is outside civil society and can be criticized by civil society, which limits the power of the state, but it seems to me that the modern state is not an entity but a nexus of projects and arrangements through which society is organized. The externality of the state is an effect of these projects. It is especially through the project of education and through legal arrangements that the modern subject is formed. As Mauss suggested, language, race, and religion are also constructed in the process of nation-state formation. This is true for both the metropolis and the colony. The moral mission of the modern state is to organize the health, wealth and welfare of its citizens, and to be able to do that, it has to get to know them through various projects of documentation, such as the census.[63] The extent to which this knowledge is gathered through religious categories and the extent to which distribution of power and services is done through religious organizations are perhaps indices of the religiosity or secularity of a particular society.

I have not dealt with this here, but it might be the case that in the twentieth century, churches and other religious organizations gradually lost their previous importance in the organization of the nation-state in

Britain as compared to labor organizations and political parties. Such a shift might be enabled by the growing centrality of scientific race theories in the definition of the British nation as compared to Christianity. Britain's growing imperial power in the second half of the nineteenth century certainly allowed for racial fantasies of superiority. Moreover, the conceit of religious neutrality that was thought essential to imperial rule (perhaps even more after the revolt of 1857 than before) made race a better marker of difference than religion. At least it allowed some government officials to steer away from the constant evangelical pressure to promote Christianity in India. These imperial designs of religious neutrality (a neutrality it did not have in the metropolis), however, did not prevent Indians from seeing it as a moral state with a definite Christian morality.

Obviously, the crucial difference between the modern state in the metropolis and in the colony is that in the former, political legitimacy is in terms of the nation, citizenship, and national identity, whereas in the latter, the subjects are excluded from citizenship, while their national identity is either denied or denigrated. Religious and racial difference are both legitimations of differences of power. That is why anticolonial nationalisms are not only struggles for power in the political arena, but also attempt to counter the cultural hegemony of the colonial theory of difference. They often do so, as in the cases discussed here, by posing an alternative interpretation of the grounds of hegemony, whether religion or race. Vivekananda posed the superiority of Hinduism's spirituality over and against Western materialism. In doing so he denied that Britain's Christianity possessed a superior morality that allowed the British to rule India. Britain's ascendancy was, in his view, only a material one, which in fact had jeopardized the spiritual value British Christianity might have had. Dayananda took the Aryan race theory over from orientalism, but instead of accepting the theory that Christianity was to redeem the "fallen state" of Hindu civilization, he proposed a return to Vedic religion, which had preceded Christianity and was the very origin of all morality.

Notes

1. Quoted in Talal Asad, *Genealogies of Religion: Discipline and Reasons of Power in Christianity and Islam* (Baltimore, Md.: Johns Hopkins University Press, 1993), 244.

2. Quoted in Keith Robbins, "Religion and Identity in Modern British History," in Stuart Mews, ed., *Religion and National Identity*, Studies in Church History, vol. 18 (Oxford: Blackwell, 1982), 465.

3. T. N. Madan, "Secularism in Its Place," *Journal of Asian Studies* 46 (1987): 748.

4. Ibid., 749.

5. Ibid., 753.

6. Ibid., 753–54.

7. Marcel Mauss, "La nation," in *Oeuvres* (Paris: Les Editions de Minuit, 1969), 3: 592–93.

8. Ibid., 596.

9. Ibid., 604.

10. Timothy Mitchell, "The Limits of the State: Beyond Statist Approaches and Their Critics," *American Political Science Review* 85 (1991): 93.

11. Jürgen Habermas, *The Structural Transformation of the Public Sphere: An Inquiry into a Category of Bourgeois Society* (Cambridge: MIT Press, 1989).

12. Margaret C. Jacob, *Living the Enlightenment: Freemasonry and Politics in Eighteenth-Century Europe* (Oxford: Oxford University Press, 1992).

13. David Zaret, "Religion, Science, and Printing in the Public Spheres in Seventeenth-Century England," in Craig Calhoun, ed., *Habermas and the Public Sphere* (Cambridge: MIT Press, 1992), 212–36.

14. John Wolffe, *God and Greater Britain: Religion and National Life in Britain and Ireland, 1843–1945* (London: Routledge, 1994), 22.

15. Élie Halévy, *The Birth of Methodism in England*, trans. and ed. Bernard Semmel (Chicago: University of Chicago Press, 1971); Edward P. Thompson, *The Making of the English Working Class* (Harmondsworth: Penquin, 1977).

16. Quoted in Boyd Hilton, *The Age of Atonement: The Influence of Evangelicalism on Social and Economic Thought, 1795–1865* (Oxford: Clarendon Press, 1988), 209–10.

17. Quoted in Hilton, *The Age of Atonement*, 210.

18. William Carey, *An Enquiry into the Obligations of Christians to Use Means for the Conversion of the Heathens* (Leicester: Ann Ireland, 1792).

19. Brian Stanley, "Christian Responses to the Indian Mutiny of 1857," in W. J. Sheils, ed., *The Church and War*, Studies in Church History, vol. 20 (Oxford: Blackwell, 1983), 278.

20. Hilton, *The Age of Atonement*, 26.

21. Ibid., 340.

22. Hugh Tinker, *The Ordeal of Love: C. F. Andrews and India* (Delhi: Oxford University Press, 1979).

23. Lynn Zastoupil, *John Stuart Mill and India* (Stanford, Calif.: Stanford University Press, 1994).

24. Samuel Taylor Coleridge, *On the Constitution of the Church and State* (London: Hurst, Chance, 1830).

25. William E. Gladstone, *The State in Its Relations with the Church* (London: Murray, 1838).

26. Gladstone, quoted in Richard Helmstadter and Paul Phillips, eds., *Religion in Victorian Society: A Sourcebook of Documents* (Lanham, Md.: University Press of America, 1985), 82–89.

27. Hilton, *The Age of Atonement*, 341.

28. Thomas Arnold, *Principles of Church Reform* (London: Fellowes, 1833).

29. Zastoupil, *John Stuart Mill and India*.

30. Robbins, "Religion and Identity in Modern British History," 470–71.

31. This section is largely based on a discussion of Irish, Scottish, and Welsh nationalisms in Wolffe, *God and Greater Britain*.

32. Ibid., 69.

33. Ibid., 37.

34. John Henry Newman, *Apologia Pro Vita Sua* (London: Longman, 1864).

35. John Wolffe, *The Protestant Crusade in Great Britain, 1829–1860* (Oxford: Clarendon Press, 1991).

36. Ibid., 309.

37. Quoted in Robbins, "Religion and Identity in Modern British History," 471.

38. Robert J. C. Young, *Colonial Desire: Hybridity in Theory, Culture, and Race* (New York: Routledge, 1995), 47.

39. Quoted in Gauri Viswanathan, *Masks of Conquest: Literary Study and British Rule in India* (New York: Columbia University Press, 1989), 19.

40. Young, *Colonial Desire*, 71.

41. Viswanathan, *Masks of Conquest*, 102.

42. Geoffrey A. Oddie, *Hindu and Christian and South-East India* (London: Curzon Press, 1991), 57.

43. Brian Stanley, *The Bible and the Flag: Protestant Missions and British Imperialism in the Nineteenth and Twentieth Centuries* (Leicester: Apollos, 1990), 61.

44. Viswanathan, *Masks of Conquest*, 117.

45. Peter van der Veer, *Religious Nationalism. Hindus and Muslims in India* (Berkeley: University of California Press, 1994).

46. Thomas R. Metcalf, *Ideologies of the Raj* (Cambridge: Cambridge University Press, 1994), 95.

47. Gayatri Spivak, "Can the Subaltern Speak?" in Cary Nelson and Lawrence Grossberg, eds., *Marxism and the Interpretation of Culture* (Urbana: University of Illinois Press, 1988), 271–313.

48. Wilhelm Halbfass, *India and Europe: An Essay in Understanding* (Albany: SUNY Press, 1988), 205–6.

49. Lata Mani, "Contentious Traditions: The Debate on *Sati* in Colonial India," in Kumkum Sangari and Sudesh Vaid, eds., *Recasting Women: Essays in Colonial History* (New Brunswick, N.J.: Rutgers University Press, 1990), 88–126.

50. Charles Taylor, *Sources of the Self: The Making of the Modern Identity* (Cambridge: Harvard University Press, 1989), 273–74.

51. Ranajit Guha, *A Construction of Humanism in Colonial India: The Wertheim Lecture* (Amsterdam: CASA, 1993).

52. David Kopf, *The Brahmo Samaj and the Shaping of the Modern Indian Mind* (Princeton, N.J.: Princeton University Press, 1979).

53. Partha Chatterjee, *The Nation and Its Fragments: Colonial and Postcolonial Histories* (Princeton, N.J.: Princeton University Press, 1993).

54. Tapan Raychaudhuri, *Europe Reconsidered* (Delhi: Oxford University Press, 1988).

55. Peter van der Veer, "Gender and Nation in Hindu Nationalism," in Hans Antlov and Stein Tonneson, eds., *Asian Forms of the Nation* (Richmond: Curzon Press, 1996), 188–213.

56. Charles Dickens, "The Perils of Certain English Prisoners" (1857), quoted in Young, *Colonial Desire*, 120–21.

57. Stanley, "Christian Responses to the Indian Mutiny of 1857" 279.

58. Ibid., 288.

59. Quoted in Metcalf, *Ideologies of the Raj*, 48.

60. See Nicholas Dirks, "The Conversion of Caste: Location, Translation, and Appropriation," in Peter van der Veer, ed., *Conversion to Modernities: The Globalization of Christianity* (New York: Routledge, 1995), 115–37.

61. Kenneth Jones, *Arya Dharm: Hindu Consciousness in nineteenth-Century Punjab* (Berkeley: University of California Press, 1976), 34.

62. Bernard Cohn, *An Anthropologist among the Historians and Other Essays* (Delhi: Oxford University Press, 1987).

63. Bernard Cohn and Nicholas Dirks, "Beyond the Fringe: the Nation State, Colonialism, and the Technologies of Power," *Journal of Historical Sociology* 1 (1988): 224–30.

3

Protestantism and British National Identity, 1815–1945

HUGH McLEOD

LINDA COLLEY in her influential *Britons: Forging the Nation, 1707–1837* argues persuasively that the most powerful factor in the making of British national identity was war against "a powerful and persistently threatening France," "the haunting embodiment of the Catholic Other that Britons had been taught to fear since the Reformation in the sixteenth century"— and goes on to cite Margaret Thatcher and her father, Alderman Roberts, as examples of the continuing vitality of Francophobia.[1] In the century following Napoleon's defeat, war bulked much less large in the national consciousness than it had in the previous century and a quarter. All of the wars in which the United Kingdom was involved took place in distant parts of the globe. None involved fighting against the French, and in the Crimea the old enemy was actually an ally. Furthermore, with the Catholic Emancipation of 1829, the United Kingdom ceased to be a Protestant state. There might therefore, seem to be good reasons to suppose that those forces that had come together in the forging of the nation were now spent, and that Britain would begin to fall apart in the nineteenth century or else that national identity would be rebuilt on new foundations.

It is evident that Britain did not fall apart, and in fact older sources of identity retained much of their force. In particular, I argue that a Protestantism defined by its uncompromising anti-Catholicism remained central until about 1860. In the period between 1860 and the World War I, Protestantism was still one of the most important components of national identity. But the nature of the Protestant faith was changing, and new foundations for national identity were emerging, sometimes in conjunction with, and sometimes in tension with, the older Protestantism. During the era of the two world wars British national identity was no longer specifically Protestant, but a more generalized Christianity remained an essential component. Finally, in the period since 1945, this Christian basis has also dwindled away.

In view of the very different evolution of the relationship between religious and national identities in Ireland, I concern myself only with

England, Scotland, and Wales, ignoring the fact that a British national identity has been, and still is, held by many Irish Protestants. I also limit myself to those aspects of national identity shared by English, Scots, and Welsh, and am not concerned with different forms British nationalism took in these three countries, or with specifically English, Scottish, or Welsh nationalisms. In spite of the cultural and institutional differences between the three countries, and the continuing importance of Welsh, Scottish, and English identities, the forces binding the three countries together were throughout the period from 1815 to 1945 considerably stronger than those that pulled them apart. These included a common Protestantism, a common investment in the empire, and loyalty to the monarchy. But a fourth factor is often overlooked, and yet is perhaps most important of all: namely the fact that until very recently the three main national political parties have been genuinely national, drawing voters and leaders in significant numbers from all three countries. The most striking example was the Liberal Party under W. E. Gladstone, the most popular political leader Britain has ever known. An essential part of Gladstone's appeal was his Britishness, symbolized by the fact that he was born in England to Scottish parents, represented Scottish constituencies in Parliament, but lived in Wales.[2] By the same token, one of the most potent factors in the recent collapse of Scottish Conservatism and in the growth of separatist feeling was the perception of Margaret Thatcher as a specifically English politician, indifferent to Scottish interests. I should add that throughout this period, with very few exceptions, social and religious conflicts within England, Scotland, and Wales were more significant than national conflicts between the English, Scots, and Welsh. The Scottish Disruption of 1843 is sometimes cited as an exception to this rule, but I am persuaded by Callum Brown's argument that the decisive role in the Disruption was played by social tensions within Scotland.[3]

One other assumption needs to be stated at the outset. The significance of the various forms of national identity lay not only in the fact that they enabled the British to define themselves in relationship to those peoples whom they fought or colonized, or with whom they competed economically. Equally important was the fact that rival conceptions of national identity enabled them to define themselves vis-à-vis other Britons.[4] And for most people most of the time the most dangerous enemies were those nearest to home. From an Indian point of view, as Peter van der Veer points out, differences between one Briton and another may have seemed of very minor significance. From the point of view of most Britons the differences between different churches or political parties, or between secularists and believers, were often of more immediate concern than relationships with other nations, peoples, or races. Although much of this essay concerns ideas, symbols, and self-images shared by most Britons, I suggest that their meaning and practical applications were often bitterly disputed.

A Favored Nation

Five definitions of national identity occur continually throughout the century after Waterloo. Britain was Christian, Protestant, prosperous, civilized, and free. Of course the relative importance attached to these different points varied over time and with the members of different social classes, political parties, or religious communities. Many Catholics, Jews, and agnostics bought part of the package, while rejecting the rest. More remarkable is how widely the whole package was bought.

Of course, identity is always defined most sharply in juxtaposition to a hostile or conspicuously alien Other, and plenty of candidates were available for this role. Rather than the French playing the role of star villain, there was now a series of villains, whose importance fluctuated. Indeed, each of the components of national identity mentioned above was defined in juxtaposition to a different Other.

One major change, which Linda Colley does not treat sufficiently, is the fact that Britain's Christianity, rather than its Protestantism, was emphasized by the contrast with France. After 1793 France was seen primarily as a nation of scoffing infidels rather than of idolatrous Catholics. This perception of France, at least in the eyes of the dominant sections of society, was further emphasized as a result of the religious revival that gripped the British middle and upper classes in the years after 1815. Weekly churchgoing became normal in those classes; such pious practices as family prayers became widespread, and the British Sunday served as a symbol of national devotion and rectitude. British seriousness contrasted with French frivolity, British rectitude with French immorality, and British faith with French skepticism. This particular form of critique of the French had a long life. It was certainly in Alderman Roberts's mind in 1940 when he claimed that the French were "corrupt from top to bottom," and it was also in the mind of a writer in the Anglican *Church Times* that same year when he began by blaming the Fall of France on "bourgeois atheism"— though admittedly he went on to place part of the blame on Catholicism and its alleged affinities with fascism.[5]

The other, and increasingly important comparison was between British Christianity and the ignorance, superstition, and cruelty of "the heathen." The first great upsurge of British interest in overseas missions took place in the 1790s and was focused on India. Interest in missions fluctuated during the nineteenth century and seems to have reached its highest point in the 1890s, by which time Africa had become a second major focus.

Throughout this period missionary propaganda highlighted not only the falsity of heathen beliefs but also the various forms of cruelty or oppression that non-Christian religions were alleged to encourage or tolerate. Around 1800, the main impetus to missionary activity was fear for the souls of those who died without Christ. Around 1900, missionary propaganda placed as much or more stress on the sufferings of the heathen in the present world and the material as well as spiritual benefits that would follow conversion. This new emphasis therefore tended to highlight the contrast between Christian enlightenment and humanitarianism, and heathen cruelty. The binding of feet in China, the killing of widows in India and of twins in Nigeria, the practice of slavery in Zanzibar, and the practice of cannibalism in New Guinea all received extensive publicity.[6]

For nineteenth-century British Protestants, the supreme embodiment of the Catholic Other was not France but Ireland. The Irish were feared and also despised. They were feared because of the possibility of armed revolution in Ireland, the threat to national security posed by Irish nationalist soldiers in the British army, the assassinations carried out by Irish secret societies, and the possibility that Ireland might provide a stepping-stone for foreign invaders. They were despised because their poverty was seen as a result of drunkenness and fecklessness. A hostile Irish stereotype became widely current in nineteenth-century Britain, which presented "Paddy" as often charming, yet lazy, dishonest, irresponsible, and potentially violent. The roots of these alleged character traits were sometimes seen in racial differences between Anglo-Saxon and Celt, and indeed cartoonists frequently underlined the alleged racial difference by drawing apelike Irish caricatures. Yet other Celts, such as the Cornish, the Welsh, or the Scottish Highlanders were seldom defined as racially inferior, and certainly never described in such hostile terms as the Irish.[7]

Although racial terminology was often used loosely in British anti-Irish rhetoric, the main basis of British attacks on the Irish was an objection to their religion.[8] Their Catholicism was seen as a false religion, which placed exaggerated stress on showy externals of piety but bore none of the good fruit of sobriety, thrift, and industry by which a true religion was to be judged. They were seen as priest-ridden. Irish nationalist electoral successes were easily written off as a product of coercion, and huge village churches towering above shabby cottages were seen as the results of priestly skills in extortion. The main root of the antagonism between British Protestants and Irish Catholics lay, of course, in the question of the political relationship between the two islands, which dominated the political agenda for much of the nineteenth century, reaching a point of maximum urgency in 1886, when the Liberal Party split over this issue. But awareness of the Irish Catholic Other was further stimulated by the very considerable Irish Catholic immigration to Britain, which peaked in the years following the Famine of the 1840s. For a century after the Famine, some degree of sectarian tension remained a normal part of urban life in most parts of Britain.

While British Protestant perceptions of Catholicism in the nineteenth century were mainly defined by reference to Ireland, the Papacy also played a part, as did Mediterranean Catholic societies, such as Spain and Italy.[9] The triumph of Ultramontanism in the nineteenth-century Catholic Church provided "No Popery" militants with plenty of ammunition. The upsurge of Marian devotion and the official approval granted to Lourdes and other shrines were taken as evidence that Catholicism was intrinsically superstitious, while examples of misgovernment in the papal states suggested that the Church was also inefficient and oppressive. Nineteenth-century examples of Catholic intolerance, such as the imprisonment of two Protestants by the grand duke of Tuscany in 1852, were seized upon by Protestant propagandists, and the Spanish Inquisition continued to be remembered and evoked long after its demise. In the eyes of many Protestants, Roman Catholicism corrupted all areas of life. An encounter with a priest in Malta in 1878 led one Protestant missionary to reflect in his journal, "What is Italy today, but what thy corrupt teaching for centuries has made it? What is Spain? What is Ireland? Even in Malta thy vileness is everywhere conspicuous. Beggary, ignorance, blackguardism, crime,—these are the characteristic marks, with filth and poverty too." And Reverend J. E. C. Welldon, who was leaving the headmastership of Harrow to be bishop of Calcutta, though he expressed himself with a slightly greater degree of urbanity, was saying much the same when he asserted that, "If it were necessary to look for an assurance of the divine favour towards the nations that have shaken off the yoke of Rome, I should find it not so much in their success as in the principles by which the success has been mainly won, in the love of truth, intellectual freedom, religious equality, the right of private judgement, and the sense of personal, direct responsibility to God, which produce a more robust and virile type of national character than has been, or can be the product of sacerdotal authority."[10]

But, while British Protestant attitudes toward the Papacy and Irish Catholicism were unreservedly hostile, there was a degree of ambivalence in attitudes toward Mediterranean Catholicism. Italy and Spain certainly evoked images of indolence, corruption, and superstitition. Yet many dour northern Protestants felt the attraction of the sun, the flowers, the buildings, the art, the music—and perhaps also a certain freshness and spontaneity, which often seemed lacking in the dark north.

This reevaluation of the Catholic south became increasingly important in the twentieth century. But for most nineteenth-century Britons the proof of their own superiority lay in the nation's prosperity. Above all, in the third quarter of the century, when Britain's continuing position of economic supremacy was combined with significant improvements in real incomes for the majority of the population, patriots perpetually boasted of this supremacy, seeing therein the supreme vindication of the nation's political and religious institutions, its policy of free trade, and its national character.

Claims to relative prosperity had an objective basis in fact, even if the explanations advanced were sometimes fanciful. Civilization was an entirely subjective concept, but it provided a major part of the rationale for Britain's empire, and it became an increasingly prominent component of national identity as the empire bulked ever larger in Britons' perception of themselves during the nineteenth century. It was particularly attractive to those who had limited faith in Christianity or Protestantism and wanted to find a new basis for Britain's national mission. This was the position of Rudyard Kipling, British imperialism's most popular apologist around 1900.[11] Civilization also worked well in tandem with the racial ideas that were increasingly fashionable and influential in the later nineteenth century. Most obviously, civilization included such things as levels of education, scientific knowledge, and technology—areas in which comparisons betwen one people and another were relatively practicable. It also included the more intangible areas of culture and manners, where it was certainly possible to make comparisons between different peoples but very much harder to show that one stood at a higher level than another. Such value judgments were hardest of all in the area of morality, though acts of violence perpetrated by the victims of British conquests, especially those that involved particular cruelty or victimized women or children, were seized upon by apologists for British imperialism as evidence of the "uncivilized" character of the conquered.[12] For instance, early-twentieth-century school books presented most non-European peoples in terms of a series of hostile stereotypes: the Chinese were "cruel and vengeful," Morocco was "a monument of barbarism," and the African was "an overgrown child, vain, self-indulgent and fond of idleness."[13]

Boasts of British freedom had played a crucial part in the development of national identity in the eighteenth century, and at the time of the threatened French invasion in 1803, it seems that even those who were skeptical of the kind of freedom that Britain offered generally regarded the prospect of rule by Napoleon as being a good deal worse. In the nineteenth century an orthodox version of English history took shape in which the leitmotiv was the battle for freedom, fought in successive generations against tyrannical monarchs and foreign would-be invaders, and reaching its culmination in the Glorious Revolution of 1688. As Hugh Cunningham and Robert Colls have shown, this history was common ground shared by members of all social classes and each of the main political traditions—

though they differed widely as to where in the nineteenth century the logic of this history led. "Nineteenth century Liberalism," writes Colls, "represented English freedom as an ideal force, deep within the national character, and capable of universal dissemination as England's special gift to the world." In the 1880s, exactly the same claim was made by Ashmead Bartlett, the Conservative politician and apologist for the extension of "the beneficent Empire of Britain," who argued that "True liberty, civil and religious, the birthright of Englishmen, has become associated with the supremacy of England in every quarter of the globe." And in the 1880s and 1890s, both Fabian and Marxist socialists saw themselves as true heirs to this great national tradition.[14] In the twentieth century patriotic Britons would be able to seize on a series of foreign dictators as vivid embodiments of everything they believed their own country to be opposed to. The nineteenth century, after the fall of Napoleon, had no Hitler or Stalin, but there were plenty of lesser tyrants. In particular, Russia served for freedom lovers as a standing example of a state built on foundations of police terror, spying, censorship, and extreme social inequality, and thus as a favorite theme of British patriotic rhetoric.[15]

A Protestant People

Throughout the nineteenth century many people believed that the five dimensions of national identity were interrelated and that the linchpin was Protestantism. Churches and chapels, Sunday schools and day schools, and wide sections of the press all contributed to sustaining this belief.

Protestant consciousness was by no means limited to active church members or regular church attenders. Claims were often made at the time, and have been repeated by historians since, that those who did not attend services were heathen, pagans, or indifferent. It is now clear that this is a considerable oversimplification. Interviews by oral historians with people born in England or Wales in the last quarter of the nineteenth century have shown that the overwhelming majority were brought up as Protestants, Catholics, or Jews, and, if Protestant, as "church" or "chapel." In Scotland, denominational consciousness may have been even stronger; in his study of Aberdeen, MacLaren cites an 1837 survey that found that despite widespread nonattendance of services, 92 percent of those questioned claimed membership of a specific congregation. My own research on working-class areas of London in the later nineteenth and early twentieth centuries, as well as that of Jeff Cox and Sarah Williams, indicates that those who seldom attended church services often had strong religious beliefs, which may have differed at important points from the orthodoxies of church and chapel but were in their own eyes equally Christian. Such beliefs were often learned from parents, but they were also partly shaped by day school and Sunday school.[16]

Certainly much of the elementary school teaching of the later Victorian and Edwardian periods was intended to instill a strong sense of national identity, often with an explicit Protestant dimension. School manuals justified the teaching of history and geography mainly because of their patriotic uses, and a study of history textbooks from the Victorian and Edwardian periods noted how "religion, politics and patriotism often seemed inseparable" and that "writers compared the state of religion and civil liberty attained in England with that elsewhere and concluded that the English were uniquely blessed by providence." The English/British (the two terms tended to be used interchangeably) national character was frequently praised, whereas the Irish tended to receive condescending treatment, and the empire was justified on the grounds of the barbarism or cruelty of many of the subject peoples. Most writers showed a strong Protestant bias, which highly colored their treatment of such episodes as the church/state conflicts of the Middle Ages, medieval monasticism, the Reformation, and the Glorious Revolution. The crimes of Bloody Mary received extended coverage, whereas persecution of Catholics was seldom mentioned.[17]

The links were even stronger in the public schools, attended by young males of the upper and upper middle classes. Since most of the pupils in these schools were boarders, the possibilities of imposing a set of values on the pupils were much more promising than in the elementary schools, where children were subject to a host of other influences, including in many cases parental skepticism about the value of any form of schooling. The dominant features of the public schools in the period from the mid-nineteenth century to World War I were Anglicanism (the great majority of headmasters in this period were Anglican clergymen), the teaching of classics (knowledge of which was seen as the hallmark of the gentleman), the cult of sport (seen as the best form of character building), and a pervasive spirit of patriotism and imperialism.[18] Daily chapel services were an essential part of the public school regime, and headmasters frequently used chapel sermons as a means of either declaring school policy on a controversial issue or defining the school ethos in more general terms. H. H. Almond, headmaster of Loretto School near Edinburgh from 1862 to 1903 preached an annual "Waterloo sermon" on the day following the anniversary of the battle, in which he expounded the worldwide role he believed God had allotted to the British people, and urged the school's pupils to assume the positions of leadership that ought to be theirs. H. W. Moss, headmaster of Shrewsbury School from 1872 to 1908, combined an emphasis on the importance of military training for the defense of the empire with a belief that England had a unique role to play in bringing the gospel to the entire world. Welldon of Harrow subscribed to an unequivocally Protestant form of patriotism, according to which England had risen to "a position of unique greatness" since, and partly because of, the Reformation: "wherever there was a country that was stationary and retrogressive it was Catholic, wherever there was a people that was progressive and Imperial it was Protestant."[19]

The Sunday schools, which were attended by the great majority of working-class children in the later Victorian and Edwardian years, contributed to the strengthening of national identity by stressing on overseas missions.[20] Missionaries were presented as heroes to Sunday school children; the fact that many missionaries came from fairly modest backgrounds, and that by the 1890s many of them were women, added to their potential as role models. Moreover, lessons about missionaries were often popular because they tended to lead exciting lives in exotic parts of the world. The numerous missionary biographies published in this period mixed the genres of adventure story and tract. The biography of A. M. Mackay, a Scottish-born agent of the Church Missionary Society who died in 1890, is typical. Chapter titles include "Heathen Superstitions," "Cruelty of the Heathen," "Fiery Trials," and "Slave Raiding and the Slave Trade." The epigraph consists of words written by Mackay shortly after his arrival in Uganda in 1878:

> It is no sacrifice, as some think, to come here as pioneers of Christianity and of civilization. I would not give my position here for all the world. A powerful race has to be won from darkness to light; superstition and idolatry have to be overthrown; men have to be taught to love God and love their neighbour, which means the uprooting of institutions which have lasted for centuries; labour made noble, the slave set free, knowledge imparted and wisdom implanted; and above all that true wisdom taught which alone can elevate man from a brute to a son of God. Who would not willingly engage in such noble work, and consider it the highest honour on earth to be called to it?

Here were many characteristic themes—for instance, the belief that Christianity went hand in hand with civilization. (Mackay had earlier written that "In England it is true that as Christianity made progress, so civilization advanced; and as civilization advanced, Christianity became more deeply rooted, and shines now as the light of an enlightened people.") His judgment of the way of life of those he had come to convert was completely negative: they were "brutes," living in "darkness." Christianity would bring a comprehensive salvation, social and intellectual as well as spiritual.[21]

Meanwhile a large section of the press maintained a strongly Protestant stance, reinforced by cartoons that presented all aspects of Roman and Anglican Catholicism in the most derogatory light. John Bull was a sturdy no-nonsense Protestant, whereas Anglo-Catholic priests were feeble and effeminate, which could be told from the fact that they were often portrayed gazing up at the ceiling with their hands clasped in front of them, and wearing an otherworldly expression. Roman Catholic priests were dirty, disreputable, and cunning, which could be determined from the fact that they did not shave properly and did not look anyone in the eye. *Punch* perpetuated these stereotypes in innumerable cartoons for the benefit of a middle-class readership, while papers like *Lloyd's Weekly Miscellany* delivered the same kind of fare to a more popular audience.[22] The spirit of Protestant nationalism was also to some extent maintained by such traditions as the annual Guy Fawkes Day celebrations, with their processions through the streets and burning in effigy of the pope, Guy Fawkes, and local politicians or clergy.[23]

There are thus considerable areas of continuity between eighteenth-century forms of British national identity, as Linda Colley describes them, and nineteenth-century forms. In the mid-nineteenth-century there were still many people who saw Britain as an elect nation, a second Israel, with a divine mission to uphold and propagate pure Christianity. They saw Britain's prosperity as a divine reward, and they interpreted such calamities as cholera epidemics as punishments for the nation's failures in living up to the demands of this mission. They read Foxe and Bunyan, and they believed that the pope was the Antichrist, whose overthrow would herald the Second Coming.[24] Indeed this particular form of militant Protestantism enjoyed a revival in the 1830s and 1840s, as a result of the fears provoked by Catholic Emancipation and the growing strength of Catholicism in Ireland, and also because of the upsurge of eschatological speculation among Evangelical Protestants from the 1820s onward. The 1820s and 1830s saw the emergence of such organizations as the Protestant Reformation Society and the Protestant Association, which combined attacks on the Catholic Church and attempts to restrict its activities with efforts for the conversion of individual Catholics. In the 1840s they seemed to enjoy a very considerable following. They were supported by such influential figures as Lord Shaftesbury, and at the 1847 election Protestant campaigners persuaded about one-quarter of English and Scottish MPs to declare their oppositon to the schemes then being mooted for state endowment of the Roman Catholic Church in Ireland ("ruling Ireland through Rome," as Wolffe calls it).[25]

By 1849 the Protectionist Party had committed itself to anti-Catholicism—not, as its leader, Stanley, explained in a letter to his colleague, Disraeli, on grounds of principle, but because of a recognition that any state support for Roman Catholicism was "revolting the feelings of a great majority of English and Scottish people," and that the party that exploited this sentiment could hope for a lot of votes.[26] For a short time it seemed he might be right. The restoration of the Catholic hierarchy in England and Wales in 1850 saw the last nationwide outbreak of No Popery. Lord John Russell, the Whig prime minister who only a few years earlier had launched the abortive scheme for state endowment of the Catholic Church in Ireland, now tried to present himself as the nation's Protestant in chief by denouncing the pope and introducing an Ecclesiastical Titles Bill. It dominated the 1851 parliamentary session, but its significance was far more symbolic than practical. In the years immediately following there was a stalemate between those parliamentary forces that wanted more stringent measures to restrict Catholicism and those that favored modest measures of liberalization, as part of a general policy of extending the rights of religious minorities. Thus a bill to introduce state inspection of convents failed to get through Parliament, in spite of considerable support, but neither did a bill to introduce state-salaried Catholic prison chaplains. In fact, the outbreak of the Crimean War in 1854 was followed by the appointment of state-salaried Catholic army chaplains and the use of Catholic nuns as nurses. Since about one-third of the soldiers were Roman Catholic,[27] there was a very strong pragmatic case for providing them with Catholic chaplains, and arguments of this kind tended to weigh more heavily with governments of the time than those derived from Protestant or liberal principle. The alliance with Catholic/infidel France and Muslim Turkey was also distressing for many militant Protestants, though most persuaded themselves that such alliances were justified in the interests of curbing Russian expansion, and they were in any case somewhat reassured by the observation that the sultan was less intolerant of Protestants than the tsar.[28]

If in retrospect the war appears as a turning point in the decline of political Protestantism,[29] this is probably more a coincidence than a direct result of the war itself. The chief cause of this decline lay in the fact that whereas prejudice against Catholics and dislike of the Catholic Church continued to be widespread in nineteenth-century Britain and are far from dead today,[30] for most people, most of the time, other issues had a higher priority, and other enemies appeared more threatening. Similarly, though Protestantism continued to be a pervasive element of national culture, Protestants were deeply divided among themselves as to the meaning of their faith, and were seldom willing to unite against a common Catholic danger.

Militant Protestantism succeeded in putting down deep popular roots only where there was a sufficiently large local Catholic population to pose a direct and visible threat. In mainland Britain, there were only two such areas, namely Lancashire and the west of Scotland, and in both of these regions militant Protestantism established itself as a major force over several generations.[31]

External manifestations of this strong sectarian consciousness included distinctive patterns of employment and voting, the formation of Orange lodges, and periodic riots. Less visible reflections included residential segregation, vigorous hostility to mixed marriages, mutual stereotyping, and a rich local folklore of jokes, chants, or offensive nicknames.[32] Separate schooling for Catholic and Protestant children was normal in nineteenth—and twentieth-century Britain, but it did not necessarily lead to overt antagonism. In Lancashire, however, local traditions prescribed that St. Patrick's Day should be observed by fights between Protestant and Catholic schools. With the rise of professional sport at the end of the nineteenth century, football teams, and the rivalry between the Protestant Glasgow Rangers and the Catholic Glasgow Celtic in particular, soon became a major focus for sectarian antagonism.[33]

In this situation certain preachers won a large personal following, becoming symbols of Protestant identity and resistance to the Catholic threat. One such individual was George Wise, pastor of Liverpool's Protestant Reformers' Memorial Church and founder of the Protestant Party, which was represented on the city council from the early 1900s to the 1960s. His populist credentials were confirmed by spells in prison, and he provided much of the inspiration for Liverpool's biggest bout of sectarian rioting in 1909, which left one person dead, at least 157 Catholic families forced out of their homes in mainly Protestant neighborhoods, and at least 110 Protestant families forced out of their homes in mainly Catholic neighborhoods. At the subsequent official inquiry one of Wise's followers, when questioned about the pastor's open-air harangues, remembered that he had called for the Jesuits to be "driven out of England," and had alleged that Cardinal Manning had once declared his "desire to bend and to break, and to subjugate this imperial race," since if it could conquer England, "Romanism would be supreme in the whole world."[34]

New Foundations

Here then in 1909 was the same Protestant language and view of the world and the same identification of England with the Protestant cause that had been familiar for three centuries. Yet after about 1870 this form of Protestantism soon came to be regarded as "extreme" and its proponents as "fanatics."[35] This was partly because of growing religious pluralism and a more gradual process by which an increasingly wide range of religious options came to be tolerated. In the earlier part of the nineteenth century, in spite of the deep split between members of the established churches and those adhering to various free churches, evangelicalism united the overwhelming majority of the latter with a very considerable proportion of the former. But after 1860, there was a substantial growth both in Anglo-Catholicism and in agnosticism, and Roman Catholicism gradually won a reluctant acceptance in most parts of the country. In 1867 a nationwide tour by the anti-Catholic lecturer William Murphy brought fighting between Protestants and Catholics in many towns.[36] But after that date, such violence was largely confined to the Glasgow and Liverpool regions. Elsewhere, although Catholics continued to to be separated by concentration in Catholic neighborhoods, by attendance at separate schools, by major cultural differences, and sometimes by strong identification with Ireland, Protestants and Catholics gradually came to accept, if not exactly to like, one another, and politics and trade unionism, as well as the mingling of the two communities caused by mixed marriages, sometimes provided common ground.[37] At the same time the Protestantism of the Church of England was being undermined by the growth of Anglo-Catholicism, the most dynamic section of that church in the later nineteenth and early twentieth centuries. And the growth of agnosticism in the same period meant that there was a small but increasingly influential section of the population for whom Protestantism was largely or wholly irrelevant, and who found their principal sources of national identity elsewhere.

But equally important were the changes within Protestantism. Characteristic of the second half of the nineteenth century was a modified form of Protestant nationalism, according to which Britain was still a favored nation but no longer a chosen people; Britain's prosperity was more a natural consequence of Protestant virtues than a divine reward for the purity of its faith; and the Papacy, though opposed to the spirit of true Christianity, was not literally the Antichrist. A typical Protestant nationalist of the later nineteenth century was Hugh Price Hughes (1847–1902), the most famous Wesleyan Methodist preacher of his day, a Welshman who lived most of his adult life in England, readily identifying himself with the people of that country, and a Liberal Imperialist. His travels on the European continent and in the Middle East had made him a keen admirer of British rule, which, he believed, meant justice and efficiency. He thought the British had brought peace to India and claimed that "British rule was the best thing that could happen in this world to the dark races." One of his major arguments in favor of the Boer War was that the Africans would receive better treatment under British than under Afrikaner rule. Indeed he claimed that the British Empire was part of the divine plan. As a fierce critic of the Papacy, he was an admirer of the Italian national movement, and during a tour of Italy he visited—and even kissed—the tomb of his hero Mazzini. Yet in some respects he had moved some way from the ultra-Protestants of the midcentury. For instance, he favored home rule for Ireland. And indeed his feelings about

Catholicism were more ambivalent than appears at first sight. In Italy he visited not only the tomb of Mazzini but also that of his other hero, St. Francis. As a fervent admirer of Italian Renaissance art and architecture, he was acutely aware of the aesthetic deficiencies of his own much loved Nonconformist inheritance. While in Italy he became very friendly with a scholar-monk, and he came to distinguish between the Papacy and the "Ultramontane ring" that controlled the Church, and "true Catholicism," a much more liberal faith, enriched by a strong aesthetic sensibility. Another sign of change since the first half of the century was that rather than focusing on Britain's unique calling, Hughes spoke of the mission of the Anglo-Saxon races, which included most notably the United States. Indeed he looked forward to the day when a federation of Britain and the United States might be in a position to "put an end to bloodshed and anarchy" across the world.[38]

So Hughes's form of Protestant nationalism included some major changes of emphasis, in spite of the apparent continuities with the older forms. While Britain still had a God-given mission, it was now shared with other nations, notably the United States. While Protestantism was still the key to Britain's greatness, democracy and good government were ends in themselves, the pursuit of which could sometimes (as in Ireland) conflict with the interests of Protestantism. There was also a growing tendency to use racial terminology, albeit, in Hughes's case, in a loose and ill-defined way. While he appears to have believed that the many virtues (as well as some defects) he perceived in British life and in British rule overseas were primarily a product of British religion, he tended at times to speak as if the peculiar qualities of the Anglo-Saxon race were also relevant. He was not consistent in this, since he argued that the decline of France could ultimately be traced back to the failure of the Reformation in that country, and he was optimistic about what the French might achieve if only they became Protestants.[39] The most interesting point, however, is the element of ambivalence in Hughes's attitude toward Catholicism, and his willingness to admit that Britain's Protestant heritage was not a totally unmixed blessing.

The British middle and upper classes were in fact going through a cultural revolution in the period from the 1880s to World War I. "Puritan," a name Hughes still pronounced with pride, was beginning to be a term of abuse. France and Italy were beginning to seduce as well as repel. Nonconformist chapels were beginning to reflect, sometimes in startling ways, a newfound yearning for the "beauty of holiness." The Roman Catholic Church benefited from a steady flow of converts, among whom writers, artists, and Anglican clergy were particularly prominent. More significant, however, as an indicator of the cultural shift, was the rapid growth of the Church of England's Anglo-Catholic wing. Anglo-Catholicism was certainly a many-sided phenomenon, combining widely different theological and political tendencies, but one of the major factors in its growth was a widespread rejection of most of the things that the evangelicals of the early and middle years of the century had stood for. Evangelicals were losing ground in all directions—to Anglican and Roman Catholicism, to liberal Protestantism, and to agnosticism.[40]

Antipuritanism and the new aesthetic sensibility combined badly with ideas of Britain as a specially favored nation. Admittedly, Britons of every religious and political persuasion could take pride in the nation's literature, and each party had its own special favorites. But in music and art Britons suffered from a serious inferiority complex.[41] Whether they looked to France, Italy, or Germany, art and music lovers generally agreed that Britain's record was inferior, and Protestantism was one of the favored scapegoats. The new mood was reflected in novels such as E. M. Forster's *Where Angels Fear to Tread* (1905), in which Italy offers the light of salvation to the benighted English.

The changing relationship between Britain and Ireland also affected the nature of British national identity. In 1886 the Liberal Party split over the issue of home rule for Ireland. Most Nonconformists chose to put their Liberalism before their Protestantism and to stay with Gladstone. In doing so, they allied themselves with the forces of Irish nationalism, and implicitly accepted that Ireland's troubles were due as much to British misrule as to the harmful influence of the Roman Catholic Church.

Meanwhile, from the 1870s onward, the empire was playing an increasingly large part in national consciousness. From this time on, Conservative politicians were increasingly identifying their party with the empire as part of their strategy of winning over the new mass electorate by undercutting the Liberals' appeal to democratic and radical feeling. By the 1890s Liberal politicians like Lord Rosebery and Nonconformist preachers like Hughes were calling for a Liberal Imperialism. A succession of colonial wars kept the empire continuously in the news, and journalists, popular novelists, writers for boys' magazines, and authors of music-hall songs all gave increasing coverage to patriotic and imperial themes.[42] The important part played by patriotism and imperialism in the schools has already been mentioned. The great expansion of Christian missions in the 1880s and 1890s, directed above all at India and at the recently conquered African territories, added to this consciousness of empire.

The effects of these developments were ambiguous. On one hand, imperialism could be seen as growing directly out of Protestant nationalism. This possibility is indicated by John MacKenzie's study of the cults surrounding the four greatest "heroes of empire." Only the last of these, Lawrence of Arabia, was not seen as a religious man. The three greatest heroes of the Victorian empire—Sir Henry Havelock, David Livingstone, and George Gordon—were all devoutly evangelical Protestants, convinced that the British Empire was an instrument of Providence. Their heroism was widely seen to be rooted in their faith, and countless biographies presented them as role models for a rising generation of Christian soldiers, missionaries, and servants of the empire.[43] On the other hand, part of the attraction of the empire as a basis for national identity lay in the fact that, at a time of growing religious pluralism, its appeal transcended differences of denomination and belief. Indeed some of the most influential advocates of imperialism at the turn of the century were agnostics, such as Rudyard Kipling; Joseph Chamberlain, the colonial secretary; and Alfred Milner, the high commissioner on the Cape. Moreover, imperialism was frequently justified by reference to "scientific" ideas concerning race that had no necessary connection with Christianity and had often been framed in conscious opposition to it. And, as I suggest later, however Christian imperialism was in theory, the relationship was often less harmonious in practice.

During this period, racial terminology was becoming widely used and there was a growing tendency to explain British achievements as much in terms of the intrinsic qualities of the Anglo-Saxon race as of the superiority of the Protestant religion. Historians and anthropologists made an important contribution to the acceptance of these ideas. The middle and later decades of the nineteenth century saw the publication of a series of highly influential histories of the English people, beginning with Macaulay's classic work. Most of these assumed a continuity since Anglo-Saxon times, resulting from race, and the persistence of certain qualities, notably the love of freedom, which were seen as inherent in the Anglo-Saxon race. From about the 1860s, anthropologists were giving scientific authority to such concepts. Admittedly many people alternated in a vague and unconsidered way between the use of racial and religious terminology, and others consciously made use of both. But racial language potentially offered a new way of defining national identity for the growing number of those for whom the old Protestant language had lost much of its force.[44] One example was Alfred Milner, one of the most prominent imperialists of the early twentieth century, who described himself as "a British race patriot." His definition of the components of British national identity drew mainly on the language of Social Darwinism, mixed with a religious terminology too vague to have any precise meaning, and including no explicit reference to Protestantism:

> I am a Nationalist and not a Cosmopolitan. . . . A Nationalist is not a man who necessarily thinks his nation better than others, or is unwilling to learn from others. He does think his duty is to his own nation and its development. He believes that this is the law of human progress, that the competition between

nations, each seeking its maximum development, is the Divine order of the world, the law of Life and Progress. . . . My patriotism knows no geographical but only racial limits. . . . It is not the soil of England which is essential to arouse my patriotism, but the speech, the traditions, the spiritual heritage, the principles, the aspirations of the British race.[45]

Another indication of this tendency was the controversy provoked by a sermon at the Church Congress of 1898 in which Dr. Welldon, the headmaster of Harrow, claimed that Britain owed its greatness primarily to its Protestantism. The *Spectator* published a series of letters on the subject, including a vigorous defense of Welldon by the later Anglican bishop Hensley Henson and an equally robust attack by the Catholic monsignor John Vaughan. The main point to emerge from the correspondence was that the most popular alternative to the theory that national character was a product of religion was the theory that it was a product of inherited racial characteristics. This was the view taken by the editor himself, who closed the correspondence with an article titled "The Relationship between Religion and National Success," in which he claimed that "England is great because of the blood of her people, their energy, their freedom, and their industry, not because of their creed." Similarly, "The north of Ireland is more prosperous than the south of Ireland, because the north of Ireland is occupied, or at all events directed, by men of the Scoto-English breed." He fully granted that Protestantism was "a more nutritive creed than Romanism" and "nearer to ultimate truth." But even the best of religions could take a people no further than "the inherent powers of the race may admit."[46]

Protestant Nationalism in Decline

A striking example both of the increasing influence of racialist ideas and of the diminishing respectability of explicitly religious intolerance was the campaign against Irish Catholic immigration pursued by an influential group of Church of Scotland ministers in the 1920s.[47] The motives for this campaign seem to have included a desire to reassert the Kirk's leadership of the nation by espousing a cause that potentially united middle class and working class, churchgoers and non-churchgoers; and a need for scapegoats on whom responsibility could be pinned for the growing social tensions and the declining influence of Sabbatarianism and temperance. Rather than blaming the Catholic religion, as earlier generations of Scottish Presbyterians inevitably would have done, the authors of a report on Irish immigration presented to the General Assembly in 1923 disclaimed any hostility to Scottish Catholics, and declared that Irish Protestants were acceptable not only on the grounds of common religion but also because they belonged "to the same race as ourselves." Irish Catholics, on the other hand, were rejected on the grounds that they were racially alien. The report claimed that "God placed the people of this world in families, and history which is the narrative of His providence tells us that when kingdoms are divided against themselves they cannot stand. Those nations that were homogeneous in race were the most prosperous and were entrusted by the Almighty with the highest tasks." Leading a delegation to Sir John Gilmour, the secretary of state for Scotland, in 1926, one of the most powerful figures in the Kirk, John White, insisted that "They desired to discuss it as a racial and not as a religious question," and in a letter to Gilmour, he described Irish Catholics as "an inferior race."[48]

The parallels with developments in Germany and South Africa during the same period are evident. In all three countries, many Protestants were adopting ideas that linked racialist versions of nationalism with claims that their church had a special responsibility for its own people, and should champion them in their conflicts with other peoples.[49] Yet in Britain, Protestantism was distinctly two-edged as a basis for any kind of nationalism. The Protestant cult of the individual conscience quite frequently found expression in a willingness to put what was seen as obedience to God before loyalty to state or nation. One example of this can be seen in the ambivalent relationship between Protestant missions and British imperialism. Missionaries frequently welcomed extensions of British rule, whether on evangelistic, humanitarian, or simply patriotic grounds.[50] But in practice, relations between missionaries and the colonial authorities were often strained. The overriding concern of the former with winning converts to Christianity frequently obliged them to defend the interests of local Christians, or even of the local population more generally, in cases of conflict with the authorities.[51] On the other hand, colonial officials, as well as British traders and farmers, often regarded missions with skepticism or even hostility—whether under the influence of racialist ideas, which insisted on the futility of attempting to convert "inferior" peoples, or because they saw missionary activity as socially disruptive.[52]

There also were deep divisions within British Protestantism. While in the Liverpool and Glasgow regions the conflict between Protestant and Catholic transcended all other religious antagonisms, in most parts of nineteenth-century Britain Catholics were relatively few: the most significant religious cleavage was that between Protestants adhering to the established churches and those adhering to free churches or chapels. Church and chapel embodied two rival understandings of Protestantism. The chapel embraced a multiplicity of denominations ranging widely in polity, in theological tendencies, in social constituency, and in degrees of political and social activism. One characteristic feature was, however, a pervasive moralism, which attempted to apply Christian principles to all areas of personal, social, and political life—often with deliberate disregard for prevailing conventions.[53] While the clergy of the Church of England and Church of Scotland were generally loyal (though not necessarily uncritical) supporters of the British cause in time of war, and of the defense and extension of the British Empire, the positions adopted by the Nonconformist chapels were much more varied. In most, if not all, of the wars fought by the United Kingdom during the last two centuries the often rather small minority of Britons who opposed government policy has included a disproportionately large number of Protestant Dissenters. Among the most recent cases was the war with Argentina in 1982: the Methodist Conference, meeting immediately after the end of hostilities, heard a scathing condemnation of the war by the conference secretary, and gave overwhelming approval to a letter sent to Margaret Thatcher, urging her in the future to seek nonmilitary solutions to international disputes.[54] Sometimes the pacifist minority was very small, as for instance in World War I, when the sixteen thousand conscientious objectors appeared almost invisible beside the more than three million who volunteered to fight or were conscripted. But it is still worth noting that a study of some twenty-five hundred objectors whose religious denomination is known found that about 95 percent were Protestant Dissenters.[55]

In the Boer War, when the volume of opposition was considerably greater, the two main sources of opposition were once again either socialist and radical politics or Nonconformist religion. While recent scholarship has tended to emphasize the extent of support for the war in all sections of the population, including organized labor and the chapels,[56] it is clear that Dissenting religion did provide a powerful source of alternative values for at least a minority of Nonconformists. As one prominent layman declared in a meeting of Congregationalists opposed to the war, "Through history God was on the side of the small peoples": the Boers were fighting for their freedom, and therefore deserved sympathy. The crusading journalist W. T. Stead, speaking in a London chapel, retained the concept of England as an elect nation, but insisted that England would only be faithful to its vocation if it renounced this unjust war. In 1901, when revelations about the British concentration camps had led to more widespread and vociferous criticism of government policy, more than five thousand Nonconformist ministers joined a call for an end to the war. My own research on the south London suburb of Lewisham showed that the Stop the War committee was based on a Methodist chapel, that most of its leading members were Methodists or Congregationalists, and that on Mafeking Night, when Lewisham vicarage was festooned with Union Jacks, a patriotic mob was smashing the windows of the home of one of the borough's Congregational ministers.[57]

In spite of the decline in Protestant church membership and church attendance in the early twentieth century,[58] the great majority of the population continued to regard themselves as Protestants. But there were other factors contributing to the declining significance of Protestantism as a basis for national identity. First, the partition of Ireland in 1921 settled for the time being the question of the relationship between Britain and Ireland, and thus removed the most potent source of anti-Catholic feeling in Britain. Second, Protestantism had become irrelevant to the various international conflicts in which Britain was involved. In World War I, religious differences had no bearing on the pattern of alliances and antagonisms. The defense of "little" Belgium was justified in innumerable sermons. David Lloyd George, addressing a rally of his fellow Nonconformists, compared Britain's role to that of the Good Samaritan. But the fact that the aggressor nation was mainly Protestant and the victim nation Catholic meant that the language of the preachers was of a more generalized Christian, rather than a specifically Protestant, kind. (Admittedly, many preachers disposed of the problem of German Protestantism by suggesting that their religion was merely nominal, and that most Germans were rationalists.) Within Britain, the Roman Catholic Church gave wholehearted support to the war, and the Catholic clergy seem to have won a reputation as brave and devoted army chaplains.[59] In 1926 a bill to abolish most of the remaining disabilities suffered by Roman Catholics was passed by Parliament with very little opposition. One of the main arguments advanced in favor was the patriotism shown by Catholics during the war.[60] (This did not simply reflect religious apathy, since the very next year the House of Commons fiercely debated, and eventually rejected, proposed revisions to the Anglican Prayer Book.)

In World War II the widespread perception that Britain was fighting for Christian civilization against the Nazi "pagans" provided a positive impetus to the making of common cause between Catholics and Protestants, and between ardent churchpeople and those on the margins of the churches. In fact Cardinal Hinsley emerged as the most straightforwardly patriotic of church leaders and was rewarded with invitations to broadcast on the radio. Many Anglican bishops were anxious to avoid the bellicosity of some of their predecessors in World War I, and accordingly insisted on a degree of independence that political leaders found irritating.[61] The war against the Nazis was seen as a war for democracy and civilization. But even those not normally noted for their piety frequently saw the war as also having a religious dimension and turned to religious language to express the scale of the issues at stake.[62] The crisis also led to widespread calls for the strengthening of the religious foundations of Britain—one of the favored methods of doing this being an enhanced emphasis on religious education in schools. The 1944 Education Act, with its provision for nondenominational religious instruction and a daily act of worship in all local authority-run schools, reflected the mood of these years.[63] Briefly, Protestant Britain had become a more inclusive Christian Britain, which found a place for Catholics and those with no particular denominational identity.

After the war, the memory and myth of 1940, of Britain standing alone against the Nazis, became the most powerful basis for national identity. The myth was acceptable to those of almost every political or religious persuasion, and in the 1960s and 1970s, when there was a substantial growth both in non-Christian faiths and in those with no religion, its specifically Christian dimension faded.

Conclusion

The debates at the 1898 Church Congress and subsequently in the columns of the *Spectator*, quoted earlier, indicated that many of the classic themes of Protestant nationalism were still espoused by leading Anglican churchmen. Bishop Welldon of Calcutta argued that England was free, prosperous, and civilized because of its Protestantism, and Hensley Henson, subsequently bishop of Durham, contrasted the level of religion and morality in Britian favorably with that obtaining in France and Italy, arguing that the "extreme and perverted sacerdotalism of the Roman Catholic Church" had led to "the great and ever waxing alienation from that Church of the best conscience and intellect of the Latin races." One of the main conclusions of this essay must be that specifically Protestant versions of national identity retained considerable vitality and influence right through the nineteenth century. However, these same debates also showed that Protestant nationalism was being undermined, partly by changes within Protestantism, partly because some of the classic tenets of this nationalism no longer carried such conviction, and partly because of the growing influence of rival doctrines. The archbishop of York gave a qualified support to these views, approving of the "deep-seated antipathy to Romanism which was happily characteristic of the great majority of the people of England," but going on to denounce the "ignorant demagogues" who exploited this antipathy. The bishop of Ripon, however, went much farther in this direction, making a generalized plea for religious toleration and welcoming "the desire for more fraternal intercourse between Christian Churches and denominations." In the debate in the *Spectator*, Welldon and Henson were attacked not only by a Catholic priest but by the editor and various correspondents with no apparent Catholic axes to grind. First, the claim that prosperity was a product of prosperity no longer fitted the facts: two of the most economically advanced parts of the world, Belgium and the Rhineland, were mainly Catholic. Second, Protestant claims to exclusive truth no longer carried so much weight: the editor granted that it was "nearer to ultimate truth" than Catholicism—but by nineteenth-century British standards that was a very modest claim. Most significant was the frequency with which race was seen as the fundamental determinant of national characteristics.

The claim that Britain was uniquely free and civilized remained essential to the national self-image until well after World War II. But the other tenets of Protestant nationalism were already losing some of their hold by the end of the nineteenth century. Britain was still by most standards prosperous, but it had already lost its dominant economic position, and fears of being overtaken and left behind by the more efficient Germany would soon become a national obsession. Following the decline of religious belief and practice in the 1880s and 1890s, Britain could also no longer claim to be uniquely Christian, even if it still seemed so by comparison with France and Germany. And Protestantism itself, and its position in British society, had changed in all sorts of ways. Protestant exclusiveness, whether vis-à-vis Catholics or members of non-Christian faiths, was being challenged both by the spirit of relativism represented by the editor of the *Spectator* and by the spirit of liberalism and tolerance represented by the bishop of Ripon. Anti-Catholic prejudices remained widespread and sometimes vehement. But attacks on Catholicism were no longer high on many people's religious or political agenda. And in any case there was by now wide acceptance for a system of religious pluralism in which a variety of forms of belief and unbelief coexisted peacefully, although with a great deal of mutual suspicion. The admission of avowed atheists to Parliament in 1886, following the Bradlaugh controversy, completed the long drawn-out process by which religious minorities were admitted to full citizenship. Moreover, the increasing divisions between Protestants as to the nature of their faith and the continuing conflict between Conservative, Liberal and Socialist, militarist and pacifist, imperialist and "Little England" versions of Protestantism considerably reduced its utility as a foundation for a widely accepted national identity. It is symptomatic that the two leading politicians who have in recent years drawn most explicitly on the nation's Protestant traditions come from opposite ends of the political spectrum—Margaret Thatcher and Tony Benn.

Notes

Acknowledgments

I would like to thank Callum Brown, Peter Marsh, and the members of the Department of Church History at the University of Helsinki, with whom I have discussed the arguments presented in this paper.

1. Linda Colley, *Britons: Forging the Nation, 1707–1837*, 2d ed. (London, 1994), 368.

2. Keith Robbins, *Nineteenth-Century Britain: Integration and Diversity* (Oxford, 1988), 105–6, 112–13; see also Robbins, *History, Religion, and Identity in Modern Britain* (London, 1993). I generally agree with Robbins's approach to these highly controversial issues.

3. Callum G. Brown, "Religion and National Identity in Scotland since the Union of 1707," in Ingmar Brohed, ed., *Church and People in England and Scandinavia* (Lund, 1996), 287–94. For a range of perspectives on this question, see Stewart J. Brown and Michael Fry, eds., *Scotland in the Age of Disruption* (Edinburgh, 1993).

4. This point is powerfully made by David Feldman, *Englishmen and Jews: Social Relations and Political Culture, 1840–1914* (New Haven, Conn., 1994), 12–15 and passim.

5. Stella Cottrell, "The Devil on Two Sticks: Franco-phobia in 1803," in Raphael Samuel, ed., *Patriotism: The Making and Unmaking of British National Identity*, 3 vols. (London, 1989), 1: 268; V. G. Kiernan, "Evangelicalism and the French Revolution," *Past & Present* 1 (1952): 44–56; Hugo Young, *One of Us: A Biography of Margaret Thatcher*, rev. ed. (London 1993), 9; Gavin White, "The Fall of France," in W. J. Sheils, ed., *The Church and War*, Studies in Church History, vol. 20 (Oxford, 1983), 435.

6. Brian Stanley, *The Bible and the Flag: Protestant Missions and British Imperialism in the Nineteenth and Twentieth Centuries* (Leicester, 1990), 65–67; Christine Bolt, *Victorian Attitudes to Race* (London, 1971), 168–69; Susan Thorne, "Protestant Ethics and the Spirit of Imperialism: British Congregationalists and the London Missionary Society, 1795–1925," (Ph.D. diss., University of Michigan, 1990), 287–88, 293–95.

7. Scottish Highland soldiers were a favorite theme of Victorian battle paintings. See Joseph A. Kestner, "The Colonised in the Colonies: Representation of Celts in Victorian Battle Painting," in Shearer West, ed., *The Victorians and Race* (Aldershot, 1996), 112–27.

8. Here I draw mainly on Sheridan Gilley, "English Attitudes to the Irish in England," in Colin Holmes, ed., *Immigrants and Minorities in British Society* (London, 1978), 81–110; and D. G. Paz, *Popular Anti-Catholicism in Mid-Victorian England* (Stanford, Calif., 1992). For the contrary view, see L. Perry Curtis, *Apes and Angels: The Irishman in Victorian Caricature* (Newton Abbot, 1971).

9. See John Wolffe, *The Protestant Crusade in Great Britain, 1829–1860* (Oxford, 1991), 267–68.

10. Mrs. John W. Harrisson, *A. M. Mackay, Pioneer Missionary of the Church Missionary Society to Uganda, by His Sister* (London, 1890), 42; *Spectator*, 22 October 1898, 557.

11. A. F. Walls, "Carrying the White Man's Burden: Some British Views of National Vocation in the Imperial Era," in William R. Hutchison and Hartmut Lehmann, eds., *Many Are Chosen: Divine Election and Western Nationalism* (Minneapolis, Minn., 1994), 29–36.

12. Brian Stanley, "Christian Responses to the Indian Mutiny of 1857," in Sheils, ed., *The Church and War*, 278–79.

13. John M. MacKenzie, *Propaganda and Empire: The Manipulation of British Public Opinion, 1880–1960* (Manchester, 1984), 184.

14. Hugh Cunningham, "The Language of Patriotism," in Samuel, ed., *Patriotism* 1: 65; Robert Colls, "Englishness and the Political Culture," in Robert Colls and Philip Dodd, eds., *Englishness: Politics and Culture, 1880–1920* (London, 1986), 30–32, 36–37; Hugh Cunningham, "The Conservative Party and Patriotism," in Colls and Dodd, *Englishness*, 297.

15. Cunningham, "The Language of Patriotism," 73–74.

16. Hugh McLeod, "New Perspectives on Victorian Working Class Religion: The Oral Evidence," *Oral History Journal* 14 (1986): 31–49; A. Allen MacLaren, *Religion and Social Class: The Disruption Years in Aberdeen* (London, 1974), 126; Jeffrey Cox, *The English Churches in a Secular Society: Lambeth, 1870–1930* (Oxford, 1982), 90–105; Sarah Williams, "Religious Belief and Popular Culture: A Study of the South London Borough of Southwark, c. 1880–1939" (Ph.D. diss., University of Oxford, 1993).

17. V. E. Chancellor, *History for Their Masters: Opinion in the English History Textbook, 1880–1914* (Bath, 1970), 112. See also Stephen Humphries, " 'Hurrah for England': Schooling and the Working Class in Bristol, 1870–1914," *Southern History* 1 (1979): 171–207.

18. J. R. de S. Honey, *Tom Brown's Universe: The Development of the Victorian Public School* (London, 1977), 111, 126–35, 313; J. A. Mangan, *Athleticism and the Victorian and Edwardian Public School* (Cambridge, 1981), passim; Mangan, " 'The Grit of Our Forefathers': Invented Traditions, Propaganda and Imperialism," in John M. MacKenzie, ed., *Imperialism and Popular Culture* (Manchester, 1986), 113–37.

19. Mangan, " 'The Grit of Our Forefathers,' " 118–20; *Spectator*, 8 October 1898, 488.

20. Thorne, "Protestant Ethics," 291–95.

21. Harrisson. *A. M. Mackay*, iv, 21, and passim.

22. Paz, *Popular Anti-Catholicism*, chap. 2. Although *Punch*'s humor had numerous targets, Anglican ritualists were regular victims. Working through the pages of the journal in one randomly selected mid-Victorian year (1865), I found two cartoons and two articles ridiculing Anglican ritualism, two cartoons attacking Roman Catholicism, and one cartoon attacking Dissent. (The latter, occasioned by alleged Nonconformist sympathy for the Jamaican rebellion, illustrates the hostility of some British patriots to the humanitarian/universalist dimension of Protestantism—a theme mentioned later in this essay.) A good example of *Punch*'s treatment of ritualism is the cartoon on the cover of Gerald Parsons, ed., *Religion in Victorian Britain*, 4 vols. (Manchester, 1988), 2. The presentation of Roman Catholicism was more varied, but an example of the scornful attitude often adopted is the cartoon in the same work on p. 1: 146. The former depicts a crowd of High Church clerics, partly hidden in clouds of incense. Their elaborate vestments, smooth and shiny hair, and supercilious expressions are all intended to indicate "effeminacy." The latter shows the "shepherd," a portly Cardinal Wiseman, playing his pipes, while his "flock" of apelike Irishmen fight. See also David Hilliard, "Unenglish and Unmanly: Anglo-Catholicism and Homosexuality," *Vic-*

torian Studies 25 (1981–82): 181–210, for the identification of Englishness with Protestantism and of Anglo-Catholicism with effeminacy.

23. Robert D. Storch, " 'Please to Remember the Fifth of November': Conflict, Solidarity, and Public Order in Southern England, 1815–1900," in Robert D. Storch, ed., *Popular Culture and Custom in Nineteenth-Century England* (London, 1982), 82.

24. See Wolffe, *The Protestant Crusade*, chap. 4.

25. Ibid., 232.

26. Ibid., 242.

27. H. J. Hanham, "Religion and Nationality in the Mid-Victorian Army," in M. R. D. Foot, ed., *War and Society* (London, 1973), 161–62.

28. Olive Anderson, "The Reactions of Church and Dissent towards the Crimean War," *Journal of Ecclesiastical History* 16 (1965): 212.

29. Wolffe, *The Protestant Crusade*, 281.

30. For anti-Catholicism in the early twentieth century, see Adrian Hastings, *A History of English Christianity, 1920–1985* (London, 1986), 131–32; and for a contemporary study that stresses the persistence of Protestant anti-Catholicism, see Joseph M. Bradley, *Ethnic and Religious Identity in Modern Scotland: Culture, Politics, and Football* (Aldershot, 1995). Although the ecumenical movement has modified Protestant anti-Catholicism somewhat, it has done nothing to reduce the attacks from a secular liberal standpoint. As one example, the appointment of a Catholic, John Battle, as minister for science in the new Blair government led to a protest by one Cambridge scientist who claimed that Battle's faith necessarily implied an antiscientific mentality. *Guardian*, 22 May 1997.

31. See, for instance, Frank Neal, *Sectarian Violence: The Liverpool Experience, 1819–1914* (Manchester, 1987); Tom Gallagher, *Glasgow, the Uneasy Peace: Religious Tension in Modern Scotland* (Manchester, 1987).

32. McLeod, "Victorian Working Class Religion," 42–43.

33. B. Murray, *The Old Firm: Sectarianism, Sport, and Society in Scotland* (Edinburgh, 1984); Bradley, *Ethnic and Religious Identity.*

34. P. J. Waller, *Democracy and Sectarianism: A Social and Political History of Liverpool, 1868–1939* (Liverpool, 1981), 10–11, 237–40.

35. Christopher Ford, "Pastors and Polemicists: The Character of Popular Anglicanism in South-East Lancashire, 1847–1914," (Ph.D. diss., University of Leeds, 1991) argues that ultra-Protestantism became gradually marginalized, after a period of intense activity in the later 1860s.

36. W. L. Arnstein, "The Murphy Riots: A Victorian Dilemma," *Victorian Studies* 19 (1975): 51–72.

37. See Steven Fielding, *Class and Ethnicity: Irish Catholics in England, 1880–1939* (Buckingham, 1993).

38. Dorothea Price Hughes, *The Life of Hugh Price Hughes, by His Daughter* (London, 1904), 404–34, 542–74; David W. Bebbington, *The Nonconformist Conscience* (London, 1982), 121.

39. Price Huges, *The Life of Hugh Price Hughes*, 292.

40. For the changes in Nonconformist aesthetic sensibilities, see Clyde Binfield, " 'We Claim Our Part in the Great Inheritance': The Message of Four Congregational Buildings," in Keith Robbins, ed., *Protestant Evangelicalism* (Oxford,

1990), 201–24, as well as many other papers by the same author; for the revolt by the younger generation of upper-middle-class Nonconformists, see Cox, *The English Churches*, 229–38; for the attractions of Roman and Anglo-Catholicism, see Gilley's comments in Sheridan Gilley and W. J. Sheils eds., *A History of Religion in Britain: Practice and Belief from Pre-Roman Times to the Present* (Oxford, 1994), 351–56. For the general theme of the growing acceptance of Catholicism, whether Anglican or Roman, and the marginalization of ultra-Protestantism, see Ford, "Pastors and Polemicists."

41. Jeremy Crump, "The Identity of English Music: The Reception of Elgar, 1898–1935," in Colls and Dodd, eds., *Englishness*, 165–66. Richard Aldington, *Death of a Hero* (1929; rpt., London, 1965), 133–34, includes a conversation at a London literary party c. 1910 where the participants pour scorn on both English art and English artistic taste: "The newest historians say that the Anglo-Saxons come from the same race as the Vandals, and I can well believe it."

42. John M. MacKenzie, ed., *Popular Imperialism and the Military, 1850–1950* (Manchester, 1992); MacKenzie, *Imperialism and Popular Culture*.

43. MacKenzie, "Heroic Myths of Empire," in *Popular Imperialism and the Military*, 109–38.

44. Bolt, *Victorian Attitudes to Race*, 7–9; Hugh A. MacDougall, *Racial Myth in English History: Trojans, Teutons, and Anglo-Saxons* (Montreal, 1982), 89–103; Thorne, "Protestant Ethnics," 169–74.

45. John Marlowe, *Milner, Apostle of Empire: A Life of Alfred George, the Right Honourable Viscount Milner of St. James's and Cape Town, KG; GCB, GCMG, 1854–1925* (London, 1976), 364.

46. *Spectator*, 1, 8, 15, 22, 29 October 1898. See also Feldman, *Englishmen and Jews*, 94–120. Noting that Liberal critics of Disraeli's foreign policy in 1876–80 often referred to his Jewish origins, Feldman distinguishes between the Congregational minister William Crosbie, who saw the roots of Disraeli's mistaken policies in certain aspects of the Jewish religion, and F. Harrison Hill, who explained them in racial terms in the *Fortnightly Review*, the main organ of intellectual secularism.

47. The most detailed account is Stewart J. Brown, " 'Outside the Covenant': The Scottish Presbyterian Churches and Irish Immigration," *Innes Review* 42 (1991): 19–45. See also Robbins, *History, Religion, and Identity*, 99–100.

48. Stewart J. Brown, "The Campaign for the Christian Commonwealth in Scotland, 1919–1939," in W. M. Jacob and Nigel Yates, eds., *Crown and Mitre: Religion and Society in Northern Europe since the Reformation* (Woodbridge, 1993), 210.

49. See, for instance, T. Dunbar Moodie, *The Rise of Afrikanerdom: Power, Apartheid, and the Afrikaner Civil Religion* (Berkeley, 1975); Robert P. Ericksen, *Theologians under Hitler: Gerhard Kittel, Paul Althaus, and Emmanuel Hirsch* (New Haven, Conn. 1985).

50. Thorne, "Protestant Ethnics," 167–68.

51. Ibid., 174–84; Karen Fields, "Christian Missionaries as Anticolonial Militants," *Theory and Society* 11 (1982): 95–108; A. E. Afigbo, "Christian Missions and Secular Authorities in South-Eastern Nigeria from Colonial Times," in O. U. Kalu, ed., *The History of Christianity in West Africa* (London 1980), 187–88.

52. Thorne, "Protestant Ethics," 179; Bolt, *Victorian Attitudes to Race*, 94–95, 113–18.

53. See, for instance, Bebbington, *The Nonconformist Conscience*.

54. *Guardian*, 1 July 1982.

55. John Rae, *Conscience and Politics: The British Government and the Conscientious Objector to Military Service, 1916–1919* (London, 1970), 250–51.

56. Michael Blanch, "English Society and the War," P. in Warwick, ed., *The South African War: The Anglo-Boer War, 1899–1902* (London, 1980), 210–38; Bebbington, *The Nonconformist Conscience*, 121–24. See also Anne Summers, "Edwardian Militarism," in Samuel, ed., *Patriotism*, 1: 236–56, which argues that militarism permeated all areas of Edwardian society.

57. Stephen Koss, *The Pro-Boers: The Anatomy of an Antiwar Movement* (Chicago, 1973), 33, 225–26, 230–31; Hugh McLeod, *Class and Religion in the Late Victorian City* (London, 1974), 178–79.

58. Robert Currie, Alan Gilbert, and Lee Horsley, *Churches and Churchgoers: Patterns of Church Growth in the British Isles since 1700* (Oxford, 1977); Robin Gill, *The Myth of the Empty Church* (London, 1993).

59. Alan Wilkinson, *Dissent or Conform?: War, Peace, and the English Churches, 1900–1945* (London, 1986), 27; A. J. Hoover, *God, Germany, and Britain in the Great War: A Study in Clerical Nationalism* (New York, 1989), 35–37; Alan Wilkinson, *The Church of England and the First World War* (London, 1978), 110–11, 118.

60. Walter L. Arnstein, *Protestant versus Catholic in Mid-Victorian England: Mr. Newdegate and the Nuns* (Columbia, 1982), 218–26.

61. Stuart Mews, "The Sword of the Spirit: A Catholic Cultural Crusade of 1940," in Sheils, ed., *The Church and War*, 409–30.

62. See the essay "Britain, 1940 and 'Christian Civilization' " in Robbins, *History, Religion, and Identity*, 195–213; also Hastings, *A History of English Christianity*, 382–400.

63. Robbins, "Britain, 1940," 201–2; Hastings, *A History of English Christianity*, 419.

4

Race in Britain and India

SUSAN BAYLY

THE ORIGINAL STATEMENT of purpose for this volume dismissed the crude dichotomies which have informed the idea of the secular Western nation-state. It rightly challenged the idea of the nation as a product of progressive and uncoercive ideals growing up in harmony with the principles of modern science. It also rejected the assumption that modern nationalisms are unrelated to the mentalities of those who bring premodern visions of so-called race genius, divine mandate, and blood guilt into the political arena. This essay was therefore conceived on the assumption that it would be instructive to make comparisons which recognize the pervasiveness of religious themes in recent and contemporary nationalist thought, and to unite metropolitan and colonial perspectives. It was also hoped that there would be much to learn about both the collisions and the interactions between the West and the extra-European world by examining nine-teenth- and early-twentieth-century concepts of race as these were applied to the experience of colonialism.

The aims of this essay are twofold. First, it asks how European theorists applied what they regarded as the scientific principles of nineteenth- and twentieth-century race theory to the understanding of contemporary religious experience in colonial India. Second, it explores what south Asian thinkers themselves said about the meaning of race as an inspiration to would-be spiritual and political revivalists in the shaping of nationalist challenges to colonial rule.

Race and the Early Orientalists

Long before the age of high nationalism and high colonialism, Western thinkers were already finding ways to "essentialize" human societies on the basis of moral and environmental typologies that prefigured the thinking of many later nineteenth-century race theorists. The earliest of India's colonial ethnographers were strongly influenced by the theorists of the eighteenth-century Scottish Enlightenment who were concerned to define the conditions under which the human character could advance to a state of civilization. These thinkers equated civilization with the formation of an ordered and beneficent polity in which individual rights and liberties were preserved, commerce and property secured, and despotic power held at bay. An equally important feature of these eighteenth- and early-nine-teenth-century writings was the belief that conditions of climate and physical environment determined which peoples were capable of achieving civilization, and which were condemned to an unfree or savage state.

At first glance it might appear that these typologies were derived from an exclusively materialist or rationalistic understanding of the laws governing human social evolution. But in fact, these early environmental thinkers placed religion at the core of their arguments. The model of despotism which the early orientalists brought with them to the Asian colonial setting was derived from seventeenth- and early-eighteenth-century Protestant political theory, in which it was the Church of Rome and the absolutist Roman Catholic monarchies of Europe which were held to have imposed tyrannical despotism on freeborn Christians, deforming their characters and making them passive, "womanish" and slavelike.[1]

Like Switzerland, Scotland, and the other favored domains of the European romantics, India was held by such commentators as James Forbes, author of the four-volume survey *Oriental Memoirs* (1813), to contain sizable groups of people who were endowed by nature with qualities of inherent nobility and manliness. Such peoples were referred to as nations and tribes as well as races, these terms being more or less interchangable in early orientalist texts. What these "noble" and "manly" Indian peoples were deemed to have in common was that they were all inhabitants of picturesque upland locales; they were energetic, enterprising, and "virile," and they cherished so-called tribal traditions of liberty and independence. In addition, these inhabitants of bracing, rugged landscapes were capable of achieving advanced forms of political awareness, meaning that they were inherently valorous and freedom-loving.[2] Above all, what distinguished such peoples as Rajputs, certain so-called aboriginals, and the peoples of the south Indian poligar chiefdoms from the supposedly effeminate, mild, and timid caste Hindus of the torrid tropical plains was the nature of their religion. Again and again in this literature, it is held to be a crucial mark of these "free" and "virile" peoples' superior moral and racial development that they had not been subjected to "brahminical fetters" and so were not the slaves of Brahman priests and Brahmanical "caste prejudices."[3]

Evangelical Christians were quick to attack such orientalists. This was not because early-nineteenth-century evangelicals saw any flaws in orientalist environmental categories. Neither did they object to the pronouncements of Sir William Jones and his followers about the fair-skinned Aryan conquerors who had supposedly brought with them from their western

Asian fatherland the primeval teachings of Hinduism. What British Protestant evangelicals did condemn was the glorification by Jones and his
contemporaries of the "purity" and "sublimity" of the ancient Sanskrit
scriptures, and the failure of orientalists to disparage what the Christian
proselytizers saw as the depravity, oppression, and degradation of Indian
social and spiritual life.[4]

At the same time, what both the early British evangelicals and Jones's
followers had in common was the view that so-called Brahmanical faith
was a powerful and pernicious feature of Indian life. Furthermore,
although these Western commentators did not see all Indians as equally
"fettered" by religiously defined caste ideologies, wherever the authority
of Brahmans and Brahmanical caste values was held to be strong, human
freedoms and liberties were believed to be extinguished, and Indians were
said to be corrupted and oppressed by tyrannical priest craft.

The model here was unmistakably the same concept of the Romish
yoke which had been so influential in earlier commentaries on the phenomenon of tyranny, both in Europe and in the extra-European world:
"Like all other attempts to cramp the human intellect, and forcibly to
restrain men within bounds which nature scorns to keep, this system
[varna] . . . has operated like the Chinese national shoe, it has rendered
the whole nation cripples."[5] In this respect these early Western orientalists
foreshadow the many later colonial commentators who drew on what
the scientific race theorists said about the subcontinent's religious values,
characterizing Indians as people who "know nothing of patriotism" and
lack political will.[6]

Race Theory in the Age of "High Colonialism"

Religion was clearly an essential component in the early orientalists' definitions of civilization and savagery. When these thinkers of the late eighteenth and early nineteenth centuries defined the environmental factors
which they regarded as allowing certain races or nations to advance at
the expense of others, they were far from indifferent to matters of faith
and priestly authority. On the contrary, these manifestations of spiritual
life were generally given a major causal role in the shaping of human
evolutionary hierarchies.

By the later nineteenth century, religion was being treated very differently by advocates of the extraordinarily influential new discipline of ethnology, or evolutionist race science. This of course was a field which grew
up in close association with the needs and anxieties of nineteenth- and
twentieth-century European empire builders, though as will be seen
below, European race theory was much more than a crudely self-glorifying

tool of colonial rule. This is not to endorse the abhorrent teachings of the Western race theorists. But it is important to note that the proponents of ethnological theories were regarded with deep ambivalence in Britain and elsewhere in Europe. This was partly because their works so often suggested that the white colonizer was in a state of ethnological danger or even outright decline. It was also because the ethnologists' ideas about the unstoppable power of blood, race, and activated nationhood were so evidently a source of inspiration to cultural revivalists and anticolonial nationalists in India and Ceylon, as well as being taken over and "indigenized" by members of many other Asian intelligentsias, including those of China, Japan, and colonial Burma.

Of course the ethnologists' assertions about the supposedly immutable facts of physiology and intellect which separate race from race have been widely discredited, and their methodologies, involving so-called anthropometric techniques of skull and bodily measurement, are now rightly regarded as grotesque and fallacious. However, it must be remembered that these theories of biologically determined race essences and blood purity were held in high esteem by Western scientists and social theorists until surprisingly recently.[7] Furthermore, their influence is far from dead. Indeed ethnological concepts of blood and race are still a powerful and pernicious force in the thinking of a very wide range of ultranationalists and ethnic supremacists both in the West and in the extra-European world. And once again, while there might seem to have been little place for discussions of religion in this avowedly modern and scientific discourse, the nineteenth- and early-twentieth-century ethnologists too attached great importance to matters of faith and worship. In ethnological arguments, however, religion tended to lose its causal role, and was commonly subsumed into the overarching concept of race. In other words a propensity toward either "savage" forms of faith or advanced "civilized" spirituality had come to be seen as a key property of every racial group, that is, as a marker of differential race essences in the ladder of human evolutionary attainment.

Ethnological Views of Nation, Faith, and Empire

With expanding European colonial power came attempts to compile an ever growing mass of statistics and ethnographic data on the subject peoples of the African and Asian empires. As is well known, the increasingly powerful and intrusive colonial regime that was created in India after the 1857 Mutiny-Rebellion found more and more reasons to count and classify the peoples of the subcontinent, and to call on Indians to report themselves as members of specific and often arbitrarily imposed ethnic and communal categories. It is also widely recognized that what we now call Hinduism and Islam, as well as the moral and occupational categories of caste, were all shaped (though certainly not invented) as indigenous Indian experiences of faith and moral order collided and interacted with these operations of the colonial state.[8]

The growing numbers of British census takers, land revenue officials, military recruiters, public health officers, and even missionaries who compiled and interpreted all this data certainly did not subscribe to any one view of the Indian social order. At the same time, much of this official and quasi-official writing was strongly influenced by contemporary Western race theory. Even when the immediate application of their work was in the pragmatic imperial arenas of policing and military recruitment, many of the most influential colonial scholar-officials were keenly interested in finding ways to apply the social statistics and other information they were gathering to contemporary British and Continental ethnological debates. These officials' attempts to analyze and manipulate what they understood as the concepts of caste, religion, and race in the subcontinent were often strongly marked by their awareness of what British and Continental scientists were saying about the history and future of humankind as a Darwinian "struggle for mastery" between higher and lower races, with the weak and inferior marked for extinction by their qualities of moral, physical, and cultural backwardness.

The surprising feature of these official and quasi-official writings in the later nineteenth and early twentieth centuries is that they did not invariably insist on hard and fast separations between white and nonwhite peoples, or between rulers and the colonized. But this is in line with what many of Britain's metropolitan race theorists were writing at this time. In a large proportion of their works, the key concern was to define the interrelated qualities of faith, intellect, and physiological development which supposedly distinguished the Briton from his rival European empire builders, particularly in the East. The Victorian ethnology journals abound in essays which purport to trace the distinctive racial heritage of the "manly" upright Briton, particularly as this was manifested in the making of empire. These works generally share the view that British conquest brought to Asia none of the dangerous enthusiasms of the decadent Iberian Catholic powers, or the unhealthy militaristic authoritarianism of the Russians and Germans, or the unbalanced nationalistic fervor of the French.[9]

This racial reading of empire was in accord with what many other Victorian writers were saying at this time about the supposed rationality and moderation of British colonialism. These were the qualities which had supposedly endowed the Briton with an inherent capacity to rule in harmony with the religious norms of nonwhite peoples, damping down dangerous fanaticisms and wild millenarian proclivities among Indians and other Asian peoples, and advancing and uplifting these favored subjects by offering them a form of Christianity that was widely characterized as moderate, civilized, and unprovocative.

Those who expressed these views exalted Christianity—or what they regarded as the moderate and rational faith of mainstream British Protestant culture—as the most notable of all human evolutionary attainments. This is certainly what the leading Victorian race theorists said. In repudiating the attacks of their anti-Darwinian enemies, the key metropolitan ethnologists were keen to ward off the accusation that their science was subversive of Christianity or "religion in general."[10] The chief British spokesmen for this new field insisted that the study of religion and morals was central to the concerns of the anthropometric data gatherers and race theorists. They claimed further that when the practitioners of these new methodologies assigned the members of different races to a particular rung on the evolutionary ladder, the test of collective "moral progress" would naturally place the modern enlightened Christian at the top of this ethnological pecking order.[11]

These views were widely shared in other arenas, and especially by those whose training in the increasingly professionalized fields of administration, medicine, engineering, and the military gave them a particular interest in imperial affairs. And far from being indifferent to matters of faith and spirituality, the writings of even the most pragmatic of these commentators—including those whose concerns are apparently far removed from organized missionary activities—are steeped in evangelical ideals and attitudes.[12] The concepts of nationality that were expressed in this period tended to be strongly marked by this perception of humane and rational faith as the hallmark of superior evolutionary development. In other words, while those who accepted the premises of the ethnologists generally agreed that nationhood was the defining quality of advanced and vigorous peoples, it was uncommon for nineteenth- and early-twentieth-century race theorists to conceive of nationhood as an expression of secular racial bonds. On the contrary, a nation was a free union of racially compatible people who had derived a sense of common truth and purpose from a bond of enlightened and untyrannical religious faith.[13]

Theories of Race Conflict and Ethnological Decline

During the later nineteenth century compilations of data on India's so-called castes and tribes became increasingly dominated by ethnological perspectives. When Western race theorists considered this Indian material, their writings contributed to much wider international debate and were not created purely or even mainly in the interests of colonial power. Everyone, said the ethnological theorists, whether they were writing about Indians, Africans, or Europeans, was subject to these same all-powerful forces of blood and race genius. The ethnologists' tracing of racial interactions presumed a landscape of danger, competition, and animosity, with all human history as a manifestation of these ceaseless strivings. The purpose of the ethnologist was not merely to rank and classify all humankind, but to edify and forewarn those who were equipped to understand its insights.

Like the earlier environmental theorists, the race theorists of the later nineteenth and twentieth centuries generally equated civilization with a bent toward libertarianism in both sprirtual and political life. But their account of the laws of evolution allowed of no security for those who had thus advanced themselves. Those races which had established themselves as rulers and civilizers were continually told that even those who were endowed with superior race qualities were eternally vulnerable, that the global struggle for mastery allowed of no permanent winners or survivors, and that degeneration, decline, and annihilation were the inescapable fate of even the most vigorous racial groups.[14]

This vision of eternal evolutionary race wars is explicitly endorsed in the work of the British scholar-officials whose writings were continually mined and recapitulated in official and quasi-official writing about both Hinduism and Islam in India. This can be seen, for example, in the work of W. W. Hunter, who established himself as one of the key Victorian authorities on the castes and tribes of the subcontinent, and who was also a major figure in the creation of the nineteenth-century myth of the backwardness of the Indian Muslim "nation." Hunter's best-known work, *Annals of Rural Bengal*, treats the Bengal region as a living battleground shaped by titanic warfare between noble, spiritually advanced Aryans and rude aboriginal races whose religious life was supposedly dark, savage, and "animistic."

In Hunter's account, Bengal's configurations of habitat and terrain marked the different evolutionary stages of this epic. He describes the Beerbhoom highlands as both an "ethnical frontier" and a theater of one of the great "primitive struggles of Indian history."[15] In these "bracing" uplands a great racial collision had occurred between the descendants of tall, "noble" invaders and the "inferior tribes," who were overrun in "the primitive time" by the bearers of superior Aryan civilization.[16] Far from serving as a static display of conventional caste relationships, Bengal's so-called human specimens provide Hunter with a picture of grim, degenerative racial catastrophe, and a tragic tale of nationhood retarded. This understanding of Bengal's race history was consistent with contemporary eugenicist views, that is, with the idea that advanced societies could survive and flourish only if they found means to protect themselves from the formation of racial "composites" through the merging of people from separate racial "stock" and "very unequal degrees of civilisation."[17]

According to Hunter, India did have a heritage of true nationhood, and by this he meant a form of "national spirit" which was rooted in a conception of superior, exalted divinity. The tragedy, as he saw it, was that only one part of the subcontinent's ancient racial stock possessed these superior qualities of faith and nationality. "Our earliest glimpses of the human family in India disclose two tribes of widely different origin, struggling for the mastery."[18] Of these primordial Indian racial groups, the one with the makings of nationhood in their ethnological heritage were of course the fair-skinned Aryans who "came of a conquering stock" and were imbued with "that high sense of nationality which burns in the hearts of a people who believe themselves the depositary of a divine revelation."[19] Hunter therefore shared with numerous other ethnological thinkers a vision of superior race qualities pitted in a long and desperate war against "savagery."[20] In Bengal, he wrote, the once noble Aryan conquerors gradually lost out and became degenerate, contaminating their enlightened Hindu faith with "degrading superstitions" absorbed from what he called, revoltingly, the "squat black [aboriginal] races," these being the ancestors of the hill and forest people who would nowadays be referred to as Indian tribals.[21]

This interpretation of the Aryan conquest myth has shaped a whole host of pre- and postindependence debates. It was obviously taken over and assimilated into indigenous concepts of blood and race by the many Indian polemicists who inverted the original premise, and then claimed primordial rights and entitlements on behalf of so-called Dravidian, non-Brahman, or pre-Aryan peoples whom they described as persons of noble race who had been degraded by Aryan invaders.[22] For Hunter and his contemporaries, however, the story of discordant racial contact was above all a story of faith deformed and nationhood degraded. Even the "national spirit" of a noble and advanced race were held to be vulnerable to these implacable ethnological forces: when radically unlike racial groups were placed in close proximity, Hunter proclaimed, the higher were always in danger of being infected by the degrading superstitions of their inferiors. At the same time Hunter also saw in Bengali religion the marks of a higher race attempting to protect itself from this collision of radically discordant racial unequals. Vegetarianism and the other ideologies of stratification and ritual purity that underpinned the high-caste Hindu lifestyle were in his view a reflection of the deep-seated abhorrence of a supposedly higher race for the "black-skinned, human-sacrificing, flesh-eating forest tribes."[23]

Repulsive as these views will be to a modern reader, it is important to understand that this idea of the corrupting consequences of interracial contact was regarded as scientific fact by a whole host of Victorian ethnological generalizers. Robert Knox, one of the most influential of these theorists, defined the central principle of humankind's evolutionary history as the "mysterious unextinguishable dislike of race to race," and regarded it as a key task of the ethnologist to warn against racial "hybridization."[24] Yet for all this, the European race theorists who held these views did not stereotype all Indians as members of an alien or racially inferior human order. On the contrary, like many of his contemporaries, Hunter made much of the idea that Europe and "Aryan" India were linked by powerful bonds of racial kinship. The same "prolific race," he said, had founded the great dynasties of ancient Persia and central Asia. Other Aryans had made their mark as early colonizers of Europe, and "Aryan speech" was "now conquering for itself the forests of the New World, and carrying Indo-Germanic culture to island empires in the Southern Ocean."[25]

On this basis it was widely held that there was a crucial message for India's white rulers in this imagined history of degeneration and race war. Hunter's version of this was characteristically insistent on the paramount role of religion. In its early pristine state, when the "Indo-Aryan race" was still a strong, fresh, and virile "confederacy of fighting tribes," the Aryans' "national mind" had attained spiritual insights that foreshadowed the truth of Christian revelation.[26] It was in comparatively recent times, Hunter argued, that this enlightened Aryan faith degenerated into the "degrading superstitions" of contemporary Hinduism.[27] Having established their dominion in the Gangetic plain, the original Aryan "fighting tribes" gradually subsided into degeneracy, becoming a society of "mild-eyed philosophers" strolling aimlessly in their mango groves, creating pointlessly elaborate rituals and wrangling over empty points of sectarian doctrine.[28] This, for Hunter, was the counterevolutionary development that produced caste in its true Aryan form, that is, as a "national code," disfiguring the strengths of unified Aryan nationhood and ruining the "Sanskrit people."[29]

It is obvious that this kind of ethnological analysis, whether applied to India or the world at large, was in large part a product of the experience of worldwide colonial expansion. At the same time it is not a reflection of complacency about European or British mastery of the world. On the contrary, in its anglophone manifestations, Western race theory derived much of its energy in the later nineteenth century from growing concerns about whether Britain was in danger of losing its collective national will and vigor, and might therefore find itself being supplanted on the world stage by Germany, France, and the various other powers which were

amassing imperial possessions in this period and threatening to outper-
form the British both economically and strategically.

Since British and Continental race theorists tended to see all human
history as a story of evolutionary warfare, their purpose as ethnologists
was to chart the rise and fall of competing peoples, races, and nations
in every part of the world. Mapping one's own ethnological story, and
discovering the message of race as it applied to one's dangerous European competitors, was just as important as comparing and classifying
the nonwhite populations of the extra-European empires. Indeed it was
part of the same exercise, to be done in precisely the same way, using the
same "essentializing" vocabulary for both white and nonwhite "types"
and "specimens."

As early as the 1860s, British theorists were speculating anxiously
about the ethnological meaning of Germany's drive for national unification, about the achievements of Germans in the sciences and the arts, and
about the expansion of Germany, France, and other European powers in
Asia and Africa. Contributors to metropolitan ethnological debate were
much exercised about the apparent vigor of "Teutonic" racial essences,
compared to the inheritance of race qualities that had hitherto given Britons their supposed evolutionary lead over other peoples. This is the background to the many discussions of these themes in the leading Victorian
ethnology journals. Typical of these is an article in the *Memoirs of the
Anthropological Society of London* on the "psychical characteristics of
the English people." The author, L. Owen Pike, uses anatomical data as
a basis for comparing the character and intellect of Englishmen with those
of their "Teutonic" rivals.[30] The evolutionary history of the British Isles,
says Pike, had endowed the English with a unique sense of decency, as well
as an innate capacity to use the intellect in a clearheaded and constructive
fashion: "the steady scientific method of the English is characteristic of
the people. . . . The English know the true value of facts; they know how
to arrange . . . , classify [and] . . . utilize them. They know also the value
of theories. . . . The Germans . . . value theories for their mysticism, . . .
rather than for their agreement with established facts."[31]

These of course are the special data gatherer's skills that were being
so enthusiastically taken over from the ethnologists for use by colonial
officials, though they also came to be used for policing and other purposes
at home in Britain. Commentators like Pike were in no doubt about the
interdependence of empire and ethnology. Ethnologists regarded the making of empire as a collective racial achievement; in their view it was as a
vigorous and racially purposeful power that Britain had subjected so
much of the globe to its commercial and military hegemony. So in Pike's
ethnology Britons are prosaic but manly and upright empire builders who
must ultimately win out against thrusting, competitive Germans: "The

Germans emigrate, but do not colonize,—precisely as they carry a new discovery to further results more frequently than they make the discovery itself. England is the great colonizer; but wherever England sends colonies, Germany sends migrants."[32]

Charles Morris, one of the key Victorian popularizers of the Aryan race myth, also extolled the special qualities of nationhood which he saw as having equipped the English to fulfill their destiny as expansive Aryans: "The England of today is extended until it has its outlying members in almost every region of the habitable earth. The other Aryan peoples . . . have lost in great measure their national migratory activity. . . . The very recent colonizing efforts of Germany are acts of Government [not the people]. . . . Only in England [of all the expanding European powers] are the people and the Government moving hand in hand."[33] So to these and the many other like-minded commentators who wrote on this topic, the English conqueror deserved his ascendancy because he belonged to a vigorous race with an "athletic spirit" and a racial predisposition to use his intellect in a distinctive, assertive, and "manly" fashion—arranging, classifying, taxonomizing.[34] But what is especially striking about this period's ethnological writing is that India had come to be so widely regarded as a terrain in which Britain's ascendancy was no longer secure. And the reasons for this impending danger were to be found in religion, or more precisely in what many British advocates of race theory understood as the ethnological meaning of India's nineteenth- and early-twentieth-century movements of religious and cultural revival.

Race Theorists and Indian Religious Revival

Victorian race theorists held that the capacity to civilize others was an essential mark of advanced ethological capabilities. And it was axiomatic to colonial thought that Britons had brought the boons of modern civilization to India, most notably through the benefits of their supposedly superior Christian values. But this was an India that was held to be inhabited by Britain's distant racial kin, their fellow Aryans, and the teachings of ethnology made it difficult to portray these descendants of superior fairskinned Aryans as being eternally condemned to the role of passive colonial subjects. Indeed by the 1880s many ethnologists agreed that "Aryan" India was beginning to live up to its ethnological heritage, and that this renewal of collective vigor and dynamism was being manifested in the so-called stirrings of the subcontinent's assertive new movements of spiritual uplift and revival. In other words degeneracy was being reversed; Aryan Indians were apparently beginning to become ethnologically dynamic again, just as they had been equipped to do by their racial heritage.

These spiritual "stirrings" were specifically referred to by ethnological theorists as expressions of national will. The British commentators who expressed themselves in these terms did not necessarily like what they were seeing, but they certainly did not write as if either the debilitating moral and mental environment of the tropics or the so-called Brahmanical fetters of caste had made all Indians safe, tame, and tractable. On the contrary, what many British commentators said at this time about the nature of nationality reflected the disquieting realization that there were increasing numbers of Asians who were forming themselves into large and assertive activist movements, most notably India's anti-Brahmanical Arya Samaj, and the anticolonial Buddhist rationalizing movements of Ceylon and Burma, as well as the pan-Islamist purifying organizations that were taking shape throughout south and southeast Asia. Many race theorists were well aware that the adherents of these organizations commonly referred to themselves as modernizers and nation builders, and that in this and other respects they were doing precisely what ethnologists said was characteristic of the most robust, advanced, and competitive human populations.

Whether they addressed themselves to people they regarded as Sikhs, Muslims, or Hindus, these self-professed Indian revivalists and purifiers of south Asian faith, and their many counterparts in other parts of Asia, generally exalted the sort of depersonalized monotheist worship that was classed by Western ethnology as the hallmark of racially advanced human "types." Both in India and elsewhere, the Asian leaders of these movements told their adherents that there was strength in unity, and that pluralities of caste, sect, or confessional allegiance were backward and baneful, and a cause of their weakness in the face of colonial conquest. In all this they were both echoing and reinterpreting Western ethnological principles, as well as synthesizing these with indigenous visions of regeneration, nationhood, and blood essence.[35]

This, said many Western ethnologists, was why Britain was facing dire ethnological danger in Asia. India's "Aryan" peoples were still widely held to be true though distant and debased kin of their British conquerors.[36] And what was being widely said by British commentators in this period was that in their newfound stirrings of activism and spiritual self-renewal, Asia's Aryans were dangerously ready to recover the vigor and competitive greatness that was implanted in their racial heritage. This was the message of Charles Morris's *The Aryan Race: Its Origins and Its Achievements* (1888). In this work the Aryans, "that great and noble family of mankind," are first encountered in ancient times "marching resolutely south, singing their stirring hymns of praise and invocation." Century by century this story of racial achievement unfolds as the white European descendants of the original Aryans bring civilization and Christian ethics to more and more of the world. Finally, says Morris, through Britain's conquest of India, "Aryan is again face to face with Aryan as in the era of the past, and as then the migratory march may end in a fierce strife of these ancient cousins for a lion's share of the spoils."[37]

Many of the nineteenth and early twentieth century's self-professed experts on the caste system shared this view that Britain was facing a moment of truth in its Asian empire. In India, they argued, Britons must find a way to build on their racial kinship with Aryan caste Hindus, helping them shape and direct this march toward moral and spiritual vigor and liberation, or risk the kind of ethnological doom that was so persistently harped on in the writings of the race theorists. The view of many anglophone ethnologists was that Britain had evolved as a nation from a favorable amalgam of Celts, incoming Teutons, and other compatible races. In contrast Aryan India had been retarded in its move toward national advancement because of this history of unfavorable racial mixing. "Two races, the one consisting of masters, the other of slaves, are not easily welded into a single nationality."[38]

But although stagnant, "effeminated by long sloth," and therefore vulnerable to conquest by their "Tartar" and "Mughal" racial "inferiors," India's Aryans were said to be still of noble stock like their British colonial rulers.[39] Hunter therefore was one of many writers who argued that under enlightened British government, these so-called Aryans could be regenerated and helped to recover their old ennobling vision of nationhood. In due course, India would overcome the debilitating fragmentation which had manifested itself for Hunter in the atomizing ideology which other theorists had misleadingly called caste. Nationhood would then be reborn in India.[40]

By the 1920s, many British commentators were inclined to take a far more pessimistic view of India's supposed Aryan awakening. One of the most revealing colonial texts of this period is *The Heart of Aryavarta: A Study of the Psychology of Indian Unrest* (1925) by the Conservative peer Lord Ronaldshay, who had been viceregal aide-de-camp during Curzon's turbulent period as viceroy, and whose term as governor of Bengal coincided with the 1919 Amritsar Massacre.[41] The term *Aryavarta* was already in widespread use among militant Hindu nationalists at this time, and Ronaldshay explains his title as a reference to the deep-seated "race genius" of India's Aryan Hindu population. The aim of the book was to explore what he saw as the dangerous new mentality of the Hindu political "extremists," whose understanding of patriotism was fatally flawed, in his view, by the immoderate and irrational religious sentiments which they attached to their idea of nationhood.

All the key Bengali Hindu nationalists discussed by Ronaldshay are to be seen as tragic figures who had rejected the notion of regenerative collaboration between Indians and their enlightened British rulers. In the teachings of Bipinchandra Pal, B. K. Ghose, C. R. Das, and other leading advocates of revolutionary nationalist activism, what to Ronaldshay had once been a healthy and progressive sense of Aryan spirituality, and a hope of achieving "national development on lines in harmony with [Aryan] race genius," had been taken over by a violent and irrational racial antagonism, and a "consuming hatred of the West."[42] All this was understandable, he said. In his view it was only natural for educated Indians to react against the ill-judged westernization of their country and the consequent loss of their "individuality of race."[43] The danger was in their supposed propensity to uncontrolled extremes, though he writes approvingly of those so-called Hindu spiritual revivalist movements which he finds healthy and positive, notably Swami Vivekananda's Rama-krishna mission.[44]

Race and the Regeneration of the Indian Nation

The Western ethnologists' picture of a weak divided India subdued by her inferiors will be familiar to Indian historians as a theme uniting an other-wise disparate array of Hindu revivalists, Gandhian nationalists, and Muslim separatists in the early twentieth century. Thus, although it has been usual to think of Third World nationalism, especially in India, as deriving from the liberal, secular traditions of Western constitutional poli-tics, the interpenetrating ethnological concepts of race and national reli-gious faith appealed very powerfully to aspiring nation builders in India, and indeed in many other parts of the colonial world. It is important to stress that racial concepts were used equally, though with different degrees of stridency, by the Arya Samaj and other "modernizing" religious move-ments, and also by their most vocal opponents, these being the organized defenders of *sanatan dharm* (literally "orthodox religion") who saw themselves as champions of established or traditional Hindu faith. Racial references are also very prominent in the writings of nationalists like Tilak, whose concept of a Western-style Indian nation-state took for granted a notion of primordial Indian racial qualities, and also in the thought of Gandhi's precursors, notably Aurobindo, who conceived of nationality as a more spiritual force but one that was still underpinned by blood and race.

However divided they were on other matters, south Asia's religious purifiers and cultural nationalists consistently invoked ethnological themes in their visions of a recovery of Indian greatness through spiritual regeneration. The writings of pre- and postindependence advocates of the Hindutva or Hinduness cause are steeped in ethnological principles.[45] The

Hindu revivalist concept of Aryavarta, the homeland of the true or pure Indian, has clear roots in an appropriated version of Western race theory.[46] Muslim polemicists too embraced many of these themes in the later nineteenth and twentieth centuries. Indeed, across a very wide spectrum of nationalist thought, Western ethnology was attractive because it told Indians with the voice of modern science that they could take pride in a heritage of classical Aryan, Sinhala Buddhist, or "Semitic" civilization.

Not surprisingly, many early Indian nationalists used what they regarded as the new and progressive science of race to oppose those colonial commentators who still portrayed India as an atomized, caste-fettered society, unequipped for nationhood.[47] At the same time, to some, though not all, of those who subscribed to its notions of blood purity and historic race essences, ethnology provided an attractively modern and scientific basis on which to stigmatize the Hindu or Muslim Other as an alien and an interloper within the national homeland. In other words there was a wide range of Hindu and Muslim polemic in both English and the vernaculars which invoked what the Western race theorists were saying about the meaning of religion on the so-called ethnical frontier. These pronouncements were then used to justify assertions that the alien Other whose faith was different from one's own was to be regarded as a person of unclean blood, and an enemy of one's race.

None of this reflected an uncritical assimilation of Western scientific thought. On the contrary, the attraction of theories of race and blood for many Indians, and indeed for other Asians, has been the ease with which the theories of European ethnologists could be made to fit and uphold indigenous concepts of blood-based community and moral essence.

Religion and Race Essence

By the early twentieth century the term *Hinduism* had come to be used in indigenous speech and writing as a territorial and ethnic category with strong polemical overtones. Its connotations were not neutral or passively descriptive; they were used instead to designate the qualities of history, blood, and intangible "race genius" which bound true Indians to their sacred homeland. Shared faith and spirituality had come to be widely seen by both Europeans and Indians as key components of this Hindu identity. Since the later nineteenth century the recovery of Hindu nationhood was a goal that had become closely tied to campaigns to codify those texts and bodies of pious obligation which could be regarded as an appropriate core of faith for the modern Hindu.[48] By the 1930s, these views had acquired an assertive new edge among many "modernizing" Hindu commentators. According to Shiv Kishan Kaul, a leading proponent of so-called Aryan Hindu regeneration, the Hindu nation had been for too long stagnant and divided. To restore the nation's greatness, every Hindu must be supplied with what he called the fundamentals or essentials of his faith. Once consolidated as a body of "essential and fundamental truths," this modern rendering of the Aryan heritage would enlighten the "mass mind." This enterprise was "in harmony with the spirit of modern science."[49] Shiv Kishan Kaul's view of Hinduism as a religion of science, power, and modernity was echoed by many other proponents of national growth and uplift in this period. And the insistence on codified faith as the key expression of modern nationhood is a central feature of these arguments. To Shiv Kishan Kaul it was through "united and uniform faith" that Hindus would acquire the power to rally, expand, and conquer. This, he maintained, was the lesson to be learned from the example of Russia, fascist Italy, and Nazi Germany. In "the current history of the world," he wrote, the force of faith had proved itself to be an ideal instrument in the making of progressive modern nationality. "Some of the most rational modern countries have perforce infused faith where reason was supreme so as to accelerate the reconstruction of society. Thus we see Bolshevism, Fascism and Nazism in their fullest force."[50]

For the many Indians who were aware of what Western ethnologists were saying about neo-Darwinian race conflicts, and about the ethnological doom that awaited the weak and degenerate, there was good reason to represent India's national heritage as much more than an array of distinctive pious obligations. The key social "reformists" of the early twentieth century, especially those who championed what they regarded as progressive social causes as members of the National Social Conference, wrote about the Indian nation as a vibrant living entity which was in the process of renewing and invigorating itself, expunging so-called social evils and superstitions from its life and thought, and recovering through the efforts of its modernizing elites a dedication to ethical purity which was the true expression of its primordial race genius.

All this was implicit in what the modern nation builder was told to understand by the term *Hinduism*. Far more than just a theological system, Hinduism was to be seen as a biological and moral order, that is, a civilization with its own self-renewing racial heritage. The social reform journals read by India's large and vocal anglophone intelligentsia were highly insistent on this theme. The anticaste campaigner Rao Bahadur M. Audinarayanana Iyer exalted Hinduism as a faith "which . . . not only enshrines the highest truths, but the traditions, the individuality, and the genius of the nation."[51] By professing their dedication to the unique "spiritual principle" of Hinduism, Iyer and his allies denied what Tilak and their other enemies from the so-called traditionalist camp said about them, which was that reformists who spoke on public platforms against the "backwardness" of Brahmanical caste ideologies were enemies of the nation and its spiritual heritage.

Both sides in these disputes therefore insisted that they were the true guardians of Hinduism. Citing both Carlyle and the Vedas, Iyer's ally T. V. Vaswani insisted that the advocates of "reformist" causes—"caste reform," female education, postpubescent marriage for women, and the remarriage of widows—were inspired by the spirit of race. "I have faith in the divine destiny of the Aryan race; I believe that every social reformer must be in tune with the genius of his nation."[52] So it was on ethnological grounds that Vaswani defended his controversial pronouncements on the evils of caste: "The social reformer seeks not to eliminate but to evolve the Idea immanent in the history, . . . thought and culture and life and age-long aspirations . . . of the Hindu race. . . . We plead for reform which proceeds along lines of our national evolution and yet seeks to adapt our social life to the requirements of modern times."[53] And the Bombay High Court judge M. G. Ranade (1842–1901), cofounder of the National Social Conference, expressed his vision of India's march to nationhood in very similar terms, that is, as a form of racial predestination: "I profess implicit faith in two articles of my creed. This country of ours is the land of promise. This race of ours is the chosen race."[54]

These self-proclaimed Hindu social reformists took a cautious line on untouchability, but argued robustly against prohibitions on intermarriage between castes and subcastes of roughly equivalent ritual rank on the grounds that these injunctions were divisive and ethnologically unsound. The influence of contemporary Western eugenics was very pronounced in these discussions, though Brahmanical concepts of purity were often held to be in harmony with what modern science was supposed to be saying about the preservation of race purity. Both child marriage and the barring of intercaste marriages were therefore attacked by reformists on the grounds that these practices promoted inbreeding and other unhealthy genetic trends, and were therefore damaging to the nation's racial "stock." There were also unmistakable echoes of the Western race theorists' claims about the superior race qualities of unfettered freedom lovers, in the Hindu reformers' insistence that to ascribe undue reverence to Brahmanical teachings was the badge of a degraded and unfree people, and that Brahmanical caste hierarchies must be dismantled if the Hindu nation were to flourish.

It was on this basis that many self-professed reformists linked the spread of caste to the supposedly debilitating and racially alien rule of both the British and the former Muslim dynasties of the subcontinent. The supposed rigidities of caste were not true features of primordial Hinduism, they said, but were irksome and deplorable accretions which had sapped the "natural vitality of the race," curtailing "man's individual lib-

erty" to a pernicious degree.[55] The result had been "the weakening of the
individual consciousness and the consequent enfeeblement of the national
consciousness. . . . A nation whose individuals are moral weaklings, social slaves and intellectual dwarfs [sic] could never . . . make a strong and
powerful nation intellectually, morally and spiritually."[56]

Keen as they were on the forms and expressions of faith that the reformists opposed, defenders of so-called dharmic Hindu convention were
equally quick to cite ethnological themes and theories in these debates
about the nation's future. In fact, far from regarding scientific modernity
as the enemy of Hindu faith and heritage, many of the most vocal Indian
opponents of the so-called reformists used the same ethnologically informed language in their defense of "traditional" caste values, and in their
advocacy for Brahmanical standards in matters of marriage and domestic
convention. This is why none of the participants in these debates should
be seen as passive recipients of a hegemonic Western scientific discourse.
Many of the same reformists who cited eugenicist theories about racial
health in their attacks on prepubescent marriage were fiercely hostile
to Risley and the other scholar-official ethnologists who said that there
was no nationhood in India because its castes were of radically divergent
racial origin.[57]

On the other side of these controversies, the reformists' Indian opponents merged scientific arguments with appeals to divine authority in their
attacks on so-called caste reform. These polemicists too addressed themselves to the cause of race purity, but in their view Brahmanical teaching
and modern eugenics were in close accord. Their writings therefore
recapitulated what Hunter and his contemporaries had said about the
supposed law of nature that decreed universal repugnance between people
of "high" and "inferior" race. Commentators like B. N. Bhajekar read
deep-seated ethnological truth into the instinctive horror which all pious
Hindus supposedly felt at the idea of "twice-born" women being "soiled"
through sexual contact with tribals or untouchables. Scripture and modern science were as one on this issue: "It is Hindu law, Hindu community,
and the British High Courts, not my poor self, who have given [the] power
of enforcing . . . moral and social rules [against such intermarriages]."[58]

The ethnologists' fear of degenerative racial catastrophe is also apparent in these writings, which told readers that there was moral and physiological doom in store for any nation that was foolish and decadent enough
to throw away its racial heritage by promoting "race blending" through
intermarriages between people of radically unequal blood. In India this
supposedly meant people of "civilized" Aryan origin and those of inferior
race, meaning those defined as impure in the sastras (classical Hindu scriptures extolling caste).

In all this one can see how readily indigenous humoral theories of health and moral essence could be assimilated into the teachings of Western eugenics and race science.[59] The other key characteristic of these writings was the view that Indians must analyze the so-called essentials of their own and other people's faith to discover the path to a healthy national future. In the case of antireformist thinkers, this often meant inverting the falsehoods that these critics claimed to have detected in the historical writing of Britons as well as reform-minded Indians.

This can be seen, for example, in the writings of the Bengali essayist Chandranath Basu (1844–1910), who was one of the earliest popularizers of the now familiar Hindu supremacist term *Hindutva*.[60] Basu, who was also a noted economic nationalist, exalted the virtues of caste as a path to sublime and selfless national morality. In this he shared common ground with many of his fellow antireformists, most notably Jogendranath Bhattacharya of the Bengal Brahman Sabha, who proclaimed in 1896 that caste was a "golden chain" which had welded the sons of the ancient Aryans into a single virtuous composite, "one race under the name of Brahmans." This exalted heritage had endowed Indians with selfless spiritual ideals which had united the subcontinent's supposedly separate races and clans, and had inspired them in their struggles against foreign domination.[61]

But while Basu cited the authority of divine will and the sacred scriptures for his view of caste as a product of unquestionable sacred mandate, he too considered it essential to tie his arguments to the known conventions of Western science and scholarship. He therefore argued that Indians had been lied to about the meaning of the European Protestant Reformation, and that far from being a triumph of virtue and libertarianism over the tyrannical Romish yoke, Europe's Protestant reformers were self-seeking materialists who had achieved a base and inglorious victory over the noble and ascetic faith of the Roman Church.[62] This is all the more striking in that Basu was one of the many "modern" Hindu nationalists who alarmed British commentators because they subscribed to a view of the divine that was held to be ethnologically advanced, that is, a God who was understood as a formless multifaceted Creator, but in whose eyes both the intermarriage of unlike castes and the marriage of postpubescent girls were un-Hindu and abominable.[63]

Both Swami Vivekananda and Gandhi made much of eugenicist themes in their arguments about the need to restore health, vigor, and social purity to the Hindu nation. Vivekananda's understanding of progressive social action as a regenerative racial panacea helped to shape the ideals of the Ramakrishna mission movement, and there were close parallels to this in the aims of Gandhi's social service organization for untouchables, the Harijan Sevak Sangh.[64] Indeed the many Hindu nationalists who campaigned for educational and social "uplift" for the untouchable or depressed castes were particularly inclined to express the goal of so-called social reclamation for these groups as a matter of desperate ethnological urgency.

These schemes of so-called uplift first began to be widely advocated in the reformist press at a time when the colonial census was reporting an alarming decline in population growth among Hindus in relation to Muslims, Sikhs, and Christians. Tilak's Congress rival Gokhale was one of many commentators who portrayed the success of Muslim, Sikh, and Christian proselytizers in attracting lower-caste and untouchable converts as a sign of Hindu weakness and racial decline: his social service venture, the Servants of India Society, was yet another movement devoted to the energizing of national spirituality through constructive social work.[65]

The fear as expressed by Hindu nationalists on this matter was that other ethnoreligious communities had become stronger and more vigorous in evolutionary terms, with higher rates of female fertility and a healthier and more active "race spirit." This was the basis on which members of the Arya Samaj were enjoined to arrest the numerical and moral decline of the Hindu nation by taking part in campaigns of *shuddhi* or reconversion so as to reclaim untouchable convert groups who had been lost to the Hindu nation through the missionary endeavors of these rival faiths.[66]

A wide range of other Hindu revivalist organizations also committed themselves to this cause on the same grounds. The Prarthana Samaj, or society of liberal religionists, which was founded in 1871 to promote ideals of transcendent monotheist divinity and all-embracing moral community for "enlightened" Hindus, was one of the earliest of these movements to invite its educated anglophone membership to commit themselves to the cleansing and regeneration of the nation by joining the "noble work" of uplift for the depressed.[67] At the other end of the spectrum was the theosophist Sons of India Order: the leaders of this group were defenders of ancient Hindu moral truths and believed that untouchables could and should be educated, but along lines that harmonized modern scientific improvement with their inherited caste qualities.[68]

But in fact whether they belonged to conservative or ostensibly liberal organizations, the architects of the new Hindu nation all set the same standards of propriety and civilized behavior for the people they professed to be reclaiming. Like comparable social service societies in nineteenth-century Britain, the energies of the depressed class missions were primarily devoted to fighting drink, "vice" and uncleanliness. But in their Indian manifestation these goals reflected a convergence of modern science with a synthesis of Victorian morality and established Hindu pious norms.

These activists made it clear that to be accepted as a worthy member of the Hindu nation, the reclaimed untouchable must become a clean, sober, and thrifty vegetarian, and an adherent of purified Hindu faith.[69] Such people were thus to behave in a way that conformed to the known codes of "pure" dharmic social convention and, at the same time, to the teachings of eugenicists and race theorists, whose writings had defined both the spiritual and the physiological attributes of advanced nations, and had made clear distinctions between healthy and unhealthy manifestations of appetite and psychic energy. In other words, it was easy for the modern Hindu nationalist to take a deeply coercive and hierarchical view of so-called untouchables, and indeed of anyone else—including Muslims—who could be seen as transgressing these notions of collective national virtue and propriety. Such attitudes could be justified on the grounds that the backward practices of untouchables and other unenlightened people were a willful violation of Hindu race genius, and a threat to the health and progress of the nation.

Conclusion

This essay has argued that an urgent and assertive concern with religion has been at the core of orientalist writing since the earliest stages of the Western colonial experience. In the age of modern empire, the concept of nationality was a central theme for the many metropolitan thinkers and colonial scholar-officials who attempted to define human societies on evolutionary racial grounds. Even in those works which professed a strictly scientific understanding of race, polity, and nationhood, matters of faith and spirituality were of critical importance. The pronouncements of the nineteenth- and early-twentieth-century race theorists were very insistent on this theme: in their view the mark of an advanced race was a strong and expansive sense of spirituality, and a devotion to national purpose which was expressed through the teachings of vigorous and rational faith, as well as an endowment of libertarian political ideals.

All these principles, which were supposedly borne out in the findings of the anthropometric data gatherers, were enunciated in an atmosphere of deep anxiety about the evolutionary future of the white "Aryan" Briton in an age of global conflict and alarming new stirrings of "race vigour" amongst Britain's so-called Aryan kin in India. Here too it was in the domain of religion that the Western race theorists believed that they could discern these dangerous new developments on the so-called ethnological frontier. And it is at this point, both in India and in many other parts of Asia, that the ideas of the European commentators met and interpenetrated with the powerful new ideological developments which were taking shape from within the indigenous societies in the late nineteenth and twentieth centuries.

A very wide range of south Asian commentators participated in the making of Indian nationalist ideologies in this period. These thinkers borrowed extensively from the writings of British and Continental evolutionists and eugenicists, but their writings were emphatically not a mere recapitulation of any one Western scientific consensus. For all their diversity, these early architects of south Asian nationality had two things in common with the British commentators whose works they assimilated into their own indigenous notions of blood, faith, and nationhood. The first of these was their insistence that nationhood was the highest of human evolutionary attainments. The second was their conviction that to achieve national fulfillment, people of common blood must find the means to realize their spiritual potential, as well as purifying themselves of the physiological and moral inadequacies defined by both God and science as harmful to the nation's health.

In the late twentieth century these are ideas that have become fully indigenized by south Asians. As in other parts of the world where very similar ideologies have been embraced, these have often been read as a message of humanity and tolerance. It is tragic yet true that in India, as in many Western societies, this synthesis of spiritual and scientific ideals has been widely interpreted as a violent and authoritarian call to arms, and an invitation to expunge the nation of its supposed racial and spiritual enemies.

Notes

1. J. Ovington, *A Voyage to Suratt, in the Year 1689* (London, 1696).

2. James Forbes, *Oriental Memoirs: Selected and Abridged from a Series of Familiar Letters Written during Seventeen Years' Residence in India, Including Observations on Parts of Africa and South America, and a Narrative of Occurrences in Four India Voyages*, 4 vols. (London, 1813); Walter Hamilton, *The East-India Gazetteer*, 2d ed., 2 vols. (London, 1828).

3. W. Ward, *A View of the History and Religion of the Hindoos, Including a Minute Description of Their Manners and Customs, and Translations from Their Principal Works*, 3d ed., 4 vols. (London: Black, Parbury and Allen, 1817–20), 3: 65.

4. On Aryan race myths, see Léon Poliakov, *The Aryan Myth: A History of Racist and Nationalist Ideas in Europe* (New York: Basic Books, 1974); Joan Leopold, "British Applications of the Aryan Theory of Race to India," *English Historical Review* 89 (1974): 578–603; and Christophe Jaffrelot, "The Ideas of the Hindu Race in the Writings of Hindu Nationalist Ideologues in the 1920s and 1930s," in Peter Robb, ed., *The Concept of Race in South Asia* (Delhi: Oxford University Press, 1995), 327–54. Because this essay contains detailed discussion

of colonial race theories, it uses many terms and phrases which will be offensive to modern readers. Even where such usages do not appear in quotation marks, there is of course no intention to suggest approval or endorsement of the racist writing and ideologies from which they derive.

5. Ward, *A View of the History and Religion of the Hindoos*, 3: 64–65.

6. Ibid., 287; see L. Ronald Inden, *Imagining India* (Oxford: Blackwell, 1990).

7. Elazar Barkan, *The Retreat of Scientific Racism: Changing Concepts of Race in Britain and the United States between the World Wars* (Cambridge: Cambridge University Press, 1992).

8. See Inden, *Imagining India*; Romila Thapar, "Imagined Religious Communities? Ancient History and the Modern Search for a Hindu Identity," *Modern Asian Studies* 23 (1989): 209–31; Gyan Prakash, "Writing Post-Orientalist Histories of the Third World: Perspectives from Indian Historiography," *Comparative Studies in Society and History* 32 (1990): 383–408; Nicholas Dirks, "Castes of Mind," *Representations* 37 (1992): 56–78; Rosalind O'Hanlon, "Cultures of Rule, Communities of Resistance," *Social Analysis* 28 (1992): 94–114; and Peter van der Veer, *Religious Nationalism: Hindus and Muslims in India* (Berkeley: University of California Press, 1994).

9. Susan Bayly, "Caste and Race in the Colonial Ethnography of India," in Peter Robb, ed., *The Concept of Race in South Asia* (Delhi: Oxford University Press, 1995), 165–218.

10. See C. Staniland Wake, "The Aim and Scope of Anthropology," *Journal of Anthropology* 1 (1870): 1–18; John Beddoe, "The Permanence of Racial Types," *Memoirs of the Anthropological Society of London* 2 (1865–66): 37–45; James Hunt, "On the Negro's Place in Nature," *Memoirs of the Anthropological Society of London* 1 (1863–64): 1–63; L. Owen Pike, "On the Psychical Characteristics of the English People," *Memoirs of the Anthropological Society of London* 2 (1865–66): 153–88; and Robert Knox, "Ethnological Inquiries and Observations," *Anthropological Review* 1 (1863): 246–63.

11. See C. Pinney, "Colonial Anthropology in the 'Laboratory of Mankind,' " in C. Bayly, ed., *The Raj: India and the British, 1600–1947* (London: National Portrait Gallery Publications, 1990), 252–63; also *Memoirs of the Anthropological Society of London*, 1870 ff.

12. See C. A. Bayly, "Returning the British to South Asian History: The Limits of Colonial Hegemony," *South Asia* 17 (1994): 1–25; also Andrew Porter, "Religion and Empire: British Expansion in the Long Nineteenth Century," *Journal of Imperial and Commonwealth History* 20 (1992): 370–93.

13. See Knox, "Ethnological Inquiries and Observations"; George Campbell, *Ethnology of India* (n.p., [1865]); and Walter Elliot, "On the Characteristics of the Population of Central and Southern India," *Journal of the Ethnological Society of London* 1 (1868–69): 94–128.

14. Daniel Pick, *Faces of Degeneration: A European Disorder, c.1848–c.1918* (Cambridge: Cambridge University Press, 1989).

15. W. W. Hunter, *Annals of Rural Bengal*, 7th ed. (London: Smith and Elder, 1897), 3.

16. Ibid., 90. See also C. Morrison, "Three Styles of Imperial Ethnography," *Knowledge and Society* 5 (1984): 141–69.

17. Hunter, *Annals of Rural Bengal*, 89. See also Knox, "Ethnological Inquiries and Observations."

18. Hunter, *Annals of Rural Bengal*, 89–90.

19. Ibid., 90.

20. Ibid., 134.

21. Ibid., 98.

22. See Bhimrao Ramji Ambedkar, *Who Were the Shudras?: How They Came to Be the Fourth Varna in the Indo-Aryan Society* (Bombay: Thacker, 1970); also Rosalind O'Hanlon, *Caste, Conflict, and Ideology: Mahatma Jotirao Phule and Low Caste Protest in Nineteenth-Century Western India* (Cambridge: Cambridge University Press, 1985); and Marguerite Ross Barnett, *The Politics of Cultural Nationalism in South India* (Princeton, N.J.: Princeton University Press, 1976).

23. Hunter, *Annals of Rural Bengal*, 131–34.

24. Knox, "Ethnological Inquiries and Observations," 248.

25. Hunter, *Annals of Rural Bengal*, 91.

26. Ibid., 92, 104, 117, and 113.

27. Ibid., 127.

28. Ibid., 97.

29. Ibid., 93–95.

30. Pike, "On the Psychical Characteristics of the English People," 185.

31. Ibid., 183–84.

32. Ibid., 185.

33. Charles Morris, *The Aryan Race: Its Origins and Its Achievements* (Chicago: Griggs, 1888).

34. Pike, "On the Psychical Characteristics of the English People," 158.

35. Compare Frans Dikötter, *The Discourse of Race in Modern China* (London: Hurst, 1992).

36. Adam Kuper, *The Invention of Primitive Society: Transformations of an Illusion* (London: Routledge, 1988).

37. Morris, *The Aryan Race*, 82, 300, and 306.

38. Hunter, *Annals of Rural Bengal*, 136 and 139.

39. Ibid., 139.

40. Ibid., 140.

41. Ronaldshay was wounded in the terrorist shooting which killed the ultra-conservative provincial governor Sir Michael O'Dwyer, who had spoken out in defense of the commander who ordered the 1919 massacre.

42. Earl of Ronaldshay, *The Heart of Aryavarta: A Study of the Psychology of Indian Unrest* (London: Constable, 1925), ix–x.

43. Ibid., 132.

44. Ibid., 203 ff. Vivekananda (1863–1902) was the renowned Bengali sage-polemicist who gained international celebrity at the 1893 Chicago World's Congress of Religions; his vision of spiritually informed national uplift anticipated Gandhi's philosophy.

45. van der Veer, *Religious Nationalism*.

46. Jaffrelot, "The Ideas of the Hindu Race."

47. Partha Chatterjee, *The Nation and Its Fragments: Colonial and Postcolonial Histories* (Princeton, N.J.: Princeton University Press, 1993).

48. Kenneth W. Jones, *Arya Dharm: Hindu Consciousness in nineteenth-century Punjab* (Berkeley: University of California Press, 1976); van der Veer, *Religious Nationalism*. Cf. Barbara D. Metcalf, *Islamic Revival in British India: Deoband, 1860–1900* (Princeton, N.J.: Princeton University Press, 1982).

49. Shiv Kishan Kaul, *Wake Up Hindus: A Plea for Mass Religion, Aryanism* (Lahore: Kaul, 1937), 56, 78, 82, 91, and 130.

50. Ibid., 95.

51. *Indian Social Reformer* (hereafter *ISR*), 3 January 1909, 207.

52. *ISR*, 18 April 1909, 390.

53. Ibid.

54. Quoted in J. C. Masselos, *Towards Nationalism: Group Affiliations and the Politics of Public Associations in Nineteenth-Century Western India* (Bombay: Popular Prakashan, 1974), 82.

55. *ISR*, 15 December 1912, 184.

56. Ibid.

57. Ibid., passim.

58. *ISR*, 9 June 1912, 486.

59. See Amiya P. Sen, *Hindu Revivalism in Bengal, 1872–1905: Some Essays in Interpretation* (Delhi: Oxford University Press, 1993), 219–26, on the scientific axioms cited by the Aryan revivalist proselytizer Pandit Sasadhar Tarkachudamani (1851–1928).

60. Ibid., 209–18.

61. Jogendra Nath Bhattacharya, *Hindu Castes and Sects: An Exposition of the Origin of the Hindu Caste System and the Bearing of the Sects towards Each Other and towards Other Religious Systems* (Calcutta: Thacker, Spink, 1896), 4–7; cf. M. G. Ranade, *Rise of the Maratha Power* (Bombay: Pubalekar, 1900).

62. Sen, *Hindu Revivalism in Bengal*, 216.

63. Ibid.

64. Mark Juergensmeyer, *Religion as Social Vision: The Movement against Untouchability in Twentieth-Century Punjab* (Berkeley: University of California Press, 1982).

65. *ISR*, 28 February 1909, 306.

66. Jones, *Arya Dharm*.

67. *ISR*, 13 December 1908.

68. *ISR*, 23 May 1909.

69. *ISR*, 18 October 1908, 78.

5

History, the Nation, and Religion: The Transformations of the Dutch Religious Past

PETER VAN ROODEN

DUTCH PROTESTANTISM acquired a national past at the beginning of the nineteenth century, during the first years of the new Kingdom of the Netherlands. From 1819 to 1827 the four volumes of Ypey and Dermout's *History of the Dutch Reformed Church* appeared, some two and a half thousand pages total.[1] Their work has not fared well. Its garrulous verbosity, weak composition, and old-fashioned liberalism have been rightly denounced. Only the four accompanying volumes with notes, more than a thousand dense pages full of facts and quotations, have been admired for their scholarship. Protestant academic ecclesiastical history prefers to trace its origin to the founding in 1829 of its scholarly journal, the *Nederlands Archief voor Kerkgeschiedenis*, by the two first occupants of the newly founded chairs for church history at the universities of Leiden and Utrecht.

Yet if we choose not to situate Ypey and Dermout's work as a contribution to academic scholarship, but rather as an expression of the self-understanding of Dutch Protestantism, then their work is very important indeed. Their book was a startlingly new representation of the church's past. The public church of the Dutch Republic had not used ecclesiastical histories to produce a past, but had linked itself to its origin by means of rituals, lists, and administrative routines. In this essay I try to show how changes in the way in which a religious past was produced were intimately linked to fundamental shifts in the location of religion in Dutch society.

Every three years from 1641 to the end of the eighteenth century, representatives of all the provincial synods of the Dutch Reformed Church traveled to The Hague, the seat of the States General of the Dutch Republic. There they inspected the chest that contained the acts of the national synod of Dordrecht. At this synod, held in 1618–19, the public church of the Dutch Republic had committed itself to a mitigated version of the doctrine of double predestination (henceforth a hallmark of orthodox Calvinism) and had expelled the Arminians. The next day the delegates of the provincial synods traveled in two boats from The Hague to Leiden, where they were received by the mayors. In the town hall they were shown

the chest that contained the manuscripts of the so-called States' translation, the Dutch translation of the Bible on which the national synod
had decided, and which had been financed by the States General. After
satisfying themselves that worms and moths had not consumed the
papers, the box was locked again, everybody had a sumptuous dinner,
and the participants sailed back. The whole outing was highly ritualized
and hierarchized, with prayers preceding and following the opening of
the chests, and occasional bickerings about precedence and sleights to
status breaking out.[2]

This visitation was the most prominent way the Dutch public church
related itself to its past. It was certainly the only national occasion at
which the ecclesiastical past was invoked. The Dutch Republic was more
or less a federation of seven sovereign provinces. All provinces upheld
the Reformed religion, as it had been defined at the national Synod of
Dordrecht. This shared confession was one of the Republic's most important symbols of unity. On the other hand, as the principle of subordi-
nation of ecclesiastical to political authority was well established and the
provinces were jealous of their sovereignty, the Dutch public church was
organized on a provincial basis. The Synod of Dordrecht was the last
national synod held during the Republic. Links between the various provincial synods were upheld by sending delegates to each other's meetings.
It would be wrong to speak of provincial churches, insofar as the of clergy's consciousness of subscribing to a common confession upheld by public authority was very strong. They knew they made up the public church
of the Republic. Yet all provinces had more or less their own church order
and administrative particularities. Movement of clergy between provinces
was comparatively rare. A national labor market for ministers did not
exist.[3] No wonder then that the only literary ways in which the public
church of the Republic constructed its past reproduced this organizational
fragmentation. In the eighteenth century provincial collections of legal
acts and decisions concerning religion since the Reformation were published.[4] In a similar way, books containing lists of ministers that had
served the towns and rural parishes since the Reformation were organized
on a provincial basis.[5] This last invocation of the past took place locally
as well. The custom of placing boards with the names of all ministers who
had served the parish since the Reformation against the wall of the parish
church stems from the seventeenth century.[6] Other local constructions of
the past centered on the sacraments. In 1729, for instance, Bernardus
Smytegelt, a minister of Middelburg, casually remarked in a sermon that
the previous Sunday communion had been celebrated for the 845th time
since the Reformation.[7]

This, I believe, is an exhaustive overview of the various ways in which
the public church of the Republic related itself to its past. Clearly, this

is not history as we now know it. This was not for lack of historical consciousness or scholarship. At the Dutch universities, during the seventeenth and eighteenth centuries some general church histories were produced. Most of these Latin works were meant for use in academic teaching and followed the conventions of Protestant historiography. They documented the gradual decay of the church from the times of the New Testament to the end of the Middle Ages and the brink of the Reformation, and defended the Reformation against the charge of being an innovation. These academic histories do not devote much attention to the Republic and its public church.[8] Some ministers of the public church engaged in popular historical writing, publishing in the vernacular.[9] Essentially, this popular historiography offered overviews of the history of the Dutch Republic, stressing its miraculous rise to great-power status. The works are full of examples of God's direct intervention in battles and sieges. The explanation of God's particular care for the Republic is found in its upholding of true religion.

In short, during the Republic, academic, general church histories, which are only marginally interested in the history of the Dutch church, stand next to confessionally inspired popular histories of the Dutch Republic, while the past of the public church is created by means of rituals and lists. These peculiar relations of history, church, and political community can be understood only if one takes into account the self-understanding of the public church of the Republic. A good place to start is Jacob Fruytier's *Struggles of Sion, or Historical Dialogues about the Various Bitter Tribulations of the Church of Christ*, published in 1715.[10] As the title indicates, Fruytier was more interested in the church's past than most other popular historical works. His book is divided in three parts. The first deals with the Reformation, the second with the Arminian troubles in the Dutch church, the third with the attacks on the church in his own day. The work assumes the form of a dialogue, in which the fictitious character Nathanael discusses the history and situation of the Dutch church with his female interlocutors, Truth and Piety. They explain to him that the crisis of the church results from various philosophers' and theologians' public attacks of the religious truth it upholds. "Public" is the central category of this analysis of the state of religion. The truth of religion is essentially a public truth; the first two parts of Fruytier's work concern the establishment of this truth as a public phenomenon. The Reformation and the Synod of Dordrecht are depicted as the founding moments of a public religious order, with the doctrine upheld at the Synod of Dordrecht as its most important element.[11] This doctrine defines the public church of the Republic; only this doctrine ought to be preached publicly.

Fruytier was not alone in locating religion in the visible, public order of society. Sermons preached at annual jeremiads, the most important civic ritual of the Republic, almost invariably ended with an overview of the duties of the bearers of authority in society: magistrates, ministers, church councils, parents, and employers.[12] Although the theologians of the public church of the Republic carefully distinguished between political and ecclesiastical authority and always upheld the theoretical independence of the latter, they conceived of society as a single body politic informed by both kinds of authority. This conception tied in rather well with the extremely decentralized and differentiated nature of the body politic of the Republic. As the Republic was imagined as a whole of interlocking ordering structures, provincial and local differences in the details of the political and ecclesiastical order were not considered to be of great importance. The same held for the presence of Dissenters and Catholics. Provided they did not encroach upon the visible and public religious order, their existence did not call into question the view of society upheld by the public church. Their encroachments upon public space, in the form of church buildings or blatantly anti-Reformed polemics, were decried, not their presence or resistance to incorporation within the public church.

I do not want to suggest that the public church of the Republic had no sense of the importance of individual commitment on the part of its adherents. On the contrary, it always upheld rather high standards for full membership.[13] Various pietistic movements, of different shapes and inspirations, were active within the church, almost from the very beginning of the seventeenth century. The practice of distinguishing between truly converted and only formal members of the church grew steadily, becoming an almost invariant feature of eighteenth-century sermons. Yet these widely shared pietistic ideas and endeavors did not influence or replace the conception that religion was preeminently present in the visible order of society. In Fruytier's dialogue, for instance, Truth repeatedly explains to Nathanael that Piety follows her, leaving if she leaves, staying when she stays.[14] Public truth precedes private belief. In a revealing passage, Fruytier states that external discipline and orderly behavior are necessary for internal conviction.[15]

Its peculiar conception of its place as part of the order of Dutch society explains why the public church of the Republic constructed its past as an origin, not as a history. The visit to The Hague and Leiden was a ritual inspection of the founding charters of the public church. The lists of ministers attested to its presence as a public body since the Reformation. Only the Republic has a history, of which the explaining factor is its upholding of the religious order.

Ypey and Dermout's work does not document an origin. It tells the development and history of the Dutch Reformed Church. Its four volumes span the three centuries from the beginning of the sixteenth to the beginning of the nineteenth century. Slightly more than half of their work is devoted to the eighteenth century. They organize their material by periods, usually of about half a century. Most transitional years between periods are derived from important turning points in the history of the Dutch Republic: 1625, 1648, 1700, 1748, 1795, 1815. Each period is treated in two chapters. In a first chapter the history of the church is told. A second chapter reviews its internal and external state. The histories mainly consist of overviews of internal dogmatic controversies. The reviews of the external state of the church offer rough estimates of its success in converting Catholics and Mennonites and descriptions of the expansion of its organization, both in the Republic itself and in the areas administered by the East India Company. The attempts to evaluate the internal state of the church are the result of a much more ambitious endeavor. In these reviews, Ypey and Dermout evaluate the piety of the members of the church for each period.

Clearly, such a structure presupposes a different view of the place of religion in society. Religion is no longer located in the structural and symbolic order of society, but in the inner selves of believers. The leading interest in the descriptions of the history of the Dutch church is its effectiveness as a means to educate the believers and mold their moral characters. Ecclesiastical conflicts are denounced as obstacles to this fundamental task of the church. Theological positions are evaluated according to their effectiveness in morally informing the believers.

This location of religion in the inner selves of believers determines the way Ypey and Dermout treat the Reformation. They make a clear distinction between the reformation of the Dutch church and the founding of a reformed church in the Netherlands, dividing these events between different chapters.[16] Already in the first half of the sixteenth century, enlightened preaching by the Dutch clergy had convinced all inhabitants of the Netherlands not tied by wordly interests to Catholicism to adopt sentiments and opinions properly called Protestant.[17] The founding and organizing of a Protestant church in the second half of the sixteenth century was, more or less, a secondary event, an external confirmation of an inner conviction already shared by the overwhelming majority of Dutchmen and -women. In their sketch of the founding of the public church, Ypey and Dermout stress its character as a societal event. They do not describe it as the result of measures by central political or ecclesiastical authorities. People found themselves in basic agreement and set up an ecclesiastical organization to suit themselves.[18]

This dialectic between internal religious conviction and its external social forms, the result of Ypey and Dermout's location of religion in the inner selves of believers, determines their treatment of the history of the

Dutch public church. They are not radical pietists, rejecting every externalization of religion. Although they express high regard for most of the pietistic endeavors within the Dutch church, as attempts to seriously educate and moralize the people,[19] they strongly condemn those revivalistic or mystic conceptions that tend to empower people in ways other than by education and civilized influence.[20] They do so for two closely related reasons. Inner piety must have a universal character, and Ypey and Dermout conceive of the universality of true piety through its links, by means of education, to the world of scholarship. Esoteric or inspirational doctrines can therefore never result in true piety. In the second place, such doctrines tend to foster separation. All religion that involves organization as a separate group within society becomes an instance of particularity, because it dissolves the distinction between inner, personal conviction and its outer, social form. Sectarians locate religion not solely in the inner selves of believers, but in their organization and group as well.

It will come as no surprise that Ypey and Dermout denounce the Synod of Dordrecht. They deplore its introduction of a rupture and an explicit formulation of particularity within Dutch Protestantism. Throughout their volumes, they describe the Arminians as part of the Dutch church and review their scholarship and piety in the overviews of the internal state of the church.[21] According to Ypey and Dermout, Arminian and Calvinist sentiments had been present within the Dutch church since the Reformation. The conflict broke out because this theological difference was taken up within a political struggle. All involvement of religion with political strife is bad, because it ensures that piety will become partisan and lose its universal character.[22] The analysis of the Arminian troubles plays a paradigmatic role in Ypey and Dermout's work. All later theological quarrels are related to political struggles as well. It is not theological difference as such, but political partisanship that destroys the proper societal role of religion. They consider it a blessing upon the Dutch church that it reached theological consensus at the end of the eighteenth century, just before the destruction of the old Republic started a whole new area of political struggle.[23]

In effect, Ypey and Dermout define true religion as an inwardness that relates itself to the nation. It is the relation to the whole nation, conceived of as a moral community of individual citizens, that ensures the universality of piety. Political partisanship introduces particular moments in piety, and thereby destroys its religious character. This religious nationalism explains the favorable judgment Ypey and Dermout pass on the involvement of political authority with the public church of the Republic. They welcome the support public authority offered to the education and disciplining of the people, and its subduing of quarrels among the theologians.[24] The state represents the nation as bearer of universality.

The location of religion in the inner selves of individual citizens of the nation has three consequences for Ypey and Dermout's conceptualization of the way religion functions in society. In the first place, it introduces a very strong process of cultural class formation. All citizens are potentially equal, because they can be morally educated. Only a minority, however, is truly educated and civilized. This is the basis for a discursive distinction between the civilized elite and the rude common people. Ypey and Dermout locate pure religious sentiments mainly in the upper middle class (the *fatsoenlijken burgerstand*).[25] Consequently, they strongly support the way in which cultural and social dominance can be translated into moral influence.[26]

In the second place, they embrace the principle of the separation of church and state, and do not wish one particular ecclesiastical body to be privileged over others. All churches should be supported by the state as they contribute to the formation of moral selves and therefore of virtuous citizens. Allowing the adherents of one particular church a monopoly on political office and on advantages distributed by political patronage corrupts piety by confounding it with secular interests. In the third place, this new location of religion immediately creates new exclusions. Ypey and Dermout evidence strong anti-Catholic sentiments. They consider Roman Catholicism the symbol of tyranny in religion, of an impure mix of power and piety.[27] It is no longer, as it had been for the public church of the Republic, a pollution of the public sphere. It is an obstacle to the proper religious and moral education of Dutch citizens.

The new vision of the place of religion in society that forms the basis of Ypey and Dermout's work was widely shared. From the 1760s on, a strong cultural nationalism developed within the Dutch Republic, stressing the duty of all citizens to be morally involved with the nation. In the 1780s, in the aftermath of a disastrous military defeat of the Republic at the hands of Great Britain, this nationalism became politicized and led to a revolution, which in 1787 was put down by Prussian regular troops.[28] In 1795, the French invaded and put the revolutionaries of the 1780s back into power. They completely overhauled the Dutch Republic, making it into a modern nation-state. One of their first acts was to separate church and state. The new Kingdom of the Netherlands, established after the final defeat of Napoleon, inherited both the ideal of the nation and the effective central bureaucracy of its revolutionary predecessors and continued their centralizing policies. Both the former public church and Old Dissent, the Mennonites, Arminians, and Lutherans, received effective organizational structures from the central authorities. Henceforth, they would be dependent not on local elites but on the central government, as mediated by strong ecclesiastical organizations, staffed by members of the clergy.

The ideological differences between the Protestants were reduced. Apart from the most traditional Mennonites, all Protestant clergy were trained at institutes of higher learning along more or less the same lines. All of them considered the Netherlands a nation of citizens and saw their own churches as means to further the welfare of this nation by morally educating its citizens. All of them received ministers of the other churches in their pulpits. In fact, the former public church together with Old Dissent had become an informal national establishment, which saw it as its task to further the identity of the Dutch nation by teaching and civilizing the common people.

Because Ypey and Dermout offered a vision of the past that fitted in extremely well with religion's modern location in the inner selves of the nation's members, their conceptualization of Dutch church history was immediately convincing. Their work created a past that was not an origin legitimating a present order but a story of the nation's continuous attempt to shape itself as a moral community, an endeavor still going on in the present. All general church histories of the nineteenth century share this conception of the church as a means to morally inform the nation, even when they reject Ypey and Dermout's theological liberalism. Such works are very much interested in the church as a teaching organization, focusing on universities and ministers.[29] The former public church itself understood its task in the nation as a continuation of older endeavors. It started to call itself the national (*vaderlandse*) church. All theological currents were united in their emphasis on the necessity of educating the people. The nineteenth and the better part of the twentieth century witnessed an unprecedented catechetical effort.

In academic church history Ypey and Dermout's vision of religion as an inner piety relating itself to the whole nation, essentially independent of formal ecclesiastical organization, translated itself into an interest in the Dutch medieval church and the early Reformation and its precursors. Ypey and Dermout had started their work with the disarming observation that it had not been sufficiently remarked that the European Reformation was due to the Dutch invention of printing, the Dutch Brethren of the Common Life, and the Dutchman Erasmus. Such presumptuous claims were not made by later Dutch church historians, but they were, until quite recently, very much interested in proving the Dutch origin of the Dutch Reformation, at least.[30]

In the last quarter of the nineteenth century, religious difference was reintroduced in Dutch political discourse, due to the rise of neo-Calvinism as political and social mass movement. This was an unexpected development. The Netherlands entered the second half of the nineteenth century as a homogeneous nation-state, with a surprisingly modern constitution but a stagnant economy and stable society, in which the cleavage between

the political and cultural elite and the common people was by far the most
important social distinction. Within this elite, a broad consensus existed
about the essentially Protestant nature of the Dutch nation. The nation
was considered to be a moral community made up of individuals. The
allegedly Protestant nature of such a conception of community was
stressed again and again. The Protestant clergy, both of the former public
church and of Old Dissent, underwrote this settlement as well.

Among the common people there was no broad-based opposition
against this conception of the nation. Only small groups of lower-class
people expressed dissent. In a steady trickle they left the former public
church, setting up churches that conceived of themselves as orthodox Calvinist. Around the middle of the century these made up about 2 percent
of the population, some 3 percent of all Protestants.[31] The slightly more
than one-third of the Dutch who were Catholics possessed a very strong
religious identity, but did not conceive of themselves as a nationwide community.[32] Their identity was a curious mix of allegiance to the pope and
strong local sentiments. Apart from their very small noble elite, they were
only loosely, perhaps not at all, integrated into the national community.

When the Netherlands entered its period of industrialization and societal differentiation in the 1870s and 1880s the country seemed posed to
follow a course that would see the broad consensus of the elite on national
identity challenged by the emergence of socialism and the building of a
Catholic subculture. Both of these would have been minority movements.
Given European socialism's notorious failure to provide a working alternative to the concept of the nation as the ultimate moral community, and
the permanent minority position of the Catholics in the Netherlands,
these challenges to the concept of the Protestant nation would probably
not have stood much of a chance.

In reality, something completely different happened. In the 1860s and
1870s Dutch Protestantism polarized both ecclesiastically and politically.
At the university of Leiden, a radical liberal theology emerged, which
denied both miracles and the inspiration of Scripture. Despite its radical-
ism, this modernism was in certain important social and intellectual
respects a continuation of the main trends of Dutch Protestantism since
the beginning of the century, especially in its close association with the
universities and its unrelenting emphasis on the necessity of educating
the common people. It easily captured control of most existing religious
organizations and the general synod of the former public church. The
orthodox opposition it engendered was forced to create its own organizational world. Especially after 1867, when church councils became elective
by all male members of the church not receiving poor relief, the battle
between modernists and their self-styled orthodox opponents took the
form of highly visible conflicts in some cases. The very great majority

of ministers, even orthodox ministers, was loath to drive this conflict to extremes. The struggle between liberal and orthodox Protestants in the church was duplicated by a conflict between liberals and orthodox in politics about the place of religion in the primary schools. Originally, these were very much debates among Protestants about the proper way in which the children of the Protestant nation were to be educated in the public school system. In both of these conflicts, the orthodox Protestants took the unity of the nation for granted. They did not dream about fissuring the moral community.[33]

Abraham Kuyper, a Leiden-trained theologian who became an orthodox minister and later a journalist and national politician, decisively changed the nature of these conflicts. Kuyper was a superb agitator and mobilizer, a natural-born mass politician. He understood both the strength of mass politics and the necessity of dramatic political stances to engender mass support like no one else in the Netherlands. Kuyper changed Dutch politics in two closely related ways. He exchanged the usual tone of Dutch politics—accommodating, consensual, unideological—for an adversarial and dramatic style. As a result of this change in political style he also involved the common people in politics, which up until that moment had been the preserve of the elite.[34]

Kuyper loved to stress fundamental oppositions, to paint world-historical perspectives, to call for earnest decisions. The most important way in which he convinced his followers of the importance of their struggle was by offering them a novel view of history. He described Dutch history as an ongoing struggle between three principles: Catholicism, Calvinism, and liberal humanism. At various moments in his long political career he could switch, as opportunity dictated, between stressing the relative equality of these three principles and claiming that Calvinism was the most important strain in Dutch national life. The essential element of this historical view was, however, first and foremost its dramatic appeal. Dutch national life was depicted as an ongoing struggle between radically different principles. Moreover, Kuyper tended to locate these principles in definite social and historical groups, Calvinism, for instance, among the common people.

For both the conflicts within the church and the political struggles about the nature of primary education Kuyper's mobilizing of broad support had dramatic consequences. In the ecclesiastical conflicts Kuyper from a very early date intended to force through a formal rupture with the former public church. Yet this was neither apparent nor, one suspects, even conceivable, to his fellow orthodox ministers. When it gradually became clear that he really meant to break with the liberal-dominated synod, almost all other orthodox ministers shied away. In the late 1880s, when the secession took place, Kuyper was followed by most of the laity involved in the orthodox organizations, but by only a small minority of the orthodox ministers.

Kuyper did everything to consolidate the identity of his followers—the members of the Gereformeerde Kerken in Nederland—from introducing a new baptismal rite to pronouncing the name of our Lord in a slightly different way. Theologically, the new church reintroduced the doctrine of the Synod of Dordrecht as the main founding symbol of its identity. Once again, the predestinarianism of the canons of Dordrecht became a means to mark fundamental differences within Dutch Protestantism. By means of ritual separation, historical mythography, and theological delineation, Kuyper's ecclesiastical creation became the core of a new moral body, fundamentally opposed to the idea of the nation as the most important moral community. Their position as a minority movement—Kuyper's followers made up only some 9 percent of the Dutch population, some 15 percent of all Protestants (although probably half or more of all involved Protestants)—fitted the romanticism of his thought very well. Kuyper's followers loved his description of them as the necessarily small core of true Calvinists, who notwithstanding their weak numerical strength were ultimately the most important or strongest part of both the nation and world history.

Even more important in the long run was Kuyper's involvement in the political struggle over primary education. Kuyper decided to forego any attempt at reforming the public school system in an orthodox direction. Instead, he opted for confessional schools, set off from the public school system. The struggle for these confessional schools became the main issue for the political party founded by Kuyper, the first modern political party in the Netherlands. In the agitation for the confessional school, Kuyper modeled his actions on the methods used by British radicals and liberals against Parliament, organizing mass petitions and rallies. In these mobilizing movements, he used the networks created during the struggle against liberalism in the church.

Concentration on the issue of the confessional school conferred a supreme strategic advantage. It made possible an alliance with the Catholics, who wanted confessional schools of their own. Kuyper's interpretation of Dutch history and therefore of the Dutch nation as made up of three different groups offered an excellent justification for this strategy. It enabled the devaluation of the public school as no more than the instrument of a particular interest group and justified the alliance of Catholics and Calvinists, with the argument that their wishes for separate schools were in accordance with the divided nature of the nation. The alliance proved singularly successful. Even during the period of a limited franchise until 1917, the Right—meaning the coalition between Catholics and orthodox Protestants—managed to gain a majority in about half of all general elections from the late 1880s on. After the introduction of general male suffrage, and especially after the extension of suffrage to women, the coalition consistently gained absolute majorities for another half century.[35]

I want to add two notes to this interpretation of the emergence of orthodox Protestantism as a separate moral community within the Dutch nation. The first concerns Kuyper. I stress more than is usual that he was a modern mass politician. I believe that his most eminent gift was his talent to create parties. It is clear from his fascination with both American Protestantism and Ultramontane Catholicism that he was deeply attached to the ideal of a Christian movement powerful in its own right and capable of dominating society without formal help from the state. It is also clear that he experimented freely with a wide range of ideological tactics. He had, for instance, a brief try at political anti-Semitism after Stöcker's first successes in Germany.[36] The ultimate nature of the orthodox movement owed as much, I would think, to this kind of experimenting as to preexisting ideals.

A second cautionary note concerns Kuyper's view of Dutch history. His tripartite vision of the Dutch people has been generally accepted. Yet it is necessary to stress that it is an invention. Kuyper did not find a preexisting religious group that he organized politically. The orthodox Protestants in the Netherlands were created by the campaigns for mobilization of support in the struggles between liberals and orthodox in the church and in politics.[37]

As a social movement, the Dutch Catholics emerged even later than the orthodox Protestants. By 1880 the Catholics had provided themselves with a great number of organizations and institutions, yet these were all narrowly religious in character. The expansion of this religious world into cultural, political, and economical domains took place only in the decades around 1900, stimulated by the example of the orthodox Protestants. Like these Protestants, the Catholics developed their own marked rituals and symbolic public presences, in order to emphasize that they were not simply Dutchmen and -women who happened to be Catholics, but rather a separate moral community.

In this way the Dutch pillarization of society sprang into being. The particular nature of this system did not consist of the emergence of more or less closed organizational worlds. After all, Catholic and socialist self-imposed ghettos emerged in other countries as well.[38] The originality of Dutch pillarization is to be found in the fact that the movements contesting the liberal Protestant nature of the nation were successful and actually succeeded in eclipsing the notion of the nation as the supreme moral community. In a certain sense the ghettos took over the nation. After 1917, even those who desperately wanted to be totalizing were forced to conceive of themselves as a particular group and not as representatives of the commonwealth. Apart from the notion that it was made up of different groups, there was almost no common view of the nation and national history left.

A perfect expression of this conception of Dutch history is to be found in the introduction of an important empirical article on pillarization written by two prominent Dutch sociologists, a Catholic and a Protestant, in the early 1960s.[39] They trace the conditions for the emergence of the pillarized system of the twentieth century to the early years of the Dutch Republic. They distinguish three parties in the religious struggles of the sixteenth century. The traditional Catholic church was challenged by a humanistic, Erasmian current, deeply rooted in late-medieval Dutch piety, that could have become the bearer of a national reformation, had it not been pushed aside during the Dutch Revolt by Calvinism. Since the sixteenth century, Catholicism, humanism, and Calvinism have formed the components of Dutch history. By the sixteenth century, they had already become deeply rooted in separate segments of the Dutch people (*volksdelen*). The authors express their impartiality by pointing out how each of these groups, when alone in power, had oppressed the other two: the Catholics in the sixteenth century, the Calvinists during the Republic, the liberals in the nineteenth century. Only with the emergence of pillarization was justice done to all.

This conception of a nation and people made up of three different religio-political groups is ubiquitous in twentieth-century Dutch political and social thought. It will come as no surprise that it played an overwhelmingly important role in the legitimation of the mobilizing and organizing activities of the Catholics and Calvinists. It is always present in the works of political scientists and sociologists studying pillarization.[40] And although no professional historian has written a general history of the Netherlands based on this tripartite division, and most of them even shy away from using the term *volksdelen*, the concept makes its influence felt in the background of most works on religion and politics, informing, for instance, the recent wave of local studies on the emergence of pillarization.[41]

Yet if we situate this conception of a nation made up from different groups as a way of producing a religious past, it becomes apparent how much it depends on the discursive space opened up by Ypey and Dermout's work. Kuyper's description of orthodoxy preserved among the common people is an inversion of the cultural class formation entailed by Ypey and Dermout's location of religion within the inner selves of the members of the moral community of the nation. Whereas this location defined the common people as lacking in knowledge, Kuyper empowers them as bearers of knowledge.[42] Moreover, the whole notion of *volksdelen* is a means of reintroducing religious difference within the public sphere, while still locating religion in inner selves. It is, in effect, this ethnicizing of religious difference that made it possible to base modern Dutch mass politics on religion.

Notes

1. A. Ypey and I. J. Dermout, *Geschiedenis der Nederlandsche Hervormde Kerk*, 4 vols. (Breda, 1819–27).

2. A. Fris, *Inventaris van de archieven behorende tot het "Oud Synodaal Archief" van de Nederlandse Hervormde Kerk, 1566–1816* (The Hague, 1991), xvi–xviii; J. W. Verburgt, "De totstandkoming van den Staten-Bijbel en de bewaring zijner oorspronkelijke stukken," *Leids Jaarboekje* 30 (1938): 138–63.

3. Peter van Rooden, "Van geestelijke stand naar beroepsgroep: De professionalisering van de Nederlandse predikant, 1625–1874," *Tijdschrift voor Sociale Geschiedenis* 17 (1991): 361–93.

4. Nikolaas Wiltens, *Kerkelyk plakaat-boek, behelzende de plakaaten, ordonnantien, ende resolutien, over de kerkelyke zaken*, 5 vols. (The Hague, 1722–1807); Johannes Smetius, *Ordre of reglement voor de classis in Gelderland* (Nijmegen, 1698); Johannes Smetius, *Synodale ordonnantien ende resolutien*, vol. 1 (Nijmegen, 1699); C. Nauta, *Compendium der kerkelijke wetten* (Leeuwarden, 1757); J. Lindeboom, "Classicale wetboeken: Een bijdrage tot de kennis van het kerkelijke leven in de achttiende eeuw," *Nederlands Archief voor Kerkgeschiedenis* 41 (1956): 65–95.

5. Martinus Soermans, *Kerkelyk register van de plaatsen en namen der predikanten van alle de classes, gehorende onder de Synodus van Zuyd-Holland, van 't begin der Reformatie, tot nu toe.* [Synod of South Holland] (Dordrecht, 1695; 2d ed., Haarlem, 1702); Melchior Veeris, *Chronologia ecclesiastica, dat is Kerkelyk Tyd-register* [Synod of North Holland] (Amsterdam, 1697; 2d ed. 1705); Henricus van Rhenen, *Lyst van de namen der predikanten die zedert de reformatie de kerken behoorende onder de provintie van Utrecht, zo by leeringe als anderzints, bedient hebben.* [Synod of Utrecht] (Utrecht, 1705; 2d ed., 1724); Arnold Moonen, *Naamketen van predikanten die van de Hervorming tot aen 1709 in de gemeenten van het Overijss. Synode het Evangelium bedient hebben.* [Synod of Overijssel] (Deventer, 1709); C. Adami, *Naam-lyst der predikanten in de provincie van Stadt Groningen en Ommelanden t' sedert de reductie tot aan 't jaar 1721. . . .* [Synod of Groningen] (Groningen, 1721; 3d ed., 1745); H. de Jongh Azn, *Naam-lyst der predikanten die in de gemeenten, gehoorende onder de IX classen van het Geldersche Synode zedert de Hervorming der Kerken tot den jaare 1750 het heilig Evangelium bediend hebben.* [Synod of Gelderland] (Leiden, 1750). In Friesland, separate books were published for the six classes making up the provincial synod by M. Laurman, J. Engelsma, W. Columba, H. Grevenstein, A. Greydanus, and H. Reinalda, all appearing in Leeuwarden in 1751–63. In Zeeland, where the Provincial Estates did not allow the meeting of a provincial synod, no lists of ministers were published.

6. C. A. van Swigchem, T. Brouwer, and W. van Os, *Een huis voor het Woord: Het protestantse kerkinterieur in Nederland tot 1900* (The Hague, 1984), 283.

7. Bernardus Smytegelt, *Keurstoffen of verzameling van vyftig uitmuntende predicatien* (Middelburg, 1765), 429.

8. The various works are reviewed by Christiaan Sepp, *Bibliotheek van Nederlandsche Kerkgeschiedschrijvers: Opgave van hetgeen Nederlanders over de geschiedenis der Christelijke kerk geschreven hebben.* (Leiden, 1886), 27–36.

9. J. C. Breen, "Gereformeerde populaire historiografie in de zeventiende en achttiende eeuw," in *Christendom en Historie*, 1: 213–42 (Amsterdam, 1925).

10. Jacob Fruytier, *Sions worstelingen, of historische samenspraken over de verscheide en zeer bittere wederwaerdigheden van Christus' kerke, met openbare en verborgen vyanden,* 3 vols. (Rotterdam, 1715).

11. Only the Arminians published books about the Synod of Dordrecht and its previous history: Johannes Wtenbogaert, *De kerckelicke historie, vervattende verscheyden gedenckwaerdige saecken, inde Christenheyt voorgevallen, van het jaer vierhondert af, tot in het jaer sesthienhondert ende negenthien* (N.p., 1646) and the magisterial work of Geeraert Brandt, *Historie der Reformatie en andre kerkelyke geschiedenissen, in en ontrent de Nederlanden,* 4 vols. (Rotterdam, 1671–1704). Theologians of the public church published refutations of these works. Attempts undertaken by the public church in the direct aftermath of the synod to publish an official history came to naught. J. G. R. Acquoy, "Mislukte pogingen der Nederlandsche kerken om hare geschiedenis te doen beschrijven," in Alistair Duke, "The Ambivalent Face of Calvinism in the Netherlands," in *Reformation and Revolt in the Low Countries* (London, 1990), 269–94.

12. Peter van Rooden, *Religieuze regimes: Over godsdienst en maatschappij in Nederland, 1570–1990* (Amsterdam, 1996), 78–120.

13. Duke, "Ambivalent Face."

14. Fruytier, *Sions worstelingen*, 177, 583, 836.

15. Ibid., 814–15.

16. Ypey and Dermout, *Geschiedenis*, 1:98–99.

17. Ibid., 1:47–160, 161–293.

18. Ibid., 1:202–3.

19. Ibid., 3:46–47.

20. Ibid., 3:114, 4:28–29.

21. Ibid., 1:474, 3:7, 49–50.

22. Ibid., 4:203–5.

23. Ibid., 2:294–95.

24. Ibid., 1:378, 2:230–31.

25. Ibid., 3:50.

26. Ibid., 1:201, 3:176.

27. Ibid., 1:24, 2:293–94, 3:6.

28. Margaret C. Jacob and Wijnand W. Mijnhardt, eds., *The Dutch Republic in the Eighteenth Century: Decline, Enlightenment, and Revolution* (Ithaca, N.Y., 1992).

29. B. Glasius, *Geschiedenis der Christelijke kerk en godsdienst in Nederland, na het vestigen der Hervorming tot den troonsafstand van koning Willem I,* 3 vols. (Amsterdam, 1842–44); B. ter Haar et al., eds. *Geschiedenis der Christelijke*

kerk in Nederland in tafereelen, 2 vols. (Amsterdam, 1864–69); G. J. Vos Azn, *Geschiedenis der Vaderlandsche Kerk: Van 630 tot 1842*, 2d ed. (Dordrecht, 1888). Cf. also van Rooden, *Religieuze regimes*, 159–61.

30. D. Nauta, "De reformatie in Nederland in de historiografie," *Serta Historica* 2 (1970): 44–71; J. C. H. Blom and C. J. Misset, "Een onvervalschte Nederlandsche geest": Enkele historiografische kantekeningen bij het concept van een nationaal-gereformeerde richting," in E. K. Grootes and J. den Haan, eds., *Geschiedenis, godsdienst, letterkunde: Opstellen aangeboden aan dr. S.B.J. Zilverberg ter gelegenheid van zijn afscheid van de Universiteit van Amsterdam* (Roden, 1989), 221–32.

31. W. Bakker et al., eds., *De Afscheiding van 1834 en haar geschiedenis* (Kampen, 1984).

32. J. A. Bornewasser, "De Nederlandse katholieken en hun negentiende-eeuwse vaderland," *Tijdschrift voor Geschiedenis* 95 (1982): 577–604; Peter Raedts, "Katholieken op zoek naar een Nederlandse identiteit, 1814–1898," *Bijdragen en Mededelingen betreffende de geschiedenis der Nederlanden* 107 (1992): 713–25.

33. C. Augustijn, "Kerk en godsdienst 1870–1890." in W. Bakker et al., eds., *De Doleantie van 1886 en haar geschiedenis* (Kampen, 1986), 41–75.

34. C. Augustijn, J. H. Prins, H. E. S. Woldring, eds., *Abraham Kuyper: Zijn volksdeel, zijn invloed* (Delft, 1987).

35. Theo van Tijn, "The Party Structure of Holland and the Outer Provinces in the Nineteenth Century," in G. A. M. Beekelaar et al., eds., *Vaderlands Verleden in Veelvoud: 31 opstellen orer de Nederlandse geschiedenis na 1500.* (Den Haag, 1975), 560–89; J. J. Woltjer, *Recent verleden: De geschiedenis van Nederland in de twintigste eeuw* (Amsterdam, 1992).

36. Ivo Schöffer, "Abraham Kuyper and the Jews," in *Veelvormig verleden: Zeventien studies in de vaderlandse geschiedenis* (Amsterdam, 1987), 159–70.

37. van Rooden, *Religieuze regimes*, 169–99.

38. Hugh McLeod, *Religion and the People of Western Europe, 1789–1970* (Oxford, 1981).

39. J. P. Kruyt and W. Goddijn, "Verzuiling en ontzuiling als sociologisch proces," in A. N. J. den Hollander et al., eds., *Drift en Koers: Een halve eeuw sociale verandering in Nederland* (Assen, 1962), 227–63.

40. For instance, Hans Daalder, "The Netherlands: Opposition in a Segmented Society" in Robert A. Dahl, ed., *Political Oppositions in Western Democracies* (New Haven, Conn., 1966); J. E. Ellemers, "Pillarization as a Process of Modernization," *Acta Politica* 19 (1984): 129–44; A. Lijphart, *Verzuiling, pacificatie en kentering in de Nederlandse politiek* (Assen, 1968); J. M. G. Thurlings, *De wankele zuil: Nederlandse katholieken tussen assimilatie en pluralisme*, 2d rev. ed. (Deventer, 1978).

41. Cf. my review article "Studies naar lokale verzuiling als toegang tot de geschiedenis van de constructie van religieuze verschillen in Nederland," *Theoretische Geschiedenis* 20 (1993): 439–54.

42. I owe this formulation to an intervention by Peter Pels at a Research Centre for Religion and Society seminar.

6

On Religious and Linguistic Nationalisms: The Second Partition of Bengal

PARTHA CHATTERJEE

The Nation at the Time of Swadeshi

It is constructive to compare the first partition of Bengal in 1905 with the second in 1947. The first partition of Bengal into two provinces—Bengal in the west and Eastern Bengal and Assam in the east—was almost exclusively the result of an administrative decision at the top. There was no mass political agitation of the kind we now associate with nationalist mobilizations, making the demand that the province be divided in accordance with cultural demography. On the contrary, the partition decision provoked what was perhaps the first mass nationalist agitation in India— the Swadeshi movement—demanding the repeal of partition on the ground that the people of Bengal were culturally one and indivisible. The reason given for the partition decision was administrative convenience: the undivided province with an area of 189,000 square miles and a population of seventy-nine million was said to have become ungovernable. But, of course, there were important political considerations that were, as Sumit Sarkar has shown in his classic study, by no means secondary.[1] The most clearly stated of these was the need to curb the growing nationalist sentiments in Bengal, which were thought to be confined almost exclusively to the Hindu middle classes: a partition of the province, the colonial governors felt, would reduce the effect that this movement, "unfriendly if not seditious in character," was having on "the whole tone of Bengal administration." As H. H. Risley, the ethnographer-administrator, put it in two oft- quoted sentences: "Bengal united is a power; Bengal divided will pull in different ways. . . . One of our main objects is to split up and thereby weaken a solid body of opponents to our rule."[2]

The political objective of the colonial administration, in other words, was preemptive: to disrupt what was seen as a growing nationalist opposition led by the Hindu middle classes. Curzon, the viceroy, stated the objective quite plainly:

> The Bengalis, who like to think themselves a nation, and who dream of a future when the English will have been turned out, and a Bengali Babu will be installed

in Government House, Calcutta, of course bitterly resent any disruption that will be likely to interfere with the realisation of this dream. If we are weak enough to yield to their clamour now, we shall not be able to dismember or reduce Bengal again; and you will be cementing and solidifying, on the eastern flank of India, a force already formidable, and certain to be a source of increasing trouble in the future.[3]

He did not forget to mention the other part of the colonial strategy: partition "would invest the Muhammadans in Eastern Bengal with a unity which they have not enjoyed since the days of the old Mussulman viceroys and kings."[4]

If the first partition of 1905, therefore, is attributed primarily to a colonial strategy of divide and rule, then that strategy can already be seen to be playing with the varying possibilities of congruence between territories and culturally marked populations. The historically significant point here is not whether there already *existed* one nation of Bengalis or two. Rather, the point is that even as the project of imagining a nation into existence got under way, it found itself on a political field where contending strategies could be devised to contest or disrupt that project by enabling the rival imagining of rival nations, one on a principle of linguistic nationalism, the other that of religious nationalism.

The first partition was undone in six years. The Swadeshi movement's success in "unsettling the settled fact" of a divided Bengal (in the celebrated words of Surendra Nath Banerjea, a principal leader of the movement) provided a major spurt to the nationalist imagination in Bengal and produced most of the ideological and organizational forms that would characterize nationalist politics there in the subsequent decades. This was the first significant occasion when the nationalist imagination in India was confronted with a concrete question about the territorial division of state jurisdictions. The idea that Bengal was one and indivisible, regardless of religious plurality, was a crucial element that shaped the notion that territory and culture were inseparably tied in a sort of "natural history" of the nation. The same natural-historical theme once again made the encompassment of Bengal within India largely unproblematic: the culture of Bengal was seen to be "naturally" a part of the larger cultural unity of the Indian nation.

The success of the antipartition movement, however, barely concealed the fault lines in this unitary conception of the nation. The nationalist political leadership in Bengal at this time was overwhelmingly upper-caste Hindu. More significantly, the nationalist imagination that flourished so spectacularly at the time of the Swadeshi movement actually naturalized a conception of the nation in history that was quite distinctly Hindu. And yet, it would be wrong to suppose that this Hindu-centered view of the nation was targeted against Muslims or that it even sought to exclude them from the ambit of the nation. It is noteworthy that even though there was little political campaigning in favor of partition, the Swadeshi movement nevertheless produced an explicit rhetoric of Hindu-Muslim unity as part of its evocation of nationhood. Bipinchandra Pal, for instance, put forward the idea of a composite patriotism and a federal India of which the units would be the religious communities—Hindu, Muslim, Christian, aboriginal tribes.[5] The idea persisted into the period of mass nationalism and was applied most famously in Chittaranjan Das's Hindu-Muslim pact of the 1920s. Alongside the conception of a natural history of the nation, therefore, articulated predominantly in terms of a Hindu religious idiom, there was also the idea of unity born out of fraternal association between Hindus and Muslims. The two ideas were perhaps best expressed in a very early nationalist text, which stretched the metaphor of natural relationship to its limit:

> Although India is the true motherland only of those who belong to the Hindu jati and although only they have been born from her womb, the Muslims are not unrelated to her any longer. She has held them at her breast and reared them. The Muslims are therefore her adopted children. Can there be no bonds of fraternity between two children of the same mother, one a natural child and the other adopted? There certainly can; the laws of every religion admit this. There has now been born a bond of brotherhood between Hindus and Muslims living in India.[6]

To sum up, the dominant form of the imagined nation produced in Bengal at the time of the Swadeshi movement contained, at one and the same time, an Indian nationalism built around a natural history of Aryan-Hindu tradition, a linguistic nationalism valorizing Bengal's cultural unity and a rhetoric of Hindu-Muslim unity. This combination was possible because neither the place of Bengal within a state structure of the Indian nation nor the place of a Hindu minority within a Muslim-majority Bengal had yet been posed as problems. The nationalist elite of Bengal, predominantly upper-caste Hindu and belonging to the landed proprietor and urban professional classes, was still comfortably ensconced in its position as leader of the nation it had imagined into existence.

Two developments threw this situation into disarray. First, the rise of nationalist mass movements all over India from the 1920s produced an entirely new organizational structure of the all-India Congress in which the place of Bengal's nationalist leadership became either marginal or oppositional. Second, within Bengal, the politics of Muslim identity found an agrarian base. The older rhetoric of Hindu-Muslim fraternity could not suffice anymore unless it was able to confront the question of agrarian class relations.

Let us begin with the second development, since this is often taken to be the most crucial element of a "structural" explanation of the second partition of Bengal.

Histories of Partition

The fact that the peasantry in eastern Bengal was predominantly Muslim and the landlords largely Hindu has long been regarded by historians, especially Marxist historians, as the crucial structural condition that allowed a class antagonism to be expressed as a conflict between religious groups and that enabled the British to manipulate the various Indian political organizations around this issue. Badruddin Umar, the radical Bangladeshi historian, for instance, states that the partition of Bengal in 1947 "became possible because of the presence of certain nonantagonistic contradictions in the country that were converted into antagonistic contradictions by the British rulers."[7] Sugata Bose provides the most carefully researched elaboration of this argument.[8] He notes that the Muslim-majority districts of east Bengal consisted of a peasantry that was little differentiated. Until the early decades of the twentieth century, this peasantry had a "symbiotic relationship" with the predominantly Hindu landlords, moneylenders, and traders who supplied the vital needs of credit in a highly monetized agrarian economy. The prolonged depression of the 1930s, however, destroyed these networks of rural credit, leading to "a decisive shift in the balance of class power in [the peasant's] favour." The rentier and trading classes

> ceased to perform any useful function. Once a political challenge came within the realm of possibility, the strength of a religious identity was exploited in a readily available and, for the privileged co-religionists, a safe ideology. To the vast mass of smallholding peasants living under similar, yet very splintered, conditions of economic existence in east Bengal, religion seemed to impart a sense of "community"; so at a critical juncture in Bengal's history, religion provided the basis of a "national bond," however stretched, and became the rallying cry of a "political organisation" demanding the creation of a separate Muslim homeland. Efforts by some Hindu and Muslim leaders to mobilise the Muslim peasantry under the banner of progressive nationalism and socialism proved abortive. Weighed under for decades by an economic, political and moral order they had long ago silently rejected, the Muslim peasantry responded to the appeals of religion and gave a powerful ideological legitimation to a breakdown in social relations that had already occurred, but which was only now being formally conceded.[9]

Agrarian class conflict erupted in east Bengal in the 1930s. "This conflict was interpreted and used by self-serving politicians for their own ends.

Operating in higher-level political arenas with communal constituencies, the gift of government's successive constitutional reforms, these politicians unflinchingly used religion to mask an essentially economic conflict."[10]

While not quite arguing that religion only provided a mask over class conflicts, Suranjan Das nevertheless points out that between the two partitions of Bengal, a significant change in the nature of Hindu-Muslim antagonism occurred.[11] After an early period in which they were relatively unorganized, less connected with the institutional politics of parties and legislatures, and strong in class orientation, communal conflicts later showed two kinds of convergences: on one hand, class and communal identities tended to converge, and on the other hand, elite and popular communalism also tended to converge. The result was a polarization of virtually the entire population around two communal blocs, each led by the respective elites but successfully mobilizing the popular masses.

What about the Hindu population? Joya Chatterji has recently made the argument that the emphasis on agrarian conflict and peasant-communal consciousness in east Bengal has tended to suggest that "communalism in Bengal was essentially a Muslim phenomenon" and that "a parallel Hindu communalism did not emerge, or . . . if it did, it was too limited and peripheral to have contributed in any significant way to the conflicts that led to Pakistan."[12] She then attempts to show how a Hindu-communal identity was built up in Bengal from the 1930s, initially as an alliance of the educated and the well-to-do landed and professional classes with the lower middle class but increasingly attempting to mobilize the "sanskritising aspirations of low-caste groups" and having as its main political objective the refusal "to accept the rule of the Muslim majority."[13]

> Bengalis were not passive bystanders in the politics of their province; nor were they victims of circumstances entirely out of their control, forced reluctantly to accept the division of their "motherland." On the contrary, a large number of Hindus of Bengal, backed up by the provincial branches of the Congress and the Hindu Mahasabha, campaigned intensively in 1947 for the partition of Bengal and for the creation of a separate Hindu province that would remain inside an Indian union.[14]

Placed alongside each other, the two histories of Muslim and Hindu communalism in Bengal seem to suggest a population divided right down the middle, cutting across classes and strata, one half asserting its political right to rule over the entire province by virtue of its being the majority religious community, the other insisting on a political division of the province in order to create (or perhaps to retain) a separate "homeland" for the minority religious community. The historiography has, it seems, conditioned itself precisely to explain the "historical inevitability" of an unfortunate event.

It seems to me especially important that when we think about the histories of an "event" such as the partition of Bengal (or of India), we take care to disentangle the many different roots of that event, running along different levels of determination and with very different temporalities. Separate narratives can be constructed for each of these roots, from that of the cultural construction of nationality, a story running over more than a hundred years, to the mobilization for a partition of the province that, properly speaking, lasted only a few months. It is the property of foundational events such as those of August 1947 in India that they supply each of these narratives with a closure that identifies it as a history of partition. But they are very different histories, in which categories such as religion or nationalism have entirely different significations.

Restricting myself to the theme of religion and nationalism, let me go through some of the narratives that might be told of the second partition of Bengal. At the level of popular beliefs and practices, we could tell a long story of the spread of Islam in Bengal, of the coexistence in the everyday life of Muslim peasants of numerous Islamic and non-Islamic practices, and of periodic attempts to "purify" Islam.[15] At another level, we could tell the story of the formation of a new middle-class Muslim elite in the late nineteenth century, the conflict between those who preferred to identify with an Urdu-speaking north Indian aristocratic culture and those who sought to build up a distinctly Bengali Muslim cultural identity, and the rapid spread of secondary and higher education in east Bengal in the early twentieth century.[16] To take up another strand, I have already mentioned the evolution in the late nineteenth century of a historicized nation whose core was supposed to consist of an Aryan/Hindu civilization. This construction went hand in hand with a new modernized hegemony of upper-caste Hindus over the entire province, as shown dramatically at the time of the Swadeshi movement. It saw little inconsistency between an Indian and a Bengali cultural identity, or indeed between its explicitly Hindu lineages and the rhetoric of Hindu-Muslim unity. This nationalist endeavor found its greatest moment of success at the time of the Khilafat-Noncooperation movement conducted by Chittaranjan Das's Congress. Riding the crest of a mass agitation in both city and country, nationalism in Bengal in the early 1920s proudly displayed the banner of Hindu-Muslim anticolonial fraternity.

It is much too simplistic to think that when Hindu-Muslim unity broke down in the late 1920s and the Congress took a much more narrowly defined position in defense of Hindu upper-caste landed interests, there was a transformation in the long-duration ideological construction from nationalism to communalism.[17] The story of this change must be sought among political strategies adopted over much shorter durations, in institutional arenas that involve only small numbers of people. One cannot tell this story without mentioning specific meetings and negotiations, without citing statements and declarations, indeed without sneaking behind particular people into particular smoke-filled offices. It is precisely because of the relevance of this level of political activity that there will always remain the possibility of telling secret histories and untold stories of events such as the partition.

To be more specific, religious identity as a demographic category became perhaps the single most crucial factor in determining the distribution of government power in Bengal under the constitutional reforms of 1935. The legislature out of which provincial ministries were to be formed was statutorily constituted so that 48 percent of the seats were reserved for Muslims (who were 54 percent of the population), 12 percent for the depressed classes (scheduled castes, who were 18 percent of the population), and 20 percent were available as "general" seats for Hindu candidates (Hindus, not including the depressed classes, were 26 percent of the population). Significantly, as many as 10 percent of the seats were reserved for Europeans, who amounted to only 0.04 percent of the population, but who could nevertheless hold a crucial balance in a communally constituted house. The "provincial autonomy" arrangements in Bengal remain one of the most obvious examples of nationalist accusations about divide and rule.

That Hindu communalism came strongly to the fore in Bengal's provincial politics in the 1930s and 1940s can hardly be denied. What is not true, however, is that organized opinion among Hindus became any less anti-British. Indeed, the allegation that the imperial power and the local British bureaucracy were promoting Muslim interests in order to curtail those of the nationalist Hindus only strengthened anti-British feelings. What is also not true is that the new atmosphere of Hindu-Muslim conflict required any significant transformation in the internal elements of the nationalist consciousness as it had been constructed since the late nineteenth century. If it was generative of slogans of Hindu-Muslim fraternity in an earlier era, it could now generate with equal ease the specter of Muslim tyranny. We fail to see the hegemonic power of the nationalist imagination as it emerged in India if we ignore the wide range of strategic political possibilities it could yield on the question of religious identity—from Hindu dominance at one extreme to varying degrees of intercommunal fraternization to an insistence on the separation of religion and politics altogether.

Not so in the case of Muslim politics in Bengal, at least not in the decades we are considering. One of the most striking features of Muslim-majoritarian politics in Bengal in the 1930s and 1940s is its singularly nonhegemonic ambition in relation to the Hindu minority. There is no way to explain this except by connecting Muslim politics in Bengal with that in India as a whole—where, of course, it had the character of the politics of a minority. There is not a single cultural or political endeavor in Bengal in the period that can be read as a hegemonic attempt to mobilize the consent of the Hindu minority for Muslim leadership over Bengali society. This absence, perhaps, was only an inevitable sign of the subalternity of the movement. It could also be said that there was little time for any hegemonic efforts to coalesce. Or, to be more careful, we could say that at the most promising moment for such an effort—the 1937 emergence of Fazlul Huq's peasant-populist Krishak Proja movement as the most dynamic political force in east Bengal—attempts to forge a political alliance between the Congress and the Krishak Proja Party were foiled, first by the unbending policy of the all-India Congress not to enter into coalitions in any province and, subsequently, by the systematic vigilance of the governor and the rest of the British bureaucracy against any intercommunal political alliance that might put Congress leaders in ministerial office during the war.[18] The only noteworthy, though entirely inchoate, intellectual efforts to present the Proja movement as a democratic upsurge holding out the promise of social and political transformation not just for Muslims but for Bengali society as a whole come from this brief period around 1937.[19] In the absence, however, of an intercommunal democratic alliance at the provincial level, local efforts by left-wing peasant organizers to build up agrarian bases cutting across the religious divide either remained confined to particular localities or were scuttled by the more resourceful and organized communal forces backed by a government bureaucracy.[20] The peasant-populist upsurge in east Bengal, with its powerful use of Islam as a religion of agrarian solidarity and justice, could not, in the end, produce a credible democratic force that might elicit the consent of the religious minority.

Strategies and Outcomes

It is also historically inaccurate to suggest that the decision to partition the province of Bengal along religious-demographic lines actually involved the participation of masses of people. As far as opinion within Bengal was concerned, the relevant decisions were made by members of the Bengal Assembly, elected on the basis of a very restricted suffrage. There was some campaigning on the issue of partition in 1947, both in favor and against, but by the standards of mass agitation of the time they involved small numbers of people. In fact, evidence from the period suggests that the incidents that most strongly framed discussion on the subject were in fact the communal killings in Calcutta in August 1946 and those in Noakhali a few weeks later. These were perhaps the most powerful mass actions, organized by Hindu and Muslim communalists, contributing to partition. Some people understood the unprecedented communal violence of 1946 as the cataclysmic sign of a general transition of power, with its associated feelings of anxiety as well as of anticipation. Others took it to mean that Pakistan, whatever its precise legal or constitutional form, was inevitable.

Reading through the political debates that took place in Bengal from August 1946 to August 1947, one cannot but get the sense that positions were being taken on the assumption that Pakistan was in the offing, that there was nothing left to be done to change that eventuality, and that all that remained was to strike the best bargain for each sectional interest, whether majority community, the minority community, or the depressed classes within the minority community. One also gets the undeniable sense that irrespective of party or community and irrespective of the stature of the organization or leader within Bengal, every statement, whether a demand or an appeal, a promise or a threat, was addressed to an external and distant group of decision makers; no one in Bengal saw himself as involved in taking the momentous decisions that would determine the future of the province. There is reason why the feeling would persist, in West Bengal as well as in Bangladesh, that in 1947 Bengal was merely a pawn in the hands of all-India players.

It is easy to demonstrate the highly contingent and strategic nature of the various positions taken on the question of religion and national status by organizations and individuals in the months preceding August 1947. Fazlul Huq, who was by then out of power and estranged from the Muslim League, had little qualms about stating that there was "constitutionally speaking, no government in Bengal," since the ministers were responsible not to the legislature but "to Mr. Jinnah as head of the Muslim League."[21] More significantly, when the debate broke out in May 1947 over the Sarat Bose-Suhrawardy proposal for a sovereign United Bengal, Abul Hashim, campaigning for the proposal from within the provincial Muslim League, sought to justify it as being consistent with the original Lahore resolution in which Pakistan had apparently been thought of as consisting of "independent Muslim states." Opposing the proposal, Akram Khan took the stand that no one in the Provincial League was empowered to make statements in this matter since negotiations were being conducted on behalf of all Muslims of India by Jinnah and the central Muslim League.[22]

As far as Hindu opinion is concerned, it was clear almost as soon as the question was raised that there would be near unanimity, at least within the domain of organized opinion, from the Hindu Mahasabha on the right to the Congress in the middle to the socialists and even communists on the left.[23] Once it became apparent that Pakistan was a certainty, and especially after the Congress high command seemed to have accepted in March 1947 the idea of a partition of Punjab, the argument became unstoppable among Hindus that Bengal too must be partitioned so that the Hindu minority would have a place outside Pakistan. Apart from the straightforward communal justifications, of which there were plenty, the position was also supported by more sophisticated arguments that said, for instance, that the Indian Union was more likely to uphold the modern democratic traditions built up through the nineteenth and twentieth centuries and therefore more likely to safeguard the rights of all communities. The United Bengal proposal found few takers and most seemed persuaded by Shyama Prasad Mukherjee's argument that if a sovereign Bengal decided, on the basis of its religious composition, to join Pakistan, the minority community would be left at that stage with no options.

Especially interesting is the debate between leaders of the depressed classes. Jogendra Nath Mandal, leader of the Scheduled Castes Federation and politically allied with the Muslim League, opposed the suggestion to partition Bengal.

> If such a thing happens, then it is a virtual certainty that Hindus from east Bengal will be forced to take shelter in west Bengal. Of course, if the leaders who are proposing the partition of Bengal intend an exchange of populations, then I have nothing to say except that only the other day the caste-Hindu leaders had vehemently criticized Dr. Ambedkar for his *Thoughts on Pakistan* and Mr. Jinnah for his suggestion that populations might be exchanged . . . If Bengal is partitioned, the scheduled castes will suffer the most. The caste-Hindus of east Bengal are wealthy and many have salaried jobs. They will have little difficulty in moving from east to west Bengal. Poor scheduled caste peasants, fishermen and artisans will have to remain in east Bengal where the proportion of Hindus will decline and they will be at the mercy of the majority Muslim community.

To this, Radhanath Das, a scheduled caste member of the Constituent Assembly, retorted:

> Today if we say to our Namasudra brothers in Noakhali that they come to west Bengal where the government of the separate province of West and North Bengal will provide them with shelter and other economic necessities, then I am prepared to swear that Jogen Babu will not be able to keep a single one of his caste brothers in Noakhali. In other words, he will not be able to make them feel secure under Muslim League rule or Muslim League protection. . . . I say the backward Hindus will be better able than others to leave east Bengal, since they have few possessions besides their tiny huts.[24]

In the end, when the votes were taken in the Bengal Assembly, only five of the thirty scheduled caste members voted against the partition of Bengal.

Clearly, when the time came for a strategic decision by a group organized as a minority within a minority, the hegemonic gestures of the Muslim League toward the scheduled castes proved inadequate.

We also get a sense of the extreme contingency within which the question of partition was talked about in Bengal from writings in nonpolitical circles. There is a small book published in April 1947 on the communal riots of the previous year titled—using the English word—*Delirium*.[25] The author, Birendranath Chattopadhyay, was a medical practitioner involved in voluntary social work, not directly affiliated with any political organization, and clearly conscious of his stature as a leading figure of the neighborhood, looked up to with respect by the working-class poor, both Muslim and Hindu, who lived in the nearby slums of the industrial suburb of Alambazar, north of Calcutta.

Most striking about the author's description of the communal riots in his area in August 1946 is the sense of assault from the outside, carried out by powerful but anonymous forces, against which the carefully nurtured bonds of neighborhood solidarity were no match. He talks of local Congress and Muslim League leaders jointly setting up peace committees as soon as news of rioting in Calcutta arrived. He himself went around the neighborhood, urging people to look out for outsiders. "We must not let these outside disturbances get into our neighborhood." And yet, before the night was over, the slums were in flames and people were killing one another with astonishing brutality.

The rest of the book is a series of arguments and counterarguments about why this happened and what was to come. It gives us a flavor of the animated conversations that took place in Hindu middle-class male gatherings. The full range of political arguments, now familiar to all students of modern Indian history, is presented here—blaming the British, blaming the Congress, blaming Muslim communalism and the Muslim League. What is remarkable, however, is the way in which an otherwise bewildering and deplorable set of events is sought to be made comprehensible in terms of historical necessity.

> All these differences and conflicts between the League, the Congress and other parties seem to me like an elaborate theatre being performed on the political stage. Mahatmaji is the playwright and director of India's freedom struggle and the others are all experienced actors. Most Indians have still not understood the mysterious way in which Mahatmaji and Jinnah Saheb have divided up their responsibilities. . . . They have together taken up the role of religious reformers and, by prevailing upon the men of religion, have combined religious preaching with the message of freedom. Thus have they built up their parties and the nation. . . . By starting an upheaval, they have sought to destroy stagnant minds and a decrepit society and to produce a renaissance among ordinary people. . . .

I do not think of these disturbances as communal. I think of this as India's last movement. . . . This is a conspiracy to eradicate for ever the demon of communalism from this country. The clashes now taking place will soon lead to a situation where people of both communities will get fed up with those who preach untouchability, communal hatred and religious hypocrisy. Perhaps then a new nation will arise in India.[26]

The rapidly unfolding political events are also seen as unreal, devoid of truth—events that must necessarily give way to "real" history.

This December [1946], the Congress has accepted the British view of things which was for so long in favour of the objectives of the Muslim League. Now the Congress will accept the division of Bengal, the division of Punjab, even the division of India. In time, perhaps every province of India will be partitioned in order to accommodate the League's demand for Pakistan. This will either lead to the strengthening of two nations, or else it will cause so much disruption in everyday life that Hindus and Muslims will come to see that by fighting each other and putting up fences all across the country neither community can live in happiness. . . . Even if partition is necessary today, the country cannot remain partitioned for ever.[27]

Historical necessity is the theme of another small book written at the time of independence and partition published in December 1947.[28] Partition had been made inevitable because of the nationalist Congress's failure to forestall the aggresive politics of a "fascist" Muslim League whose ideology was that of "modern totalitarianism in the garb of medieval bigotry."[29]

In truth, the failure is of the Congress, the success of the Muslim League. As a matter of fact, Congress's efforts in the last two years to avoid the partition of India were not very conducive to maintaining unity. . . . [Mountbatten] has only done that which was inevitable, because every effort to avoid that eventuality had led to miserable failure; he has merely resolved the problem with the surgeon's scalpel.[30]

Having thus condemned the all-India nationalist leadership for failing to resist an aggressive religious nationalism, the writer then takes a wistful look at the other failed possibility—that of linguistic nationalism.

Bengal, which had once energetically and courageously foiled Lord Curzon's plan to divide it, is now, in 1947, proceeding to implement another plan of the same kind. Such is the irony of history! In 1905, the leadership mainly came from eastern Bengal, now it is from western Bengal. In 1905, the organizer was the Government of India, now the organizers are the Bengalis themselves. In 1905, the problem was political, now it is communal. The movement of 1905 spread the consciousness of undivided nationality throughout India; now

Bengal is eager to sacrifice that glorious tradition as it looks upon others to come to its rescue.[31]

Wistful evocation of linguistic nationalism is the predominant mood of Chunilal Gangopadhyay's portrait gallery of individuals whose convictions had crumbled as a result of the partition.[32] Written between 1946 and 1950 as a series of letters, one of his sketches is that of Khadim Islam, lifelong supporter of the Muslim League, who now says, "It is through my fault that the land of my birth is being divided and subdued. . . . Hindu-majority West Bengal will now be separated from Muslim-majority East Bengal and turned into a colony of north India." Zainul Kabir says, "The conspiracy of the League and the English will now turn East Bengal into a colony of Aligarh and West Bengal into a colony of Banaras. . . . When will Bengal, the land of Raja Ganesa to Subhas [Chandra Bose] and of Sultan Ilyas to Titumir, rise up again from the depths of time?" Sunil Sen of Purulia realizes in April 1949 that the rulers of Patna will mistreat the Bengalis of Bihar: "His so-called 'Indianism,' fondly nurtured throughout his life, is suddenly washed away. . . . Having neared the end of his life, he realizes that he has no bonds of imagination or need with the Hindus of Punjab or the Muslims of Peshawar. Rather, he is tied by ideal and interest with the Hindus of Bankura and the Muslims of Barisal."

Read historically, this can only appear to us as a fanciful evocation of what might have been, a sign once again of the unacceptability of the truth of partition rather than an assertion of a new linguistic nationalism. Even the most recent historiography in West Bengal, self-consciously seeking to avoid the inherited demonologies of Indian nationalist history, is forced to conclude that the story of partition can only be read as a Greek tragedy:

> Like insects drawn to the flame, our characters are driven by an invisible hand towards inevitable tragedy. . . .Why else should the leaders of India's freedom movement, who were all [including Jinnah] resistant to the idea of partition, behave in the final act of the transition of power in such a way that partition would become inevitable?[33]

Curiously, as the trauma of partition was gradually overcome and a massive uprooted population managed to resettle and restart their lives, the nationalism that came to predominate in West Bengal, in the period of Congress rule as well as later under the Left, was precisely the nationalism of the Swadeshi era: an Indian nationalism rooted in a Hindu civilizational past, a sense of Bengali identity firmly anchored within that nationalism (no matter how strained its strategic relations with the political center), and a rhetoric of Hindu-Muslim unity (now called the politics of secularism). Partition, in this historiography, became an aberration, a

mark of loss and of failure, and was attributed in the main to communalism, imperial machinations, and the inadequacies of the nationalist leadership. The durable construct of the imagined nation resumed its position
of hegemony, claiming to have within itself a secure place for religious
minorities, while allowing for a considerable range of communal discrimi-
nations, animosities, and strategic conflicts to be played out in the public
arena of national life.

Across the border in the other half of Bengal, the curious development
was the rise to dominance, over the next two and a half decades, of a new
linguistic nationalism that took as its foundational moment not August
1947, the birth of Pakistan, but February 1952, the beginning of the
movement for recognition of the Bengali language in Pakistan. The nationalism that became hegemonic in Bangladesh after 1971 spoke on
behalf of a national community united by language and cutting across
religious divisions. There too the partition of Bengal in 1947 became an
aberration, a mark of loss and failure, brought on by the obduracy of
Hindu leaders and the manipulations of the British.[34] The hegemonic
move that was missing in the decade before partition was successfully
made in the 1970s, but only in a territory already truncated by a division
along religious lines.

Despite the rejection of religious nationalism, however, there has been
no significant move made on either side of the border for a reunification
of Bengal and none is likely to be made in the foreseeable future. Perhaps
what this demonstrates is that an event brought about by extremely contingent and short-term actions can in turn decisively and permanently
shape the forms of social structures and political imaginations. I have
shown that historical memory in both West Bengal and Bangladesh strenuously seeks to deny the truth of the second partition of Bengal; yet the
renewed possibility of nationalist imaginings unrestricted by religious
identity is crucially conditioned by the very consequences of that partition.

The case of Bengal seems to point to one aspect of modern nation-state
formations that has been little recognized in the literature on nationalism.
This relates to the frequent, but necessarily subterranean, presence of religion as a cultural-demographic element in the formation of hegemonic
national ideologies. Religion does not sit well with the various classifica-
tory categories with which a "population" is defined as the target of the
government activities that provide legitimacy for the postenlightenment
state. After all, of all contemporary nation-states today, only Israel and
Pakistan explicitly claim a basis of nationality located primarily in religious identity. Yet it is possible to cite numerous instances of nationalisms
in which a dominant religious identity has provided a major element
in the cultural construction of the national identity. Indeed, one of the
most surprising features of the recent emergence of scholarly interest in

nationalism is the sudden discovery of religion as a constituent element of the supposedly secular nationalisms of Western European countries.[35] Perhaps nationalist ideologies lodge themselves most effectively in the body of the modern state when they are able to relegate religion to the secret history of its birth, when they can transform the gross facts of religious majoritarianism into the benign cultural common sense of everyday national life. That perhaps is the condition in which the nation-state can make its most magnanimous gestures toward religious minorities by offering them the promise of universal bourgeois citizenship, even if it is by recognizing and protecting their identities as minorities. To create that condition, a selective erasure from public memory of certain kinds of narratives appears to be a major task of nationalist historiographies.

Notes

1. Sumit Sarkar, *The Swadeshi Movement in Bengal, 1903–1908* (New Delhi: People's Publishing House, 1973).
2. Cited in ibid., 17–18.
3. Cited in ibid., 19–20.
4. Cited in ibid., 18.
5. Ibid., pp. 420–24.
6. Bhudeb Mukhopadhyay, "Svapnalabdha bhāratbarṣer itihās" (1876), in Pramathanath Bisi, ed., *Bhūdeb racanā sambhār* (Calcutta: Mitra and Ghosh, 1969), 341–74.
7. Badruddin Umar, *Baṅgabhaṅga o sāmpradāyik rājnīti* (Calcutta: Chirayata, 1987), preface.
8. Sugata Bose, *Agrarian Bengal: Economy, Social Structure, and Politics, 1919–1947* (Cambridge: Cambridge University Press, 1986), esp. 181–232.
9. Ibid., 231–32.
10. Ibid., 277.
11. Suranjan Das, *Communal Riots in Bengal, 1905–1947* (Delhi: Oxford University Press, 1991). Taj ul-Islam Hashmi also makes the argument that there was a "communalization of class politics," a takeover of the peasant movement in east Bengal by the better-off tenants, and finally a takeover of the communalized Proja movement by urban elite political groups represented by the Muslim League. *Pakistan as a Peasant Utopia: The Communalization of Class Politics in East Bengal, 1920–1947* (Boulder, Colo.: Westview Press, 1992).
12. Joya Chatterji, *Bengal Divided: Hindu Communalism and Partition, 1932–1947* (Cambridge: Cambridge University Press, 1995), 152.
13. Ibid., 228.
14. Ibid., 227.
15. Richard M. Eaton, *The Rise of Islam amd the Bengal Frontier, 1204–1760* (Delhi: Oxford University Press, 1994).
16. Rafiuddin Ahmed, *Bengal Muslims: The Quest for Identity, 1876–1906* (Delhi: Oxford University Press, 1982); Tazeen M. Murshid, *The Sacred and the*

Secular: Bengal Muslim Discourses, 1871–1977 (Calcutta: Oxford University Press, 1995).

17. Joya Chatterji makes this argument about a shift from nationalism to communalism: "Nationalism was directed against imperialism, and gave top priority to anti-British action. The communalism of the bhadralok was directed against their fellow Bengalis. History for the one was the struggle against British rule; for the other, it was the celebration of British rule as an age of liberation from the despotism of Muslims. Its key political objective was to prevent this 'despotism' from returning when the British left India, and to deny that Muslims could be Bengalis, and by extension Indians" (*Bengal Divided*, 268). She marks this "shift" from the 1930s and emphasizes it to argue that "far from being a helpless pawn in the endgames of empire," Bengal was divided because large and powerful sections of the Hindu population, in town and countryside, actively fought for the province's partition. Her argument seems to me to flow from an astonishingly naive view of nationalist politics.

18. Both these sets of facts are well documented: Shila Sen, *Muslim Politics in Bengal, 1937–1947* (New Delhi: Impex India, 1976); Kamala Sarkar, *Bengal Politics, 1937–1947* (Calcutta: Mukherjee, 1990); Leonard A. Gordon, *Brothers against the Raj: A Biography of Sarat and Subhas Chandra Bose* (New Delhi: Penguin Books India, 1990).

19. See in particular Humayun Kabir, *Muslim Politics, 1909–1942* (Calcutta: Gupta, Rahman and Gupta, 1943), and Nareschandra Sengupta, *Yugaparikramā*, vol. 2 (Calcutta: Firma K. L. Mukhopadhyay, 1961), esp. 178–253.

20. This has been well documented for the districts of Tippera and Noakhali in Bose, *Agrarian Bengal*, 181–232.

21. Cited in Kalipada Biswas, *Yukta bānlār śeṣ adhyāy* (Calcutta: Orient Book Company, 1966), 386–90.

22. The debate is extensively quoted in Umar, *Baṅgabhaṅga*, 46–68.

23. Most communists later confessed that in 1946–47, the pressure to recognize the inevitability of a communal division was overwhelming. See the survey of communist literature and reminiscences in Amalendu Sengupta, *Uttāl calliś: Asamāpta biplab* (Calcutta: Pearl Publishers, 1989).

24. The debate is reprinted in Jagadischandra Mandal, *Baṅga-bhaṅga* (Calcutta: Mahapran Publishing Society, 1977).

25. Birendranath Chattopadhyay, *Ḍiliriyām (sāmpratik haṅgāmā)* (Alambazar: Databya Bibhag, 1947).

26. Ibid., 18.

27. Ibid., 47–48.

28. Satyen Sen, *Paneroi āgaṣṭ* (Calcutta: City Book Company, 1947).

29. Ibid., 63.

30. Ibid., 95.

31. Ibid., 87–88.

32. Chunilal Gangopadhyay, *Bhāṅgan diner kathāmālā* (n. p., n. d., possibly 1952).

33. Saileskumar Bandyopadhyay, *Jinnāh, pākistān: Natun bhābnā* (Calcutta: Mitra and Ghosh, 1988), 302–3.

34. A large unanimity on this has emerged among Bangladeshi historians. An officially sponsored history, for instance, deplores the scuttling by "obstinate Bengali Hindus" of the "noble plan" of Suhrawardy and Abdul Hashim for a sovereign United Bengal. It also criticizes the British for giving equal weight to majority and minority opinions in granting the partition of Bengal. Mohammad Waliullah, *Āmāder mukti-saṃgrām* (Dacca: Bangla Academy, 1978), 411–12. Badruddin Umar, arguing on Leninist grounds that only a genuinely democratic federal solution could have struck an acceptable balance between communal and regional interests in a multinational country like India, blames the Congress, the Muslim League, and the British for the partition (*Baṅgabhaṅga*, 104–5). Harun-Or Rashid ends his study of the demise of the Proja movement and the rise of the Muslim League in the 1940s by talking of how the all-India Muslim leadership subverted the project of an independent Bengal: "the victory of the Khwaja group . . . including the central League leadership was not to last long. With the removal of the fear of Hindu domination, Bengali subnationalism came to be asserted more prominently in the post-1947 Pakistani polity . . . culminating in the emergence of Bangladesh as an independent state in 1971, which is the partial fulfilment of the 1940s dream of an independent Greater Bengal." *The Foreshadowing of Bangladesh: Bengal Muslim League and Muslim Politics, 1936–1947* (Dacca: Asiatic Society of Bangladesh, 1987), 346.

35. For instance, Linda Colley, *Britons: Forging the Nation, 1707–1837* (New Haven, Conn.: Yale University Press, 1992).

7

Nationalism, Modernity, and Muslim Identity in India before 1947

BARBARA D. METCALF

> If there is one other sin with which I charge
> Great Britain, in addition to the charge of
> emasculating India, it is the making of wrong
> histories about India and teaching them to
> us in our schools.
> *(Mohammad Ali, "Speech to the Plenary
> Session, November 19," 1930)*

THE STUDY of nationalism as a phenomenon has changed profoundly in recent years, in part because of a focus on world history that not only encompasses multiple areas but also looks afresh at the processes and interrelations among those areas. In the case of nationalism, the conventional assumption has been that metropolitan developments flowed from a center to a periphery: thus, that nationalism arose in Europe and was transplanted elsewhere. Instead, recent work by Benedict Anderson and others has placed metropolitan and colonized areas into a single historical space where many processes, in fact, have turned out to be simultaneous and the product of complex interactions.[1] The most fundamental institutions of society and economy, even the very concept of the nation, along with gender, class, and caste, prove to have been constituted as part of these interactions. One dimension of this is that terms that have been used as scientific categories, not least *modernity* and *secularism* on one side, and *tradition* and *religion* on the other, are increasingly studied as political categories dependent on each other.

I want to illustrate this by some comments on Muslims in northern India in the 1920s and 1930s, focusing on a pietist movement called Tablighi Jama'at that has typically been taken—and indeed takes itself—as "traditional" and "apolitical." This is an oblique perspective from which to raise issues related to nationalism in contrast to a focus on the Indian National Congress or the Muslim League, which were centrally involved in the nationalist movement.

But Tablighi Jamaʿat, in fact, participates in characteristics shared by both these movements as well as by other movements typically glossed as "modern" or "social reform." Calling Tablighi Jamaʿat traditional, however, served its participants to confirm their authenticity, much as nationalism, however modern, must always seem timeless .[2] And calling Tablighi Jamaʿat traditional or fundamentalist or reactionary—allows opponents to constitute themselves as modern and, indeed, nationalist—adherents of a nationalism that sees itself justified in implicitly excluding certain categories of people from true citizenship, among them those relegated to the category of traditional or obscurantist. We need therefore to question the meaning of binaries like traditional and modern, yet, simultaneously we need to recognize the necessity of the dichotomy for creating the very categories, they purport to describe.

Mohammad Ali's comment at the beginning of this essay is an invitation to rethink the place of movements like Tablighi Jamaʿat in our telling of twentieth-century Indian history. The sections that follow attempt, first, to open up the description of the activities of a movement like Tablighi Jamaʿat in order to appreciate its complexity; second, to recognize Tablighi Jamʿat's own implicit contestation with the narratives into which it is placed; and then, in the final section, to tease out dimensions of the intimate and interdependent relationship between movements and approaches that are not the dichotomies they purport to be.

Tablighi Jamaʿat: Social Reform, Political Silence

The Tablighi Jamaʿat movement enters most historical narratives as part of a mutually aggressive communal reaction to the failure of the Khilafat and Noncooperation movements of the early 1920s. Alliterative pairs are often counterposed: Tabligh and Tanzeem of the Muslims, Shuddhi and Sangathan of the Hindus. The area of Mewat associated with the early period of the Tablighi Jamʿat movement was, in the 1920s and 1930s, in fact rife with competing proselytizing movements both Hindu, including the Arya Samaj,[3] and other Muslim movements (among them others named "Tabligh").[4] This was where the mass contact movement of the Congress, with the enrolling of "4 anna" members from 1920 on, took place. These movements were clearly not all the same. Thus, in the case of the Tablighi Jamaʿat, rather than see it as simply competitive with external groups, one can equally see it as a vehicle for social mobility and community, geared not at all to external confrontation but to internal issues very much like those of concern to the reform movements glossed as modern.

Here is an excerpt from an Urdu history of the movement, describing one of its founding moments:

Thanks to the deep relations Maulana Muhammad Ilyas [d. 1944] had with the people of Mewat, in August 1934 a *panchayat* was held under his chairmanship in the qasba of Nuh. In it were gathered *chaudhuri, miyan ji, zaildar, in'amdar, nambardar, subahdar, munshi, safeed poosh*, and other forward-looking (*sarbárawarda*) people of the region of Mewat [those listed are government functionaries, hereditary headmen, individuals with claims to some book learning and piety]. Their number was approximately one hundred and seven. First off at this meeting, the importance of Islam was discussed and then a compact (*ahd*) was made of total adherence to the pillars of Islam, of collective work for spreading religion, and of creating *panchayat* for furthering this work. The pact entered into was for the matters noted below:

1. Correct recollection of the *kalima* (the attestation of faith)
2. Adherence to the canonical prayer
3. Attainment and spread of education
4. Islamic appearance and demeanor (*shakl o surat*)
5. Adoption of Islamic customs and elimination of unfaithful customs (*rusum-i shirkiyya*)
6. Adherence to modesty (*parda*) among women
7. Performance of marriages in an Islamic style
8. The custom of Islamic dress among women
9. No abandonment of any Islamic belief and no acceptance of any noncanonical conduct (*ghair mazhab*)
10. Protection and safeguarding of mutual rights (*bahami huquq*)
11. Inclusion of responsible dignitaries in every meeting and gathering
12. No provision to children of worldly education without religious education
13. Effort and work for *tabligh* (preaching, proselytizing) of religion
14. Consideration of purity
15. Protection of each other's dignity and honor

It was also decided in this *panchayat* that *tabligh* was not only the work of the religious scholars but a duty of all Muslims and, so that we all should undertake it, all that was decided was written down. This *panchayat nama* was compiled and the participants all affixed their signature . . . the message of faith was to be spread to all classes of the *millat* . . . temporarily leaving one's homeland was deemed necessary for this. . . . [Among the injunctions was to] act toward ordinary Muslims with extreme consideration and kindness; speak to them gently and adopt a kindly manner. Look at no Muslim with contempt or hatred, and especially do not stint in respect and honor for the scholars of religion. . . . On one occasion Maulana Ilyas proclaimed, "The real purpose of this movement is that the *ummat* be shaped by the full intellectual and practical system (*nizam*) of Islam."[5]

In describing the modus operandi of the Tablighis, the author further explains that "Maulana Ilyas had prepared maps of all the *tahsil* subdivisions of Mewat as well as of the whole district of Gurgaon, set directions and routes, wrote out guidance for the preachers, as well as population of the villages, and the distance and the names of the *nambardars*; he thus established a proper system for *tabligh*."[6]

The vignette of this meeting recalls nothing more than the caste-uplift movements that proliferated across India in these decades. Groups of barbers or petty traders, led by their *panchayat*, the traditional "five" who adjudicated disputes and led activities, would meet and pledge a range of behaviors that would bring them into conformity with the respectable in a process sometimes called "sanskritization" or "ashrafization." The targeted behaviors invariably included greater control over women, since the presence of women in public space was regarded as typical of the lower orders, and restrictions on their dress. Also, as here, there was typically a move to rationalization of expenses on such events as marriage that came to be seen as "extravagance" once social relations were constituted on new grounds. These are movements that discourage custom in favor of more universally held norms; and they respond to broader social networks defined by behavior and achievement, not only by birth.

Not only were compacts signed but they were often reproduced on lithograph presses, a brittle, yellowed copy still occasionally to be found. Injunctions, as evident here, ranged from fidelity to the holiest practices of the faith to everyday domestic practices. Thus women, who were encouraged from the beginning to go out in groups for *tabligh*, were, for example, to stay in houses with indoor toilets, a custom then unknown in Mewat but now common, as one history writes, "through the blessing of *tabligh*,"[7] thus replacing the rural custom of nighttime trips to the fields with the interior toilets of the urban and respectable.

Tablighi Jama'at is notable for its generalization of leadership to lay participants,[8] a transition shared by many South Asian movements in the twentieth century. This characteristic is evident even in this early list above, not only in the guidelines for inclusiveness in relation to all potential participants but in the respect accorded to the most humble. The authority attributed to single elders now is diffused into the charismatic body of the group acting in concert. This movement provides a particularly far-reaching example of the larger move in religious organization from a vertical to a horizontal structure with the new emphasis on lay leadership.

Thus what is presented in the larger Tablighi Jama'at literature as a timeless reappropriation of pristine behavior clearly has the push to shared, respectable norms of behavior in an increasingly integrated and mobile society as one of its building blocks. The notion of *panchayat* with its lineage and village connotations soon gave way to the term *jama'at*, or association, which, like the *anjuman* that proliferated in this era, meant a voluntary association, albeit in this case notably loose in its organization.

Like the other revival and self-help movements of the day, Tablighi Jama'at drew on new modalities of communication, not least print;[9] note here the reference to maps, statistics, and local officials, all of course intrinsic to colonial culture. Tablighi Jama'at leadership has often been drawn from the bureaucracy and the army, the latter in particular credited in recent years with the careful organization of the hundreds of thousands, even millions, who attend annual meetings.

Two further characteristics of this movement resonate deeply with fundamental shifts evident in other settings in this period, both deeply affecting individual behavior and consciousness. One is the central focus on time, on managing time, measuring time—not wasting time—setting aside time for what is valued. A second is the interiorization and individualization of religious practice, for although participation in the group is central, participants also abjure the local customs of shrines and life-cycle ceremonies, minimize the role of the hierarchy as mediators, and have no expectations that social and political institutions will foster a moral life. That is left to the individual in such a way that—like speaking prose unaware—the Tablighi, living his everyday life in society, can be construed as truly "secular." In all these ways, a movement seen as "traditional" is strikingly new: new in its reach, new in its lay organization, new in its intensity, new in its modes of communication and organization, new in its self-consciousness as it deliberately strikes a "counterculture" relationship to economic and political life. Tablighi Jama'at takes hold in profoundly different local settings and means different things at different times, but the themes emphasized here have been pervasive throughout.

Politics between Khilafat and Partition: Competing Historical Narratives

The absorptions of Tablighi Jama'at in fostering individual Islamic self-fashioning, and eschewing participation in public life, are more remarkable in the context of north India in this period. The 1920s ushered in an unprecedented period of religious violence, competition for leadership, and the decisive emergence of mass politics. This was specifically when competing historical genealogies of Muslim history gained currency, usually summarized as the "nationalist" and the "communalist" interpretation of Muslim identities, histories that increasingly legitimated divergent ideologies. Tablighi Jamaʿat leadership simply ignored these issues despite the fact of being led by the same kind of people who joined the association of ʿulama (Jamiyat Ulama-i Hind) allied with the Indian National Congress, and, in the 1930s, supported the state-oriented Islamist movement of Maulana Maududi (1903–79).

All the movements of this era, including, notably, the Gandhian movement, included a spectrum of activities from what can be called the "guidance-oriented" at one end, with its focus on individual moral improvement, to the state-focused, political end, concerned with shaping and controlling public life, on the other.[10] Widespread assumptions about Islam suggest that Muslim movements invariably seek that kind of political control. In fact, there are long and pervasive orientations within Islam that have precisely focused on the individual end of the spectrum, not least those associated with Sufism. Although in the quotation above about the purpose of Tablighi Jamaʿat, Maulana Ilyas speaks of an Islamic *nizam*, a word that takes on new meaning in the twentieth century with the Islamist movements of Hasan al-Banna (1906–49) in Egypt and Maulana Maududi in India, Tablighi Jamaʿat ideology has not even posited a staged program with a focus on individual regeneration as a prelude to a changed society. The reorganization of society was simply left to some unknown future.

There was, moreover, a significant stream of thought, even among those engaged in the negotiations and competition of public life, to propose a vision of identity without territory. As Peter Hardy's study of the ideology of the Khilafat movement, and the subsequent proposals of the Jamiyat Ulama-i Hind have shown, the ʿulama who were engaged with Congress favored a kind of community federalism far more concerned with legal guidance and education than with state institutions. Joined to the Congress leadership by a common desire to remove the British from power, they envisaged an independent India comprised of religious communities whose own leaders would provide a framework for justice, education, and welfare—a kind of "jurisprudential apartheid." In basic ways this was reminiscent of earlier polities, like the Ottoman *millat* system, whose leaders served as intermediaries in regimes defined by relationships of loyalty and protection, not universal citizenship and land.[11] Thus the apoliticism of the Tablighi Jamaʿat—far from being peculiar to itself—is in fact not all that unlike the high politics of Muslim activists on the national stage.

When we turn to one critical dimension of defining community, that of constructing a historical genealogy, we also find a way of reconfiguring what are often taken as opposites. The usual binary has been drawn between those who, like Muhammad Ali Jinnah (1876–1948), pursued separate Muslim political interests and those who cooperated with the Congress, "from Azad to Rafi Ahmad Kidwai," about whom, Mushirul Hasan, for example, has written "there was no trace of "Muslimness" in their public life, except during the Khilafat movement."[12] On the contrary, I would argue, virtually all participants in public life worked from the assumption that "India" was a natural entity, inhabited by communities defined above all by religion. This perspective puts Jinnah and Congress on one side, the Tablighi Jama'at which opts out of a territorially based, national response, on the other.

The shared discourse is evident throughout the writings and speeches of the two great exemplars of what are, I suggest, wrongly taken as antithetical perspectives. Thus in a speech chosen almost at random given in 1941, Jinnah recounted the narrative of Muslims as a nation, once great and now fallen:

> [A] nation must have a territory. . . . Nation does not live in the air. It lives on the land, it must govern land, and must have territorial state. . . . It is the biggest job . . . since the fall of the Moghal Empire. . . . We come under the category of the fall. We have seen the worst days. . . . Our demand is not from Hindus because the Hindus never took the whole of India. It was the Muslims who took India and ruled for 700 years. It was the British who took India from the Musalmans. . . . Our demand is made to the British, who are in possession. It is an utter nonsense to say that Hindustan belongs to the Hindus.[13]

Maulana Abu'l Kalam Azad (1888–1958), in his celebrated address as Congress president at Ramgarh in 1940, assumed the same narrative line of India, invaders, and Hindus and Muslims, albeit to a different conclusion:

> It was India's historic destiny that many human races and cultures and religions should flow to her, finding a home in her hospitable soil. . . . One of the last of these caravans . . . was that of the followers of Islam. . . . This led to a meeting of the culture-currents of two different races. . . . We brought our treasures with us, and India too was full of the riches of her own precious heritage. . . . We gave her, what she needed most, the most precious of gifts from Islam's treasury, the message of democracy and human equality.[14]

This assumption of separate communities as the fundamental building blocks of Indian society is equally evident in the language of Gandhi and even of Nehru. It continues in Pakistan, not surprisingly. It continues unquestioned, despite a constitution based on universal individualism, in what might be called the official discourse of the government of India. Considerable recent scholarship has problematized this narrative, locating its origin in British histories and practice, and demonstrating the anachronism of reified religious communities in the precolonial period.[15]

The Tablighi Jamaʿat ideology is in this regard strikingly distinctive because it puts no gloss on the history of India at all, rather steeping its participants in historical examples drawn from the earliest days of Islam. The emphasis is less on history in the sense of tracing change over time than in historical exemplar, the lives of the Prophet and his companions as models in behavior and morality for Muslims living today. This is mythic history in which there are overlays, replications, of the past. Thus Tablighis tell the story of their efforts for the "internal conversion" (to use Geertz's term)[16] of Mewat as nothing less than that of the conversion of the Arab Bedouins from the ignorance of the pre-Islamic period toward the truth of Islam, for example, in writings of Maulana Maududi (who initially admired the Tablighi Jamaʿat) in his description of the Mewatis with their ignorance of prayer, idols, and tufts of hair.[17] Little matter that later Mewatis have countered with a history of Islamic learning and spirituality in their area[18] or that sociologists have offered a much later timetable for change.[19]

A variation of the shared linear history dwells on imagined places outside India. Faisal Devji, for example, has described the new *marsiya* of the nineteenth century, the mourning elegies of the Shia, which develop a presentation of unfolding dramatic scenes, depicting the moral drama of Karbala as a story of a people's political loss.[20] Later in the century, novelists like Sharar turned to historical novels, nostalgically re-creating past settings of Muslim worldly glory.[21] Similarly, the poet Muhammad Iqbal (1876–1938), returning home from one of the Round Table Conferences, stopped at the mosque of Córdoba and wrote one of his greatest poems, a meditation on the flow of time, interrupted, as it was there, by creative genius, now lost.[22] These writings "straddle" the imagination of a linear narrative of India and the imagination of a recurrent mythological moment of Islam. Yet, I would suggest, they are fundamentally about the British and about the experience of loss, even though that transition is played out in a non-Indian setting.

It is tempting to write the historical imaginings set outside the subcontinent into a teleology that culminates in Pakistan. But they are not fundamentally about geopolitics; they are not irredentist statements. They are in the end about the colonial predicament. Gandhi could embrace the Khilafat cause not only out of expediency but because imagining Istanbul as a site of British perfidy was another way of imagining India.

These various histories, the secular, the communal, and the Pan-Islamic, thus share fundamental characteristics as nationalist and territorial. Both before and after partition, the single story, with its competing variants, has dominated public debate. Histories like that of the Tablighis have operated in a different sphere. The Tablighi Jamaʿat itself, a minor movement until the postindependence periods, in India in particular, has simply been assimilated to evidence of Muslim difference.

In retrospect, however, it is useful to show that there were and are alternatives to the pervasive framework of history and nation that is taken as natural, among them identity constituted without reference to territory, as in Tablighi Jamaʿat. Even here, however, the Tablighi's Jamaʿat typological history takes as a given the shared question of all twentieth-century Muslim leaders: what is the cause of Muslim degeneracy and its cure?[23] The answer from the Tablighi Jamaʿat was not that of the Muslim "leaders" concerned with negotiating representation in electorates, councils, education, and so forth. Yet their historical imaginings too, even though the issue is often represented by silence, were responses to the colonial situation and thus part of a shared modernity. The Tablighi Jamaʿat is not an anachronistic fossil; it, with other Islamic movements, is grounded in the context of Indian nationalism and modernity.

Islam, Identity, and Nationalism

British nationalism and identity are inextricably linked to the encounter with what are considered non-British lands and ways of living. Britain is a "green and pleasant land" only because there are jungles and wilderness out there; Britain is enlightened and modern only because other societies are constructed as benighted and like Britain's own past.[24] As in Britain itself, however, Indian nationalism has its own internal foils for identity, among them in some contexts Muslims, including the kind of Muslims represented by the Tablighi Jamaʿat.

Muslims are, in this imagination, the limiting case of "religion." Religions, Nehru writes, have "tried to imprison truth in set forms and dogmas . . . discouraged [man] from trying to understand not only the unknown but what might come in the way of social effort. . . . As knowledge advances, the domain of religion . . . shrinks.[25] He continues that India must lessen its "religiosity" and turn to science, himself implicitly accepting the orientalist stereotype of India as a place dominated by outdated modes of thinking, hence religion.

> The rules and regulations of the kitchen dominate [the Hindu's] social life. The
> Moslem is fortunately free from these inhibitions, but he has his own narrow

codes and ceremonials, a routine which he rigorously follows, forgetting the
lesson of brotherhood which his religion taught him. *His view of life is perhaps
even more limited and sterile than the Hindu view.*[26]

Such a perspective ignores the relationship between nationalism itself and
many dimensions of religion and religious movements in the twentieth
century as products of the same historical forces, and implicitly reveals
an intimate relationship in which the modernity of nationalism is defined
by the presumed archaism of religion. This angle on Muslims was reinforced by the perception of nationalist leaders, like Nehru, that the Muslim leadership, above all the leadership of the Muslim League, represented
the "feudal" landlords who would stand in the way of centralization and
socialism in the independent state.[27]

The Muslim League leadership of course insisted equally on the distinctiveness and community identity of Muslims, but with a striking difference. Jinnah argued in his well-known presidential address of 1940 that
Islam was *not* a religion, perhaps his own gesture, stemming from the
cosmopolitanism and isolation from mainstream religious practice he
shared with Nehru, toward self-presentation as "modern." Thus the Muslims were a nation, not a religion.

> The problem of India is not of an inter-communal character but manifestly of
> an international one, and it must be treated as such . . . the only course open
> to us all is to allow the major nations separate homelands by dividing India into
> "autonomous national states." It is extremely difficult to appreciate why our
> Hindu friends fail to understand the real nature of Islam and Hinduism. They
> are not religions in the strict sense of the word.[28]

Despite Jinnah's efforts, the distinctiveness of Muslims was in fact construed internally as well as externally as religion, and the role of key spiritual leaders in areas of Sind and Punjab was critical to Muslim League
success.[29]

There is thus a long genealogy for the current Hindu nationalism of the
Bharatiya Janata Party in insisting that they are not a religious movement
but a cultural movement; to be "religious" is to be medieval. "Islam," as
they conceive it, is what they are not. Even Nehru, despite his subtle and
informed analysis of historical parallels and background, gave "purdah"
importance "among the causes of India's decay in recent centuries"—and
linked it to the presence of Muslims.[30] Just as for the British the presumed
Indian male treatment of women was a central legitimating argument for
their rule, so among Hindu nationalists, as debates over the Shah Banu
decision and subsequent legislation in 1986 attest, the status of Muslim
women is used to bolster their cultural superiority. The displacement of
gender issues onto a presumed retrograde Other deflects attention from

fundamental issues related to women and simultaneously suggests a contrast between oneself as enlightened and the Other as backward.[31]

Equally critical in this economy of meaning has been the definition of the Muslim as the one irreducibly inassimilable group marked precisely by religion as the essentialist base of all difference. Nehru, again the more interesting for his own cosmopolitanism and subtlety, can only introduce the subject of Muslim dynasties in the subcontinent by entitling that section of his book "New Problems."[32] The focus on Muslims in twentieth-century India has helped obscure social differences, starting in the 1930s debates on untouchables and continuing in the escalation of the anti-Muslim movement to destroy the mosque at Ayodhya precisely when, in 1990, opposition to the Mandal Report (expanding entitlements for the "backward") got out of hand. Especially with the creation of Pakistan and the political reality of separate nations, it could be seen—not always or in all contexts but clearly so in the early 1990s—as "legitimate" to denounce Muslim difference, thus directing attention away from the legally illegitimate but pervasive differences of hierarchy based on birth.

Muslim Identity before Partition

This sketch thus far suggests at least three arguments concerning modernity, nationalism, and identity, particularly in relation to Muslims.

1. The decades preceding partition were a remarkably active and transformative period for religious life, above all in terms of institutional change and the spread of normative practices. Although I have illustrated this process with one Islamic movement, the same kind of process was widely evident. The Tablighi Jama'at illustrates a characteristic transition to lay participation and leadership and a diffusion of normative practices.

The social context that gave rise to such movements is, broadly speaking, the same as that which gave rise to nationalism. Central are the sense of decline and the perceived need for change on one hand and the stimuli of travel and communication on the other. Mines's work on south Indian villagers exemplifies this transition: villagers, indistinguishable as Muslims at home, dress, eat, and identify as Muslims when they go to the city, thus securing a basis for community in a context of physical dislocation.[33]

By stressing movements like this as a kind of social reform, and with the allusion to Mines who grounds the evolution of such new organizations in a functionalist interpretation, I write the Tablighi Jama'at into a narrative of social change. I do this in part to problematize the place of religion as foil in narratives of modernity and nationalism. But my narrative is partial, and meaningless to the participants who would prefer, of course, to see themselves as representing what is timeless and free of social contexts.[34]

2. While many of the *anjuman* and associations like the Tablighi Jamaʿat conceived of themselves as apolitical, they by their very existence represent political positions. They are often written into the ever present and conceptually "natural" narrative of nationalism: a kind of cultural "prenationalism" awaiting fulfillment as a Muslim nation or interest group. This, is, indeed, how they often are viewed in contemporary India. Politically active or not, the Tablighi Jamaʿat in India has made Muslims into a more visible and culturally distinct "ethnicity." At the least, moreover, a movement like the Tablighi Jamaʿat delegitimizes nationalist claims that the nation is a natural and inalienable part of identity. Tablighis are widely criticized in contemporary Pakistan for not helping "build" the nation, even while political leaders in recent years praise their Islamic commitments. Tablighi Jamaʿat activities may, in fact, in India or Pakistan, be facilitated by political parties or government officials who see its apolitical stance as something to be encouraged. In India, Congress supporters identify Tablighi Jamaʿat with the politically active Deobandi ʿulama allied with them.

Tablighis implicit counternarrative to nationalism, above all its marked aterritorialism, has taken on new salience with the Muslim diaspora in North America and Europe. Indeed many of the spatial imaginings of Muslims—of Karbala, of Córdoba, of Mecca and Medina, even of Istanbul—are significant not because they suggest an extraterritorial identity, as nationalism would require—but because they suggest an identity spatially located nowhere. With today's transnationalism and movement, it is easier to see this pervasive impulse in twentieth-century Muslim thought as potentiality rather than as failure.

Such aterritorialism was also an element, as noted above, following the work of Peter Hardy, in the participation of ʿulama in the Indian nationalist movement. No spokesman was more articulate on this than Maulana Husain Ahmad Madani, who engaged with Iqbal and others, in pamphlets and letters, on the subject of common nationalism (*muttahidah qaumiyyat*) as distinct from *millat*: the latter he identified as a community based on shared textual tradition, the former on shared residence. Thus the *hindustani qaum*, he argued, bore no reference to religion. He made this latter judgment, he explained on one occasion, on the pragmatic basis of having lived abroad for sixteen years and knowing how the designation was used in the world at large[35]—a reminder that his position came from someone cosmopolitan and well traveled. For him the term *qaum*, far from having religious implications, could be applied either to descent or behavior; and he listed a variety of uses for the term: language, region (ʿarab, ʿajam [non-Arab; Irani]), nation (*irani, misri* [Egyptian]), descent (*sayyid, shaikh, mochi* [shoemaker]), color (*gora* [white], *kala* [black]), even occupation/lifestyle (*sufiyoon ki qaum* [Sufis], *dunyadaroon ki qaum*, [worldly people]). *Qaum*, the nation, was based on territory, *watn*, but since the central issues of everyday concern were to be handled by constituent groups, the *qaum* was little more than an empty space free of intrusive imperial rule.

Madani's impulse mitigates against such concerns as competition for entitlements in voting and employment since the regulation of the *millat* is ultimately internal. Its orientation to imagined spaces beyond geopolitics extends to withdrawal from competition over local place, like Ayodhya, in a later era, as well. In its expression in the Tablighi Jama'at movement, this aterritorialism is as widespread, and as detached from the state, in the so-called Islamic Republic of Pakistan as it is in the secular state of India. Can one write a narrative that makes Tablighi Jama'at postmodern, transnational, before its time?

3. Current revisionist scholarship on partition emphasizes far more ambivalence on the part of the Congress leadership in favor of partition than the nationalist myths of either India or Pakistan allows.[36] Muslims, Parama Roy argues, were taken to be an obstacle to all a leader like Nehru wished to build in terms of a secular, socialist state, so that separating off a large share of their population and leadership had certain advantages. Muslims and Islam have continued their role in the non-Muslim political imagination in India, not least in the ideology of Hindu nationalist movements like the Rashtriya Swayamsevak Sangh (RSS).[37] One tantalizing probe into the complexity of the place of Muslims in the nationalist imagination—most intimate of relationships—is Roy's study of the film superstar Nargis, whose "(absent, ephemeral, discreet) Muslimness" is intrinsically linked to her classic role in *Mother India*: "If Mother India is, at least partially, an allegory of the repudiation of Muslim difference, and of becoming a Hindu, then only a Muslim can assume the iconic position of that maternal figure."[38] The image of a Muslim as Mother India can serve as metaphor for the way Muslim movements have been part of the same modern transitions as other social and political movements in this century, at once integral yet a foil.

Notes

1. Benedict R. Anderson, *Imagined Communities: Reflections on the Origin and Spread of Nationalism*, 2d ed. (London: Verso, 1991).
2. Ibid.
3. Partap C. Aggarwal, *Caste, Religion, and Power: An Indian Case Study* (New Delhi: Shri Ram Centre for Industrial Relations, 1971).

4. Majid Hayat Siddiqi, "History and Society in a Popular Rebellion: Mewat, 1920–33," *Comparative Studies in Society and History* 28 (1986): 442–67; Gail Minault, *The Khilafat Movement: Religious Symbolism and Political Mobilization in India* (New York: Columbia University Press, 1982), 193–98; Shail Mayaram, *Resisting Regimes: Myth, Memory, and the Shaping of Muslim Identity* (Delhi: Oxford University Press, 1997).

5. Muhammad Ayyub Qadiri, *Tablighi Jamaʿat ka tarikhi jaʾiza* [A historical survey of the Tablighi Jamaʿat] (Karachi: Maktaba Muʿawiya, 1971), 91–97.

6. Ibid., 99.

7. Miyanji Muhammad ʿIsa Firozpuri, *Tabligh ka maqami kam* [The local work of Tabligh] (Delhi: Rabbani Buk Depo, n.d.), 105.

8. Barbara D. Metcalf, "Living Hadith in the Tablighi Jamaʿat." *Journal of Asian Studies* 52 (1993): 584–608.

9. Barbara D. Metcalf, "Remaking Ourselves': Islamic Self-Fashioning in a Global Movement of Spiritual Renewal," in Martin Marty and Scott Appleby, eds., *Accounting for Fundamentalisms: The Dynamic Character of Movements* (Chicago: University of Chicago Press, 1994), 706–25.

10. Ahmed Mukarram, "The Tabligh Movement and Mawlana Abul Hasan Ali Nadwi: Guidance-Oriented Strand of Contemporary Islamic Thought," typescript (Oxford University, 1991).

11. Peter Hardy, *The Muslims of British India* (Cambridge: Cambridge University Press, 1972), 190–91; Peter Hardy, *Partners in Freedom—and True Muslims: The Political Thought of Some Muslim Scholars in British India, 1912–1947* (Lund: Studentlitteratur, 1971).

12. Mushirul Hasan, ed., *Islam and Indian Nationalism: Reflections on Abul Kalam Azad* (Delhi: Manohar, 1992), 5.

13. Muhammad Ali Jinnah, *Speeches and Writings of Mr. Jinnah*, ed. Jamil-ud-din Ahamd, 2 vols. (Lahore: Mohammad Ashraf, 1968), 1:236–39.

14. Abuʿl Kalam Azad, "Presidential Address to the Indian National Congress" (1940) in *India's Partition: Process, Strategy, and Mobilisation* Mushirvi Hasan, ed., (Delhi: Oxford University Press, 1993): 67.

15. Barbara D. Metcalf, "Presidential Address: Too Little and Too Much: Reflections on Muslims in the History of India," *Journal of Asian Studies* 54 (1995): 1–17.

16. Clifford Geertz, " 'Internal Conversion' in Contemporary Bali," in *The Interpretation of Cultures: Selected Essays* (New York: Basic Books, 1973), 170–89.

17. Abu'l-ala Maududi, Maulana, "Ihya-i din ki jidd o jahd ka sahih tariqa aur ek qabil-i taqlid namuna" [The correct means of struggle for the revival of religion and an example worth imitating], in Muhammad Manzur Nuʿmani, ed., *Tablighi jamaʿat, jamaʿat-i islami aur barelwi hazrat* [The Tabligh Jamaʿat, the Jamaʿat-i Islami, and the Barelvi Gentlemen], (Lucknow: Al-Furqan Book Depot, 1939), 25.

18. Qadiri, *Tablighi Jamaʿat ka tarikhi jaʾiza*, 54–63.

19. Aggarwal, *Caste, Religion, and Power*, 1971.

20. Faisal Devji, *Muslim Nationalism: Founding Identity in Colonial India* (Chicago: University of Chicago, Department of History, 1994), chap. 1.

21. Muhammad Sadiq, *A History of Urdu Literature*, 2d ed. (Delhi: Oxford University Press, 1984), 430–35.

22. Barbara D. Metcalf, "Reflections on Iqbal's Mosque," *Journal of South Asian and Middle Eastern Studies* 1 (1977): 68–74.

23. Maulana Ihtishamu'l-Hasan Kandhalavi, "Muslim Degeneracy and Its Only Remedy" [Musalmanon ki maujuda pasti ka wahid ʿilaj], in Muhammad Zachariyya, ed., *Teachings of Islam: Tablighi Nisab No. 1*, p. 10 (Delhi: n.p., 1939).

24. Linda Colley, *Britons: Forging the Nation, 1707–1837* (New Haven, Conn.: Yale University Press, 1992).

25. Jawaharlal Nehru, *The Discovery of India* (New York: Anchor Books, 1956), 389.

26. Ibid., 393–94, emphasis added.

27. Ibid., 301.

28. Jinnah, *Speeches and Writings*, 1: 168–69.

29. David Gilmartin, *Empire and Islam: Punjab and the Making of Pakistan* (Berkeley: University of California Press, 1988); Sarah F. D. Ansari, *Sufi Saints and State Power: The "Pirs" of Sind, 1843–1947* (Cambridge: Cambridge University Press, 1992).

30. Nehru, *The Discovery of India*, 144.

31. Asghar Ali Engineer, ed., *The Shah Bano Controversy* (London: Sangam, 1987).

32. Nehru, *The Discovery of India*, 129–97.

33. Mattison Mines, "Islamisation and Muslim Ethnicity in South India," in Dietmar Rothermund, ed., *Islam in Southern Asia: A Survey of Current Research*, (Wiesbaden: Steiner, 1975), 55–57.

34. Cf. Majid Hayat Siddiqi, "History and Society in a Popular Rebellion: Mewat, 1920–33," *Comparative Studies in Society and History* 28 (1986): 442–67.

35. Sayyid Husain Ahmad Madani, "Maslah-yi fitna-yi qaumiyyat: ʿAllama iqbal ka i'tiraz aur hazrat maulana madani rahmat allah ka jawab" [The problem of the dispute over "Qaumi yat" (nationalism): The objective of ʿAllama Iqbal and the answer of the Hazrat Maulana Madani, on inborn be peace], in Ahmad Salim, ed., *Khutbat-i madani* [Sermons of Madani], (Lahore: Nigarishat, 1990), 169–77.

36. Ayesha Jalal, *The Sole Spokesman: Jinnah, the Muslim League and the Demand for Pakistan* (Cambridge: Cambridge University Press, 1985); Asim Roy, "The High Politics of India's Partition: The Revisionist Perspective," *Modern Asian Studies* 24 (1990): 385–415.

37. Paola Bacchetta, "Communal Property/Sexual Property: On Representations of Muslim Women in a Hindu Nationalist Discourse," in Zoya Hasan, ed., *Forging Identities: Gender, Communities, and the State in India* (Boulder, Col.: Westview Press, 1994), 188–225.

38. Parama Roy, "The Spectral Nargis," typescript (University of California, 1995), 17.

8

Memory, Mourning, and National Morality: Yasukuni Shrine and the Reunion of State and Religion in Postwar Japan

HARRY HAROOTUNIAN

IN 1995, the year devoted to commemorating the fiftieth anniversary of the end of World War II and the dropping of the atomic bombs on Japan, the rush to remember often appeared as a desperate attempt to make contact with momentous events of a half a century ago as if there were imminent danger that knowledge of them might disappear, as if it might be forgotten they ever took place. In the endless process of recalling, the emphasis, more often than not, focused on the figure of war and loss, the necessity for remembrance and grieving, the prices paid for peace. What seems to have happened was a celebration of memory and monumentalizing, as such, people individually or collectively remembering the war, not as a historical production but as a sign of memory, an exercise voluntarily recalling a moment now passed. Yet during the spectacular commemoration in Hiroshima in August 1995, only the mayor of that troubled city, among most participants, reminded the gathered audience (and those like myself who had watched it on CNN) that it was necessary to also remember the conditions and circumstances that led ultimately to the dropping of the atomic bomb and to recall Japan's own historical complicity in the destruction that originated in imperial military adventures in Asia that had taken the lives of untold millions and destroyed cities and communities even before the Pearl Harbor raid. Even before this timely reminder that memory and history were distinctly different perceptual operations, the city of Hiroshima added a wing to the Peace Museum to display the narrative of Japan's war in Asia that led to the wider conflict in the Pacific. What this narrativizing restored, deliberately I think, was the role played by the Japanese state as the principal agent in bringing about the war and the means it had employed to mobilizing an unsuspecting population to make the supreme sacrifice to die for the nation in order to become "heroic spirits" and gain entry into Yasukuni Shrine, the central custodian of national memory and mourning commemorating Japan's war dead.

Until recently it has been evident that both the state's role in the war and memory of the conflict have been safely suppressed or indeed displaced in the process of self-victimization accompanying a peace movement centered on Hiroshima and the experience of having been the first, and as of yet only, national group made to suffer nuclear destruction. The nuclear destruction of Hiroshima and Nagasaki was refigured to exonerate Japan, the state and population, from actually accepting responsibility for causing the war, by placing the event of nuclear experience at a higher level on the scale of moral valuation. Fighting a war that may or may not have been justified, occupying and devastating Asian societies in the name of antiwhite colonialism, was ultimately seen as less important than the heroic experience of suffering the destruction inflicted by the atomic bombs. However inhuman the Japanese conduct during the war, the atom bombs introduced new and even more unimagined forms of inhuman terror, even though they were designed to bring an end to the war Japanese had undoubtedly started. A generation of Japanese have thus matured free of guilty memories of the war and dedicated to maintaining Japan's peace constitution (forbidding war). Even though Chinese and Koreans have punctually reminded Japan that it needs to actually recall and rewrite its history to account for the role of the imperial state in Asia and the destruction it caused, most Japanese have found it easier to acknowledge Japan's brutality toward Asia in the past and forget the history of the episode as a kind of bad dream that happened long ago. But they are equally quick to point to the nuclear bombing of Hiroshima and Nagasaki as an experience that sets them apart from the very peoples of Asia they brutalized.

Although the Japanese government has moved, from time to time, to satisfy Chinese and Korean complaints and to offer qualified and even guarded apologies, the fiftieth anniversary, as it turned out, was not the occasion for cathartic reconciliation. Nor did it manage, in fact, to induce the state to apologize for having mobilized a population for "total war," as it was called by fascist theorists and military high command, and imbuing them with a religio-political ideology demanding self-sacrifice as the price for national deification. Far from offering the desired apology, the call for an expression of public remorse catalyzed a coalition of forces, long active in trying to resuscitate state Shinto and restore the cozy relationship between polity and religion, that opposed the very idea of an apology. According to the *Economist* of 12 August 1995, more than a million people, a quarter of the members of the Diet, signed a petition aimed at preventing any resolution calling for an apology. Moreover, an "astounding 70% of the Diet members belonging to the Liberal Democratic Party (LDP)," which dominates the current coalition government, supported this campaign to thwart issuing an official apology for causing the war. Instead, a diluted expression of remorse for the suffering of the

war squeaked through the Diet and reflected a long-standing conceit both
to refuse accepting responsibility for the war and to emphasize that Japan
was not the sole aggressor, as if this fact would console Chinese and Koreans by explaining that they were made to suffer because Japan was involved in a rivalry with the United States and Great Britain.

It is interesting to note that in the 1950s, intellectuals, writers, and
scholars produced an immense discourse devoted to this issue that eventually was drowned out by the student movement of the 1960s, calling for
other things, and Japan's middle-class affluence in the 1970s. The concern
for war responsibility slipped into its reverse, which has been the steadily
strident mobilization of opinion that disavows Japan's role in the war and
denies the destruction the Imperial Army inflicted on subject populations
throughout Asia. What this refusal to accept war responsibility revealed
was an even deeper conviction that because Japan had waged war against
Anglo-Saxon imperial modernity, sloganized during the war as "overcoming modernity," its involvement in Asia was somehow necessary rather
than imperialistic and aggressive, emancipatory rather than oppressive.[1]
Not too long ago, the now former prime minister Murayama Tomiichi,
a socialist, announced that Japan's seizure of Korea in 1910 had been
legal. These and other examples too numerous to enumerate here disclose
not simply collective amnesia or denial but rather a complex relationship
between contemporary political culture in Japan and the history of prewar society. In this connection, there is probably no better illustration of
this relationship than the postwar movement to reunite the state to the
Yasukuni Shrine and to once more make it the official place of national
memory. For many ordinary Japanese, Yasukuni Shrine has become the
place that houses the memory of Japan's wars and the heroic spirits who
gladly gave their lives to the nation. At Yasukuni, nobody ever asks why
a war was fought or if it was a "just war," because all of Japan's wars
have been "just." A newspaper article published a few years before the
war reminded its readers that "the wars of Japan are carried on in the
name of the Emperor and therefore are holy wars."[2]

One of the genuine ironies of Japan's postwar experience (senso taiken)
was that the very effort by writers, intellectuals, and scholars to strenuously promote discussion on war responsibility and guilt in the late 1940s
and 1950s to construct a new political subject capable of acting autono-
mously was literally forgotten in the 1960s and after in the student movement's impatience with the wartime generation's effort to establish a
social democracy. Together with this momentary move to a student-led
Left and its repudiation of social democrats was the LDP's commitment
to a policy of modernization that called for high economic growth and
income doubling, a program that promised to offer material rewards as
a substitute for genuine political involvement that easily muted political

criticism by the 1970s. While many thoughtful people believed that everyday life would yield responsible political participation, the policies of the LDP worked to rob it of this political purpose by replacing it with the incentive for consumption. Throughout this period the state appeared as a benignly recessive facilitator of economic recovery, by virtue of the discrediting of the prewar state's role in the recent war and the accompanying transformation of Japanese from the status of victimizers to victims induced by the experience of Hiroshima and Nagasaki. Yet the role of the state was quickly expanded by the LDP to promote accelerated economic growth and manage Japan's reemergence as a major global trader. With the careful construction of the "expected ideal Japanese" (*kitai sareru ningenzo*) by the Ministry of Education, the state aimed at producing a generation of disciplined workers and consumers that contributed greatly to both the disappearance of considerations associated with war responsibility and the creation of national amnesia concerning the past. This move also set the stage for regaining control of the collective memory by grounding it in national morality and mourning.

In the historical conjuncture of the 1960s and 1970s a movement was launched to have the Diet pass a bill that would make the state, once more, responsible for maintaining the Yasukuni Shrine. Although this effort to reinstate the prewar relationship between polity and religion, state and shrine, as it were, was clearly unconstitutional, it nevertheless represented a moment of repetition as if to deny the passage of historical time and the irretrievability of the past. If it constituted the sign of repetition, it also signified a return of the repressed, now out of time and place, a temporality stripped of its historical markers, what Freud once identified as the "uncanny," *unheimlich*, a ghost that has erupted from a surplus of what had been suppressed to trouble the stable boundaries between past and present.[3] At the heart of this repetition is the imperial house and its god-man emperor, who is descended from Amaterasu, the sun goddess. Instead of executing the emperor as a war criminal, the U.S. Occupation resuscitated and transformed him into the figure of a bourgeois family man no longer divine. But this role was simply superimposed on the older figure like a palimpsest that allowed older associations of divinity and authority to filter through the overlay. If, moreover, the imperial line emblematized Japan's uniqueness, it also guaranteed claims of ethnic homogeneity and social cohesion. Reinstating the link between state—the old imperial bureaucracy—and the Yasukuni Shrine, devoted to preserving the spirits of Japan's war dead, meant returning Japan to a time when people were socialized into performing unhesitant service to the emperor. The very people who campaigned loudest against an apology are the same people who have promoted the move to persuade the state to assume responsibility for managing the Yasukuni Shrine, to reconcile polity and religion as it was envisaged by the Meiji state in the nineteenth century in the figure of an emperor who authorizes but does not rule directly.

It is interesting to note that despite the nineteenth-century desire everywhere to sever polity from religion, in order to construct the modern nation-state, and Hegel's anxiety that such a division "has been a monstrous blunder of our times,"[4] the Japanese modernizing experience early showed the indissoluble link between the modern nation-state and religion. It should be recalled that the Meiji Restoration of 1868, inaugurating Japan's entry into modernity, was in large part seen as a religious event, a repetitive event outside time and distinct from the secular narrative that brought Japan to make this momentous decision, which subsequently guided the nation on its modernizing itinerary. In its refiguration of the emperor, epiphanizing the imperial line in invented ceremonies and rituals and establishing state-sponsored shrines like Meiji and Yasukuni in Tokyo, Japan seemed to confirm Hegel's worst fears that "religion was . . . something desirable perhaps for strengthening the political bulwarks but purely subjective in individuals."[5] Yet far from confirming the "monstrous blunder," the Japanese historical experience shows how the vitality of the religious has been able to survive in new guises, propel a repetition compulsion, and return to the surface when conflicts become so acute as to produce cracks in the edifice of the state. This is not to argue, as do many, that the appearance of religious impulses in modernizing societies represents a repudiation of modernity or that religion has been transmuted into nationalism.[6] What I want to emphasize is that the rearticulation of a religious memory in institutional form constituted a condition of modern, secular society, not a rejection of it. Such moves calling for commemorative acts in the present at sacred sites aim to promote the illusion of effacing mundane time, denying temporal difference, which, after all, is what marks modern societies for a realization of the same, unchanging, and truly authentic reality. Both the massive effort to reinstate Yasukuni Shrine to its place of national prominence and the desperate attempts of new, syncretic religious organizations like Omoto-kyo or the more recent Aumshinri-kyo's alleged effort to sow dissent through acts of terror show religion's resilience to appear as a force in, rather than as the handmaiden of, politics. The resurgence of the religious Right in the United States speaks this truth more loudly than better publicized instances of Islamic fundamentalism.

Yasukuni Shrine occupies a large chunk of real estate in the Kudan district of central Tokyo, within earshot of the Imperial Palace. Its name means "peaceful country shrine" and it is classed as a "protector of the nation shrine (*gokoku jinja*)."[7] Located near the center of symbolic, material, and political power (Barthes's notion of an empty center simply ignores or overlooks what constitutes central Tokyo around the Imperial

Palace), the shrine precinct is marked off by an imposing torii that serves as the gateway, a singular symbol of Shinto, filled with cherry trees—signifying the beauty and fragility of a short, hopefully heroic life—and large stone lanterns lining and illuminating the walkway to the central shrine, and presided over by outsized statues of historical heroes like the early Meiji minister of war, Omura Masajiro that dwarf the visitor. Besides the shrine there is a museum filled with exhibits of military uniforms and other military paraphernalia, such as suicide weapons: a torpedo guided by a human crew; a mine attached to bamboo that was hand-delivered by a diver; a variety of kamikaze airplanes; bloodied bandannas, last testaments to dying for the emperor, and more. (It still houses the only public museum displaying military paraphernalia in Japan.) A shrine inscription announces that the six thousand men who gave their lives in suicide missions, using a variety of contraptions, were "incomparable in their tragic bravery" and "engulfed the entire country in tears of gratitude." Before the war, soldiers were told that they would become national gods of the ancestral land (*sokoku kuni*) and worshiped at the shrine if they gave up their lives serving the emperor in war. To be made a deity inhabiting the Yasukuni Shrine was a special honor bestowed only on national heroes. In 1938 the chief priest of the shrine explained that "those who rendered valuable services with silent efforts and whose achievements constituted a cause of the increase of national prosperity and the enhancement of the imperial fortunes, must not be left to remain in obscurity."[8]

After the war the U.S. Occupation briefly closed the shrine and decreed that its militarism must be tempered. Once the Occupation ended, the shrine returned to business as usual. Bronze engravings celebrating Japanese military victories were restored, and the spirits of Japan's executed war criminals were enshrined. These class A war criminals were specially designated as "martyrs of the Showa era." In fact, the majority of spirits have been enshrined since 1945.[9] It should be pointed out that registration of the war dead as deities requires priests to acquire the necessary information certifying the date and place of birth and how the candidate died. Apparently, the Yasukuni Shrine made such a request privately to the Ministry of Welfare for assistance in gathering the necessary information and, according to Helen Hardacre, the ministry responded by supplying intelligence on thousands of war dead at no expense, when in fact its policy, until 1971, had always been to deny such requests from other religious organizations.[10] An inscription honoring the act of self-sacrificing suicide was put up in 1985 to mark the war's fortieth anniversary. Prime Minister Nakasone Yasuhiro visited the shrine in 1985 to commemorate the same anniversary. In 1994, a year before the fiftieth anniversary of the end of the war, Yasukuni issued a book of poems written by soldiers at the front.

One, dated 1944, expresses "pleasure" in serving the country and prom-
ises to "color history with our blood." From an earlier collection called
Letters of the Peasant-Soldiers, a twenty-five-year-old noncommissioned
officer in the paratroops declares: "My body is not mine alone. . . . I will
become a blossom in the enemy sky; thereafter I will become a god and
continue my service for my country."[11]

Yasukuni Shrine, from its beginning in the Meiji period, was designated
as the central place for national memory. It is, in fact, *the* place of memory,
principally because it enshrined and deified the heroic spirits (*eirei*) of the
nation's war dead, those who gave service and life to the emperor.[12] Unlike
the great Shinto shrine at Ise, housing the spirit of the sun goddess, Yasukuni was a product of Japan's modernization and national formation in
the nineteenth century. Founded in 1869 after the Restoration civil wars
and the capital's move from Kyoto to Tokyo, the shrine was dedicated to
housing and commemorating the spirits of the dead who had given their
lives serving the imperial house in its struggle against Tokugawa loyalists.
If the purpose of the shrine was to provide sanctuary for the war dead
who had given their lives for the nation's "protection," it was also true
that enshrinement constituted a reward for loyal service to the emperor.
In this way, the shrine was, from its inception, an overdetermined place
of memory that made no distinction between service to the nation and to
the emperor. The shrine, like all shrines, was a constant reminder that
ceremony (religion), in the form of commemoration, was the same as governance, that politics and religion were one, or as the tradition of Shinto
constantly upheld, politics was a ceremony (*matsurigoto*). In the modern,
bureaucratic politics of imperial Japan, shrines like Yasukuni stood
as powerful markers of the identification of polity and religion and the
practices of a past that derived from the beginnings of the race. In this
connection, the emperor, as manifest deity in the prewar period, was the
agent of ceremonies that were neither political or religious but both at the
same time. This identification was reinforced by its classification. Yasukuni belonged to the category of "special shrines" and occupied a principal position in a formidable network of lesser, local shrines scattered
throughout the country called *shokonsha* or *gokoku jinja*, "nation-pro-
tecting shrines."[13] In time, there were 117 such shrines, usually devoted
to a single hero. Only Yasukuni, which commanded almost as much respect as Ise, housed all those who died for the imperial cause. Beyond
focusing attention on the identity of emperor and nation and the necessity
of serving this unity, Yasukuni managed also to reinforce the solidary
identity between national community and the ancestral, imperial land,
eliding the substantially different temporalities between an archaic priest-
king executing rituals belonging to an ancient, agrarian community and a
modern, bureaucratic state dedicated to instrumental rationality, between

past and present. In this sense, Yasukuni functioned as the place for mourning and expressing national morality, yet it was situated in a modern, bureaucratic society where such considerations were often recessive in view of interest, utility, and rational necessity.

One of the very interesting aspects of the shrine is that while it was a modern construction, serving a modern society, it riveted attention to the indeterminate past and the religio-polity of *matsurigoto*. It was the institutional representation of the revenant, enshrining the ancient figure of a political theology that made no distinction between ceremony and governance. Yet it was also a repetition of what modernity has, by necessity, repressed but returns, nevertheless, to "haunt" the present. By "haunting," I am referring to its capacity to keep the aura of an archaic experience before the population. In this respect, Yasukuni was a religious force that constantly reminded contemporaries—moderns—that politics was religious ceremony and vice versa, and that there was no easy way to rationalize these into separate, differentiated arenas. This meant that in the effort to mobilize the population to support the reunion of state and shrine in the 1960s and 1970s, the appeal was thus both religious and political, or the political masked by the religious call to mourning and morality. By keeping this identity between religion and politics ambiguous, the supporters of the shrine movement were able to enlist a much larger segment and sentiment of the population than if they were simply concerned with war rituals as religious, or the politics of shrine upkeep. Yasukuni provided the site to constantly bring to life this national community, where the aura of the past coexisted with the present, through acts of public mourning and remembering the dead. With this move came the classic conflation dreamed by late Tokugawa nativists between "ceremony and governance" (*saisei itchi*), religion and polity, pursued momentarily by the Restoration government in 1869 but abandoned for more modern forms of bureaucratic specialization. In a certain sense, Yasukuni was a lasting trace of the older nativist (*kokugakuron*) vision that formulated the ideal of Restoration. For modern Japan, Restoration was precisely the revenant momentarily actualized, a timeless figure recruited from the cultural unconscious to reconfigure and reactivate history, and would thus become the unassimilated past that the modern present hoped to repress.

The creation of shrines like Yasukuni, which called attention to and cemented the auratic memory of an archaic practice in a modern society, also reminded the population of the emperor and the state that administered his realm. Just as the emperor, a "manifest deity," worked to reinstate an ancient aura in the modern present, so shrines like Yasukuni, devoted to the inseparability of religion and politics, stood as permanent representations of this archaic ideal. While Yasukini, from its inception,

was seen as the focus of the most intense expression of patriotism before
the war, it was, nonetheless, a religionized nationalism that embraced
both politics and religion. For this reason, Yasukuni, before and after the
war, could be mobilized by the right-wing but, in the experience of modern Japan, this capacity to enlist it for conservative and reactionary causes
did not make it less religious. To offset the politicization of shrine Shinto,
the native ethnologist Yanagita Kunio and his followers in the folk-
loric movement sought to appeal to the tradition of tutelary shrine worship that avoided associations with the sun goddess, the imperial house,
and the nation for a tradition (popularized by nativists in the late Tokugawa period) that privileged the primacy of the folk over the imperial
house and emphasized the identity of shrines with local deities that anchored social solidarity in a region.[14] It is interesting to note that this
inflexion has increasingly disappeared in postwar Japan, especially as the
accelerated process of emptying out the countryside has left open a "religious" space for state shrines like Yasukuni to occupy once more without
fear of competition. In contemporary Japan, national and formerly state-
run shrines like Yasukuni supply contact with an absent past more powerfully than they did before the war, now that the countryside has virtually
vanished.

Before the war, Yasukuni Shrine was administered by the Ministries of
the Army and Navy, and its head priests usually received the rank of colo-
nel. Its special status was affirmed by the emperor through punctual visits
to pay respect to the spirits of the war dead. When the emperor showed
up, the shrine's head priest handed him a twig of the sacred *sakaki* tree,
which he held like a wand, eventually returning it to the priest, who placed
it on the altar. But it is important to add that enshrinement at Yasukuni
transformed spirits into national gods, in sharp contrast to folk practices
that believed departing family members became guardians who protected
the living survivors. In the interwar period, native ethnologists deployed
this belief as an alternative source of authenticity to challenge the state's
appropriation of Shinto practices and its designation of an official place
of memory. By proposing that the spirits remained in the village community to protect the surviving family, native ethnologists were able to project both an alternative space of daily life to the nation-state and a different object of service focused on the family rather than the emperor. After
the war, Yanagita Kunio summoned this sense of religious practice as a
replacement for a discredited state Shinto. When, in 1946, Yanagita called
for the reinstatement of tutelary shrine worship as the religious and moral
basis of the Japanese, he was returning to this alternative version of everyday life that, he believed, had endured throughout Japan's history.[15]
Yanagita's message became increasingly less relevant in Japan's postwar
economic transformation, and by the 1970s, mourning for the war dead

became a national (and religiously based) morality that would lay claim to all Japanese, not only those who had lost a loved one in the war. The vanishing of rural Japan, as it were, eliminated the claim of folklorists like Yanagita who invested authority and authenticity in local tutelary gods and regional shrines as the place people gave respect and acted out their moral obligations to their ancestors and the spirits of the dead.

During the late Meiji period the shrine fixed collective memory on war and heroic death. At the beginning of the Russo-Japanese War (1904) the emperor Meiji inaugurated the conflict with a visit to the shrine; after victory a celebration took place in its precincts in which troops in Tokyo and a representative of every military unit participated. Meiji also visited Yasukuni seven times in his lifetime; his successor, the short-lived and disabled Taisho, visited twice; and Hirohito, until 1945, visited twenty times uniformed as supreme commander.[16] By the early twentieth century the shrine had become the fulcrum of national consciousness as defined and authorized by the state, and what once had been a sanctuary of the military became a collective symbol reminding people that "every subject is a soldier."[17] People, and schoolchildren especially, were encouraged to fasten their attention on the shrine and its rituals, in order to incorporate the realization that everyone might one day be called on to die for the imperial nation.

Immediately after World War II the U.S. Occupation began to dismantle the structure that had bonded polity to religion, state to Shinto. The Occupation moved swiftly to end all state patronage of Shinto that resulted in severing the financial and administrative ties yoking shrines like Yasukuni to the state. Religious freedom and the separation of religion and government were mandated by the new constitution. Shrines were made legal corporations, like other religious organizations, and lost public financial support and their hold on the general public's obligatory participation during the performance of rituals. In fact, the symbolic edifice of emperor, cabinet, and military that participated in annual ceremonies at the Yasukuni was dissolved. Deprived of its religious legitimation, the new government sought first to recapture the lost unity by rehabilitating the economy under a "dedivinized emperor" who was, according to the new constitution, the "symbol of national unity" of the Japanese people. The presence of the emperor, however altered the figure, still recalled an instance of the archaic chiasmus between politics and religion, where political power becomes interchangeable with religious authority. Even more, the emperor's power to represent Japanese identity was never far from his staus as a figure who represented power. In postwar Japan the Imperial Palace and Yasukuni Shrine continued to be more than neighbors on the same block.

Reconfiguring the emperor into both the principle and principal of cultural identity was the background to Japan's meteoric transformation into a global economy in the 1950s, 1960s, and 1970s. After the oil shock of 1973 and the gradual slowing down of economic growth, the state turned to finding a representation for itself, making itself visible, as it were, when before it had remained safely in the shadows of American power as a faceless bureaucracy facilitating recovery. In this historic conjuncture, leading elements within Japanese society combined to restore the symbolic unity of prewar Japan represented by the Yasukuni Shrine. By inaugurating a movement aimed at inducing the Diet to pass a bill to put the shrine under state protection, a coalition made up of the LDP, Shinto organizations, and bereavement societies has sought to bring an end to the "postwar" by returning to the structure of symbolic unity marking prewar Japan since the Meiji era.[18] This effort has metamorphosed from the singular effort to persuade the Diet to pass a bill to the development of a rather large movement with an identifiable social base, as manifest most recently in the "no apology" campaign. While this repetitive gesture has sought to restore the conditions of prewar unity, it has also aimed to eliminate the historical memory of wartime oppression at home and abroad, especially the state's responsibility in this narrative, and a postwar experience dedicated to transforming Japan into a genuine social democracy under American tutelage.

Since the war most prime ministers (LDP) have attended festivals marking the autumn and vernal equinoxes; in 1976 Prime Minister Miki Takeo went a step further by visiting the shrine on 15 August, the anniversary of Japan's surrender, but as a private citizen. Since the late 1950s there has been a growing controversy over the meaning of visitation by public officials who also claim the status of private citizens.[19] Moreover, the issue has been linked to considerations of constitutional revision of the peace clause, article 9. Articles 20 and 89 of the constitution separate religion from politics and proscribe both official tribute, or the expression of tribute by an official, and financial assistance. The problem is tricky. If a prime minister visits the shrine as an official, he risks violating the law; if he attends as a private person, he affirms the religious status of the shrine that proponents of the shrine bill advocate to make their case for "state protection."[20] Who drives the car and who owns it makes the difference between breaking the law and upholding it. In recent years this issue of state funding of religious ceremony was violated twice, when the government sponsored the funeral of the Emperor Hirohito and the ascension rites (*daijosai*) of his successor, Akihito, the reigning Heisei monarch.

The argument for the Yasukuni Shrine bill has rested on the following principal stipulations: "its status as a religious corporation is based on the imperial will of the 'peaceful country' (*yasukuni*) proclaimed by the Meiji Emperor; it is dedicated to men who have given their lives for national affairs, conducting Shinto ceremonies, broadening its divine virtue, nourishing and educating the bereaved families of the enshrined, and contributing to the good fortune of society. It aims to conduct business in order to achieve the goals of the main shrine and others."[21] Yasukuni was presented as a luminous religious organization with the sole purpose of educating the bereaved families of the enshrined deities. Yet we can see from this statement that the supporters of legislation were interested in something more ambitious than the passage of a bill in the Diet, and had their sights on "educating" the bereaved (virtually every family in Japan) and contributing to society's good fortune (which in Shinto invariably meant returning to an arrangement where ceremony and governance were one [*saisei itchi*]). The actual bill was presented during the centenary anniversary of the Meiji Restoration in 1969 and turned back to committee. Throughout the 1970s it was presented four more times and turned down, owing to an opposing coalition of opposition parties, labor groups, other religious organizations, and citizens' groups. But in this time, the demand for a Yasukuni Shrine bill was transmuted into a broader appeal for the establishment of a social movement pursuing an ideological closure to the reunion of polity and religion.

There are three moments in this narrative: (1) the late 1950s (1956), in which the LDP was invested in discussions on the draft outline of the Yasukuni Shrine bill subsequently presented in 1969; (2) the late 1960s, marked by the drive for a bill that would be sanctioned within the framework of the constitution and ended with its first presentation and defeat; and (3) the late 1970s, during which this initial failure led to the demand for the realization of "manifest respect for mourning for the spirits" and "public rituals."[22] When the third stage is compared to the first, the difference is between the development of a broad movement concentrating on national "discussion" leading to constitutional revision and an inaugural desire for legislation consistent with the constitution.

The move calling for state protection of Yasukuni Shrine was prompted less by any strongly articulated desire by the population than a theory promoted by conservative politicians of the LDP, several Shinto organizations (the Association of Shrines, Jinja honcho), and bereavement societies to reconfigure state, emperor, and shrine into a new unity.[23] It is important to recognize how supporters of the bill were able to transmute bereavement for fallen family members into "exaltation" of "heroic spirits." More significantly the resulting propaganda campaign in the 1970s ultimately managed to bond bereavement to patriotism and nationality morality.

Before the bill was presented to the Diet in the late 1950s, the Bereavement Society of Japan (Nihon Izokukai) initiated a petition demanding renewed state support of the shrine. This demand was accompanied by a request, now backed by conservative politicians from the LDP, inviting the Self-Defense Force, the prime minister, and the emperor to attend the spring and autumn festivals held by the shrine.[24] Soon after, the LDP launched discussions on a draft outline that might be presented to the National Diet, which turned out to be the same as the bill drafted by the legal department of the House of Representatives. Diet commissions also examined the constitutional constraints that might be circumvented and proposed that the Yasukuni Shrine should be stripped of its religious personality as a condition of nationalization. Specifically, this meant eliminating those Shinto rites and rituals and accoutrements that signified a religious ceremony. In this way the bill might pass and avoid constitutional revision. Yet as early as 1955 the chair of the National Society of Shrines and Temples in Defense of the Fatherland and the head of the Association of Shrines, conferring with the Bereavement Society on the "public character of maintenance," called for the "promotion of a movement that would eliminate" the necessary wording in both clauses 20 and 89 of the constitution "as a condition for anticipating realization."[25] Another study from the lower house proposed that because the shrine did not sell Shinto talismans and refrained from providing instruction in a doctrine, it already was a nonreligious institution.[26]

The upshot of this discussion over the proposed bill resulted in two, somewhat contradictory positions: (1) if the nonreligious personality of the shrine was not clarified, there would be the risk of a constitutional crisis; and (2) if ritual and worship were continued and "enshrinement clarified," Yasukuni would, nevertheless, remain a nonreligious personality. Clearly, the latter position dismissed the reality of the shrine as a religious entity, a *jinja*, "deity assembly," and risked forfeiting the religious empowerment always associated with Yasukuni, whereas the former wanted to actively pursue a course that might definitively determine the status of the shrine and avoid a wider struggle over revising the constitution. Some form of resolution came with a theory that held that the country had to express the idea of bereavement toward the war dead publicly because it was an acknowledgment of national sentiment. Ultimately, the logic informing the bill was premised on this idea of national sentiment and the subsequent conviction that it was necessary for the people to give expressions of respect for the heroic spirits who died for national affairs.

The shrine bill was presented in 1969 and stipulated that Yasukuni should offer rituals for the spirits of the war dead out of respect; it also proposed that the shrine was not a religious personality, even though the Religious Jurisdiction Law had defined *religious* as "performing rites and ceremonies." As mentioned earlier, the initial bill failed passage principally because of this contested definition of the religious and its incapacity to resolve opposing views. Four subsequent failures turned its promoters to another strategy.

The new strategy, mounted in the late 1970s, abandoned the limited problem of the status of the Yasukuni Shrine for a more expansive program aimed at restoring the unified body of state Shinto through constitutional revision.[27] If it was not always pushing for revision, it consistently sought to challenge the religious definition authorized by the constitution by arguing that its wording referred to sects and denominations and the shrine was neither. Because Shinto was a common national belief without sects, it was not a religion according to the constitution's definition. Moreover, this phase saw the articulation of concrete demands for respecting the departed war dead, public forms of worship, and a public debate on what needed to be done. Mediated by groups like the People's Cooperative Deliberative Society for the Protection of Yasukuni Shrine, the campaign requested "punctual observances devoted to mourning for the spirits, the realization of public rituals in which the emperor, cabinet, and 'national guests' participate," and the convening of "A Great National Ceremony for Mourning the Spirits in Yasukuni Shrine." In the wake of legislative failure, groups like the Society for Answering the Heroic Spirits (Eirei ni kotaerukai) called for a national movement pledged to mobilizing wide-scale support and an "expansion of affairs related to the war dead and heroic spirits," in order "to construct a social base for realizing state support of Yasukuni Shrine." Specifically, the society hoped for an "enlightened proclamation" demanding the expression of visible concern for the "heroic spirits," "manifest observances of bereavement for the war dead at Yasukuni Shrine," "realization of public rituals at the shrine," "daily regulated memorial services for the war dead," "the completion of collecting the remains of the war dead," and the carrying out of "necessary business for the accomplishment of the society's goals." This document, and others produced in the latter part of the 1970s, not only advocated, in general, the actualization of state maintenance of the shrine; it also began to point to concrete goals concerning how best to realize the performing of public rituals and to define the relationship between the state and "manifest observances of bereavement for the heroic spirits." The achievement of public ceremonies devoted to mobilizing the masses, and punctual observances constituted an "expression of national sincerity of feeling and respect toward the heroic spirits." Accordingly, this act of sincerity could be accomplished only by the nation and its people.

The movement, then, was created by linking bereavement and respect together in public ceremonies capable of mobilizing national opinion for the purpose of establishing an identification between the punctual performance of such practices and the articulation of collective sentiment. This move toward the naturalization of public ceremonies was illustrated spectacularly by Prime Minister Nakasone's decision to pay tribute at the

shrine on the occasion of the ceremony commemorating the spring equi-
nox in 1983. It should be pointed out that long before Nakasone was
prime minister, he was on record for supporting the reinstatement of Yasukuni as a central place for national ceremonies. His visit, ambiguously
represented as neither public nor private, invited subsequent conservatives
to reiterate their support for nationalizing the shrine. A year later the
cabinet secretary convened a fifteen-member advisory committee to study
the Yasukuni Shrine problem. Made up of members mostly outside government it produced a split report. Regardless, the government was apparently determined to use it as justification for permitting cabinet members
to make formal tribute at the shrine during the anniversary of the surrender on 15 August, 1985. Despite the absence of consensus in the report,
the government moved ahead to pay formal tribute at the shrine. The visit
brought a rather muted criticism from within Japanese society, suggesting
the degree to which the normalization of public ceremonies honoring the
war dead had become common sense. Asian presses denounced the episode as a thoughtless return to Japanese militarism and as an affirmation
of the prewar state. In response, the government has proposed that the
shrine be made to represent a symbol of peace and international understanding under the sign of what it calls the "new nationalism."[28] Helmut
Kohl, accompanied by Ronald Reagan, at Bitburg; Nakasone Yasuhiro at
Yasukuni: the same war is commemorated, and the two similar regimes
responsible for bringing it about are now exonerated of guilt and made
to look benign, almost like victims.[29] The Japanese state's active involvement in orchestrating public ceremonies to mobilize national sincerity and
respect was dramatized in the production of the two spectacles relating
to Hirohito's death and Akihito's ascension to the throne. Criticism of
these two events in the Japanese press was even more muted.

The real effect of the Yasukuni Shrine problem was to allow the state to
commemorate the war dead, who gave their lives for the imperial nation,
without holding the prewar state responsible for inaugurating the war. In
accomplishing this, the postwar state has been able to form a continuity
with its prewar predecessor and affirm its role in the narrative of Japan's
modernization. What this means is that the postwar state has increasingly
seen itself continuing the work of modernization started earlier, facing the
same kinds of problems and obstacles that invariably pushed Japan into
war, yet building upon the base constructed earlier. The same men who
ran the imperial bureaucracy before the war became the leaders of Japan's
postwar governments; the same emperor who presided over this imperial
bureaucracy has become the emperor who represents the "symbol" of
national unity.

Repetition always comes with a difference. In this most recent repeating
of the prewar unification of state and shrine, politics and religion, the

difference is reflected in the kind of society that existed then and now. Contemporary society is putatively democratic, even though single-party democracy and state bureaucracy are actually improvements over their prewar predecessors; the emperor is still around, more powerful than ever before as the symbol and fulcrum of cultural identity and ethnic homogeneity. Yasukuni Shrine is still the place of national memory, but this time resting on the identification between mourning and bereavement—the expression of national sentiment—and a national morality cemented by the regular performance of public ceremonies—spectacles in this age of electronic reproduction—that are eagerly consumed to reinforce ideological assent. When contrasted to the noisy threats of violence and terror of militarists and fascists and the practice of coercive social obligations demanded by the prewar state to induce assent, we can see the difference repetition invariably introduces. Yet the specular indeterminacy of a factual present and an absent past that is constantly being summoned constitutes not so much a resistance to modernity in Japan but the principal condition of what it means to become modern; contemporaneity and the appeal to the timelessness of memory invariably disclose a structure of deferral and desire that repetition seeks to resolve while managing only to stimulate even greater anxiety.

Notes

1. Hiromatsu Wataru, *"Kindai no chokoku" ron* (Tokyo, 1980), 65–90. Minamoto Ryoen, "The Symposium on Overcoming Modernity," in James W. Helsig and John C. Maraldo, eds., *Rude Awakenings: Zen, the Kyoto School, and the Question of Nationalism* (Honolulu, 1994), 197–229.

2. The quote is from D. C. Holtom, *Modern Japan and Shinto Nationalism: A Study of Present-Day Trends in Japanese Religions* (Chicago, 1943), 54; see also Murakami Shigeyoshi, *Kokka Shinto* (Tokyo, 1971), 186–87. I have relied on Murakami's book for the historical account of the Yasukuni Shrine, as I have on Oe Shinobu, *Yasukuni Jinja* (Tokyo, 1984).

3. I am indebted to Marilyn Ivy for this interpretation. See *Discourses of the Vanishing: Modernity, Phantasm, Japan* (Chicago, 1995), 80–92. The argument is presented in different form in my "Figuring the Folk," in Stephen Vlastos, ed., *Mirrors of Modernity* (Berkeley, 1998).

4. Quoted in Claude Lefort, "The Permanence of the Theologico-Political," in *Democracy and Political Theory* (Minneapolis, 1988), 214.

5. Ibid.

6. See Talal Asad, "Religion, Nation-State, Secularism," in this volume. Also, Paul Connerton, *How Societies Remember* (Cambridge, 1984), 54 ff., for a brilliant account of how modern societies seek to reenact older narratives in the modern present.

7. Holtom, *Modern Japan*, 45–54; Helen Hardacre, *Shinto and the State, 1868–1988* (Princeton, N.J., 1991), 32, 38, 90–92; Murakami, *Kokka Shinto*, 184–87.

8. Holtom, *Modern Japan*, 47.

9. Hardacre, *Shinto*, 148; also Miyaji Masahito, "Handoka ni okeru Yasukuni mondai chi-i," in Yamaguchi Keiji and Matsuo Soichi, eds., *Sengoshi to hando ideorogi* (Tokyo, 1981), 97–98.

10. Hardacre, *Shinto*, 148.

11. *Economist*, 12 August, 1995.

12. Murakami, *Kokka Shinto*, 184–85.

13. Ibid., 186. Also, Hardacre, *Shinto*, 90, and Oe *Yasukuni Jinja*, 104–37.

14. See my "Kindai Nihon no keikin ni okeru kokugaku to sono kioku," in Nitta Yoshiyuki et al., eds., *Datsu sei-o no shiso*, Iwanami koza *Gendai Shiso* 15 (Tokyo, 1994), 169–90.

15. Harry Harootunian, "Disciplinizing Native Knowledge and Producing Place," in Thomas Rimer, ed., *Culture and Identity* (Princeton, N.J., 1990), 111–13.

16. Hardacre, *Shinto*, 91.

17. Ibid.; Holtom, *Modern Japan*, 54.

18. I have relied on Iguchi Kazuki, "Yasukuni jinjasha mondai no 'ronri,' " in Yamaguchi Keiji and Matsuo Soichi, eds., *Sengoshi to hando ideorogi* (Tokyo, 1981), 118–41; and Miyaji "Handoka," 91–117.

19. Hardacre, *Shinto*, 144; Iguchi, "Yasukuni," 119–20; and Nakajima Missenko, "Seiji hando ni okeru shukyo kyodan no yakuwari," in Yamaguchi and Matsuo, *Sengoshi*, 159.

20. Hardacre, *Shinto*, 144.

21. Iguchi, "Yasukuni," 126.

22. Ibid., 135–39.

23. Ibid.

24. Hardacre, *Shinto*, 144.

25. Iguchi, "Yasukuni," 135; Jinja Honcho, *Jinja honcho nenshi* (Tokyo, 1956), 299–300.

26. See Hardacre, *Shinto*, 146.

27. Iguchi, "Yasukuni," 127–35.

28. Hardacre, *Shinto*, 151–52.

29. The pairing is Hardacre's but I share her sentiments. Ibid., 152.

9

Papists and Beggars:
National Festivals and Nation Building in the
Netherlands during the Nineteenth Century

FRANS GROOT

RAIL TRAVELERS tend to spread themselves and their luggage all over the compartment. For the time being, they regard it as their "property." They are visibly disturbed when new travelers come in and sit down. These are accepted only with difficulty. The remarkable thing is that these newcomers, in their turn, tend to regard the compartment as their domain. They are just as unwelcoming to the next group of newcomers. The German writer Enzensberger uses this "parable" to establish a relation between group formation and demarcation of territory: even though the occupants of the compartment are strangers to each other, they nevertheless have the tendency to unite and defend their territory against newcomers. As a consequence of this simple mechanism, immigrants have a weak position in the country where they settle.[1]

In the process of nation building, people not only become attached to a geographical area but are also provided with a political and cultural background. Nation building is a particularly complex variant of group formation. Nevertheless, the analogy of the railway journey seems applicable to the process of nation building that took place in the Netherlands during the nineteenth century. New groups demanded a place on the national train. The established elite of liberal and conservative politicians, for the most part from Protestant backgrounds, were confronted with new groups demanding influence in the Dutch nation. These new groups comprised an orthodox Calvinist movement that manifested itself more and more clearly, and a substantial Catholic minority that demanded a place for itself, first in religious, and then in political, affairs. New balances of power between the established elite and the Calvinist and Catholic outsiders still had to mature. When, toward the end of the nineteenth century, these newcomers had achieved a certain power base in Dutch society, another group appeared: the socialist movement demanded its own right of existence. The workers' movement of the Left was greeted in a decidedly unfriendly manner by the liberal, orthodox Protestant, and Catholic leaders. Marriages of convenience were made to counter the "red peril." Not until just before the outbreak of World War II (1939) were the socialists invited to participate in government.

Central to this essay is the manner in which the Catholic section of the population, as newcomer, integrated itself into the Dutch nation. Linking into the theme of this volume, I concentrate on the interplay between nation building and religious pluriformity, reviewing the role of national festivals in process of nation building. With little exaggeration we can say that nation building and religious pluralism were imported into the Netherlands in 1795 as fruits of the French Revolution. In the years after 1795, the seeds of a national learning process were sown. This was stimulated deliberately by the government and by political elites, for example, through the institution of national festivals as a means "to promote a sense of unity among the citizens, and to bind this with the Constitution, with the Laws, with the Fatherland and Freedom."[2] Furthermore, they began to give the churches equality under the law, a process that gained momentum under the liberal constitution of 1848. As a result, the privileged position of the Calvinist Reformed Church gradually came to an end, and the small Protestant denominations, the Jews, and the Catholics gained the opportunity to develop as they wanted. The Catholics, in particular, formed a very extensive minority (about 40 percent of the Dutch population) that clearly showed its presence in religious affairs, built up a school organization in competition with the government schools, around 1870 and won a large number of seats in Parliament.

The Catholic expansion encountered considerable distrust in Dutch society. The Catholic elite adopted a cautious approach, for Protestant sensibilities had to be handled delicately. While they were building up a Roman Catholic bastion, they played up their loyalty to the Dutch nation. This nation, however, fostered definite Protestant traditions. Many Protestants traced the roots of the Dutch state back to the struggle against Spanish oppression and the Inquisition in the sixteenth and seventeenth centuries. How could Catholics demonstrate their allegiance to the nation without compromising their own convictions?

In the second half of the nineteenth century, tension grew between the process of nation building and the movement toward religious pluralism. As in other European countries, liberal politicians had the wind in their sails. However, they encountered an interesting problem. The concept of the liberal nation was based on the assumption that the citizens were free and responsible; but what was to be done when a substantial proportion of these citizens harbored religious and political views that seemed to threaten the nation? How could the citizens be inculcated with a primary loyalty to the nation, for the good of all? How could they be instilled with "social sentiments without which a man cannot be a good citizen or a faithful subject"?[3] In this learning process, commemoration days and other festivities could fulfill an important role alongside public elementary schools and the national museum, for example. They could function as rituals for integrating the different parts of the population into the community.

National Festivals

In the second half of the nineteenth century, a number of European countries began celebrating annual national festivals. In 1880, the French began celebrating the Fourteenth of July in commemoration of the storming of the Bastille (1789). In 1871, the German Empire instituted commemoration of the victory over the French at Sedan (2 September 1870) as an annual ritual. The Dutch experimented with commemorations of historical events. Eventually, at the end of the 1880s, the birthday of the young princess (and, since 1890, queen) was chosen.

In these years traditions were established en masse. Hobsbawm speaks of "invented" traditions. He associates this development with the increasing participation in politics and the extension of the franchise in this period.[4] National feeling was made concrete, tangible, audible, and visible, by means of public addresses, patriotic songs, processions and parades, display of flags, and the wearing of national colors. For a day, the masses were absorbed into a huge national pageant. People dressed up to provide a picture of the glorious past in numerous processions. Parading soldiers represented the current martial reality. The festivals not only had the effect of bringing people together; they also brought out points of difference. Commemorations of historical events had a tendency to expose sensitive nerves.

The French Fourteenth of July was primarily intended to strengthen the legitimacy of the young Third Republic, but for the monarchist and clerical opponents of the regime, this was not a festival of liberation. For them, the Fourteenth of July 1789 was a day of rebellion and murder. As good patriotic citizens they were supposed to have a selective memory. They were expected to "remember" the freeing from the Bastille of the manacled prisoners, and to have "forgotten" the death of more than one hundred citizens during and after the storming (when representatives of the ancien régime were horribly murdered). The commemorations implied the existence of patriotic feelings in the past. The enemies of 1789 were retrospectively labeled national brothers. Since, from a national viewpoint, the dead were victims of "fratricide,"[5] it was essential that the commemorations should have a cleansing and healing effect. They had to convince the people that past differences had been overcome. But, unfor-

tunately for the well-intentioned nation builders, the injuries of the past
were not in the least forgiven and forgotten. They were a time bomb that
could disrupt the process of nation building.[6]

The Dutch Eighty Years' War

Comparable problems arose in the Netherlands around the commemoration of events in the Eighty Years' War (1568–1648). In the years following 1868, a series of "tercentenaries" of high and low points of the war
were celebrated in the Netherlands. The history of the Eighty Years' War
was seen as the story of the creation of the Dutch nation. The Republic
of the Seven United Provinces had been formed during this large-scale
political and religious conflict between the Spanish monarchy and the
autonomous Dutch regions. During the seventeenth century, the Republic
underwent a period of unheard-of economic and political development.
Protestant intellectuals, of both conservative and liberal persuasion,
looked back on this period with satisfaction. They regarded the Republic
as the foundation on which the Dutch unitary state and monarchy were
built after 1813. The members of the House of Orange provided the binding link between these two forms of government. At that time they were
stadtholders, and in the nineteenth century they were the princely figure-
heads of the small kingdom. Thus, King Willem III (1849–1890), who
caused numerous notorious political incidents and led a dubious married
life, was put on a par with his illustrious ancestors who were heroes in
the fight against the Spaniards.

The religious aspects of the war especially led to much discussion in the nineteenth century. Many Protestants regarded the Republic as an oasis of religious freedom in a repressive Europe. The Eighty
Years' War brought an end to the Spanish Inquisition. During the seventeenth and eighteenth centuries, the Republic was the only European state
in which religious pluralism was tolerated. Churches of smaller Protestant
denominations, Catholic "clandestine" churches, and Jewish synagogues
were allowed alongside the dominant "public" Calvinist Church. Nineteenth-century Catholic intellectuals looked back on this period with less
satisfaction. They emphasized the second-class position assigned to the
Catholic Church at the time of the Republic. For example, Catholics
could not hold positions in government. More dramatic was the fact that
dozens of Catholic priests had died at the hands of Calvinist rebels. In
the nineteenth century, these religious figures were honored as martyrs
for the Catholic faith. A number of them were canonized in 1867. Processions and pilgrimages to the places where they were killed were organized.

In this way, the Dutch Catholics, who had enjoyed full recognition only since 1853, achieved their own sense of identity within the world Catholic Church.

In the context of the "invention of tradition," it is interesting that the Catholics drew the sense of their own identity from the Middle Ages, which were viewed as a period in which the Catholic faith had flourished. The numerous Catholic churches built after 1853 were given neo-gothic exteriors. The triumphal vertical construction of these churches directly recalled the time when the Catholic Church organization was dominant. Catholic intellectuals also expressed the opinion that the cultural heritage of the Middle Ages was their contribution to the Dutch nation.

A key problem in these Protestant and Catholic views of sixteenth- and seventeenth-century history was (just as in the French situation) the element of fratricide. While the Protestants mourned the numerous victims burned at the stake by the Inquisition, Catholics looked back with indignation on the outrages perpetrated against their priests by the Calvinists. When the pope officially reinstated the Netherlands Church Province in 1853, he imprudently referred to "the fury and the sword of the Calvinist heresy" under which Catholic laymen and priests had suffered for several centuries. In reaction to this papal act, a stream of antipapist pamphlets flooded the country. Protestant pamphlet writers warned of the dangers of the Catholic Inquisition. They saw before them Catholic domination and terror: "But the Dutchmen did not struggle for eighty years against the Inquisition and sanguinary edicts of Rome, only to bend the neck once more under the staff of the man on the other side of the mountain [the Pope]."[7]

The Sea Beggars at Den Briel, 1572–1872

The most turbulent commemoration of the Eighty Years' War was the three-hundredth anniversary in 1872 of the taking of Den Briel.[8] In 1572, a group of Dutch privateers, the "Watergeuzen" or Sea Beggars, sailed from the English ports and anchored off Den Briel, a small place near Rotterdam. At that moment, there was no Spanish garrison in the town. With relative ease, the Sea Beggars were able to ram the town gate and occupy the town. Their original intentions were only to plunder the town, but after some discussion they decided to remain in occupation. Den Briel was the first in a long series of places drawn onto the side of the prince of Orange. In 1572, the rebels acquired a base in the watery northwest of the Netherlands. The region was subsequently successfully defended against the well-armed and numerically stronger Spanish mercenaries.

In nineteenth-century eyes, this was the perfect story of David and Goliath: a small group of Calvinist exiles had taken the mighty Spanish army by surprise, and not with force, but with cleverness. This was a source of encouragement to a small country that felt somewhat insecure after the creation of the German Empire in 1871. During the commemoration of 1872, national independence was an important theme, as was the centuries-old link with the House of Orange and freedom of religion. However, the religious issue was a source of discontent. A less pleasant side to the events in Den Briel was the murder by the Sea Beggars, in July 1572, of nineteen Catholic priests (the martyrs of Gorcum, who were canonized in 1867). It is thus understandable that the Catholics did not react enthusiastically to this commemoration: "Must we, sons and descendants of the sixteenth century Dutch Catholics, joyfully celebrate events which led to our ancestors being persecuted . . . , thrown out of the Government; robbed of their rights; to our religious leaders being exiled, many even murdered; our Churches taken from us; our Abbeys confiscated; we ourselves were robbed of all political rights, for more than two centuries long, merely tolerated; not treated as equals?"[9]

Attempts to Undo the Damaging Effects of the Past

For months the newspapers were filled with controversy over the form and content of the commemoration. Remarkable in these discussions is the fact that each of the parties expressed a national point of view. Catholic intellectuals presented themselves as patriots. They were keen to demonstrate their loyalty to the fatherland, but they had a definite revulsion against the Sea Beggars. The organizers of the festival went to a great deal of trouble to make the commemoration acceptable for Catholics. It was decided early on not to erect a statue of a Sea Beggar, since this would resurrect the bloody past. The effigy of a water nymph was chosen, to serve as the messenger of freedom. In this respect the idea resembled the statue cult that developed in France from 1875. There, the peaceful image of Marianne was given preference to the sansculotte (the prototype of the violent revolutionary) as a means of propagating the élan of the Third Republic. There, too, they chose femininity rather than combativeness, and a timeless symbol rather than a historical figure that would recall the turbulent past.[10]

When, after all, this plan led to dissent, it was decided that a sailors' home should be built next to the effigy. Attempts were made to make the question less of a political issue by giving the commemoration the air of a charitable event. This was an attempt to give something back to the seamen, the "descendants" of the Sea Beggars, who had done so much for the "nation." The sailors' home was a gift, just as the capture of Den Briel had been a gift.[11] In this way, the historical event of 1572 was presented to posterity as a "fact," as a rounded and completed whole, to be accepted with thanks. When receiving such a gift, it is inappropriate to criticize parts of it. In view of these attempts at reconciliation, it was difficult for the Catholics to sustain their rejection of the festival.

But the official organizing committee did much more to make the celebrations acceptable to the Catholic section of the population. For example, they abandoned the idea of a historical procession in Den Briel. Instead, they chose an allegorical form. Providing the moving climax of the procession were busts of King Willem III and his wife, Sophie, which had been adorned with laurel wreaths. The Sea Beggars were assigned a subsidiary role. At the request of the organizing committee, the official speaker changed the title of his speech, "A Celebration of the Sea Beggars" to a more neutral "The Liberation of the Netherlands." He did refer to the Sea Beggars, but tried to do so in a balanced fashion. On the negative side, he mentioned "the stains left by the blood of innocent priests," and on the positive side, "the beneficial consequences of the battle against the country's enemy, fought so boldly and with such an outcome."[12] Thus, the Sea Beggars were forgiven their sins and were granted a modest place in the history of the nation. This history was a rather abstract story, consisting of free improvisations on the theme of 1572. In a politically correct, neutral composition, past history was supposed to bind Protestant and Catholic brothers to each other.

Some Catholics could appreciate this neutral approach and were willing to take part in the celebrations. They were certainly not happy about the events of 1572, but the commemoration had taken on such an innocuous character that they were willing to join in. Tactical considerations played an important part in their decision. It was not only the discussion in the newspapers that led to hesitation in the Catholic camp; the fear of violence also played a part. "I know our history," wrote the Catholic historian W. J. F. Nuyens at the end of December 1871 to his bishop. "We'll be having demonstrations against 'the Papists' in April if we don't find a solution."[13] Both supporters and opponents of the commemoration were aware that the "people" or the "masses" could play their own, uncontrollable part in the festivals. It could well be difficult to prevent "spontaneous" actions against Catholics. While the organizers were trying to minimize the role of the Sea Beggars, many Protestants felt themselves strongly inspired by their soldierly actions. For the Protestant rank and file, the Sea Beggars in particular were a very attractive national symbol. During the festival, houses were decorated with scenes of Sea Beggars in action, and children dressed up as Beggars. The Sea Beggars were "real men," who had fought the enemy with only ax and dagger. This passionate feeling for the fatherland made it difficult to predict how the festival would turn out. The general fear was that the revelers would want to literally reenact the militant past.

The Catholics were deeply divided about what strategy to adopt. In the southern provinces of Brabant and Limburg (which were almost 100 percent Catholic), the decision was easy. They took no part in the festivities. In the other provinces, the Catholics were a minority. Some, despite all the controversy, saw the commemoration as a festival of liberation. Many decided, in order to preserve their window glass, to put out the flag and take part in the commemoration. Others rejected this out of hand as pure expediency. The bishops gave inadequate leadership in the matter, because they regarded it as a political affair (and also because they had no ready solution). In the absence of clear guidelines, the priests and leading Catholic citizens had to devise their own local strategies. In many cases things went wrong.

Local Incidents

By way of example I consider, in more detail, the events in Naaldwijk, a village of market gardeners between The Hague and Delft. The Catholic community (about 40 percent of the population) had, since 1870, the use of an imposing church in neo-Gothic style, which put the Protestant churches in the shade. This expansion of the church apparently went too fast, because the church tower was soon leaning by half a meter. The tower played a crucial part during the commemoration.

During the preparations for the festival, groups of revelers went from house to house to encourage everyone to put out the flag. In some villages, such excursions became a babel of noise; houses were surrounded, crowds chanted derision, and the occupants were "invited" to accede quickly to the demands of the unwelcome visitors. In many cases, the revelers were groups of young people, who went about their task in a spirit of fun. It was like this in Naaldwijk. But things went wrong at a farm occupied by a Catholic widow and her four sons. The occupants refused to do what was demanded and became belligerent, making use of pistol, gun, and flail. One of the sons had had some military experience in the Pope's army. The consequence of these actions was that all the windows of the farmhouse were smashed, and several people were arrested. This did not help the atmosphere in the village. Tension increased when some Catholic parishioners removed the flag from their church. The priest had originally had this flag hoisted, but gave in to the parishioners' wishes. The Protestant revelers saw this as an insult, because their procession came past this church. The rest of the day was overshadowed by that single flag missing from the church tower. Over the course of the evening, several hundred Catholics armed with clubs gathered by the church. They had heard that the Protestants wanted to organize an assault on it. Protestant groups gathered around the bars but were warned by the mayor to keep the peace. The nocturnal happenings were limited to a sparring match in which the parties did not venture beyond their own lines. Peace returned at about one o'clock in the morning, after the mayor had emptied the inns with a "Long live the king."

The accompanying map shows that similar disturbances and incidents occurred mainly in small places in the middle of the country, but hardly at all in the completely Catholic provinces of Brabant and Limburg, or in the almost completely Protestant provinces of Friesland, Groningen, and Drente. Particularly in the middle of the country, there was a mixture of mainly Protestant and mainly Catholic places. This led to the biggest conflicts of opinion. In many cases, the disturbances represented a struggle between religious minorities and majorities, fought out in relatively close-knit communities. Militant forms of Catholicism and Calvinism came to the surface here, fed by past martyrdom and heroism.

The involvement and excitement during the festivities among broad layers of the populace is remarkable. How can we explain the enthusiasm, for, and revulsion against, an event that took place three-hundred years earlier? To begin with, we may assume a certain amount of knowledge about the history of the fatherland among the populace. This knowledge was supplied through various channels. At the beginning of the nineteenth century, only about 50 percent of children between the ages of five and fourteen attended elementary school. By 1870, school attendance had risen to 76 percent. It increased particularly strongly between 1850 and 1870.[14] The schools conflict played an important part in this. In the 1860s, state education was challenged by orthodox Protestant organizations and by the Catholic bishops. The number of Protestant and Catholic schools grew rapidly. The trademark of these new schools was religious education; but, at the same time, they prided themselves on their individual approach to other subjects—in particular, history. From 1857 on, history was a compulsory subject at elementary schools. It is therefore reasonable to assume that the younger generation had an acceptable level of knowledge of Dutch history, albeit biased, according to their religious background.

For the older generation, books, brochures, and newspapers were an important source of information. An enormous quantity of literature, including very cheap booklets and pamphlets, rolled from the presses around the time of the commemoration. An Amsterdam catalog lists

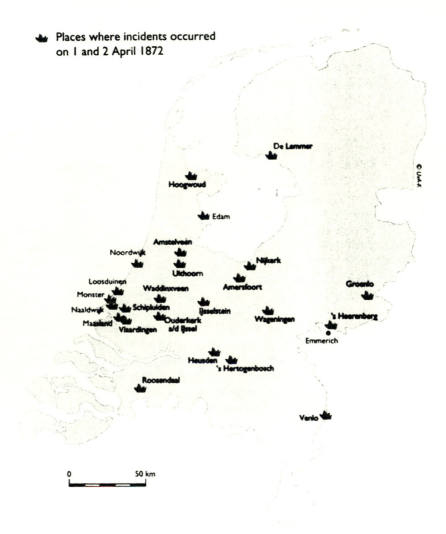

Places where incidents occurred
on 1 and 2 April 1872

De Lemmer

Hoogwoud

Edam

Amstelveen

Noordwijk

Nijkerk

Uithoorn

Loosduinen

Amersfoort

Greenlo

Monster

Waddinxveen

Naaldwijk

Schipluiden

IJsselstein

's Heerenberg

Maasland

Ouderkerk
a/d IJssel

Wageningen

Vlaardingen

Emmerich

Heusden

's Hertogenbosch

Roosendaal

Venlo

0   50 km

seven-hundred items. The increasing importance of the daily press is of
particular interest. The tax on newspapers, the newspaper stamp, had
been abolished in 1869. This stimulated a rapid expansion of the newspaper industry. National newspapers could appear in a larger format, and
regional papers became a viable proposition. As a result, newspapers entered the homes of much of the population, and played a crucial part in

the discussions leading up to the commemoration. They published points of view on the pros and cons of the festivities, guidelines for the revelers, and informative historical stories. Finally, many people acquired their knowledge from the churches. While the Catholic Church was expanding in the 1850s and 1860s, the Dutch Calvinist Church was the victim of internal polarization exacerbated by the militant tendencies primarily of the orthodox churchgoers. Clergymen and priests produced various publications about the commemoration and without a doubt would also have addressed the matter in their sermons. It is therefore understandable that religious sensitivities were so prominent in 1872.

So the people were informed and mobilized in various ways. Can we really, with Hobsbawm, speak of "mass producing traditions"?[15] We get the impression that the message did reach the masses. We may assume that attending school, reading newspapers, and going to church were in vogue, especially among the middle classes. These groups also had an important share in the festivities. But the press regularly reported that even the poorest of the poor decorated their streets, hoisted the flag, and joined in the festivities, sporting orange caps. Such reports had a propagandist element. It is certain, however, that the better-educated sections of the working class shared in the festivities. Artisans who valued their position in society, and wanted to demonstrate their trades to town or village, objected to the middle-class character of the festivities and demanded their own place in the program.[16] As already mentioned, both Protestant and Catholic leaders feared excessive religious involvement or rejection among ordinary people during the festivities.

The explosive character of the Protestant-Catholic divide in the smaller towns and villages is fascinating. In many places, the attempts to make the festivities neutral and unbiased proved a failure. Where Protestants had the upper hand, Catholics were forced to take part in the celebrations. Elsewhere, Catholic majorities forced the Protestants to take down their flags. How were such conflicts able to occur? The events in Naaldwijk provide a good example. For a long time, the Catholic minority had lived together with their Protestant fellow villagers without problems. From a churchgoing point of view, they were two clearly separated groups. A clear segmentation could also be seen in private life. There were scarcely any marriages between Catholics and Protestants. However, business contacts were good. There was no question of religious tensions until the 1870s. Around 1870, the local peace was disturbed by outside influences. Through the process of nation building, religion became more and more a political issue. This showed up, for example, in the schools conflict. In the 1870s, much effort was put into modernizing state education in Naaldwijk. As a reaction, both the Catholic parish and several orthodox

Protestant groups prepared to set up their own schools, to the dissatisfaction of the liberally oriented mayor, who saw this as a serious threat to the local community. For many parents, the upbringing and schooling of their children was a tangible and constant problem. They therefore felt heavily involved. Religious questions became important, not only in the privacy of church or home, but also increasingly strongly in village politics. On top of this, the commemoration of 1872 brought the problem of religious differences into day-to-day life.

Protestants compelled their Catholic fellow villagers to put out the flag so as to publicly demonstrate their loyalty. This was not an attempt to change the persuasion of the Catholic minority. Rather it was a method of making clear who had the upper hand at the local level. The Protestants marked out their territory symbolically. By hoisting the flag, the Catholics made a gesture of submission. (It makes one think of the traditional Protestant Orange parades through Catholic neighborhoods in Northern Ireland. This is a symbolic show of strength to register Protestant views on the division of power at the local and national levels.)

These were not large-scale religious wars. Nobody was killed. What did perish were the reputations of priests and mayors who had not reacted adequately to the incidents. Relations between the denominations were also disturbed in the affected places. A typical example from Naaldwijk was prompted by the opening of a Catholic barber's shop. On the village pump could be read: "If you don't want to be skinned by the Beggars, then go to Servaas Nederpelt for a good shave."[17]

Methods of Enforcement

If the opinions in the Dutch press were anything to go by, all these incidents had pushed national self-confidence off balance. The papers spoke of "bitterest religious hate," of a threatening "religious strife" that could split the country into two hostile camps, of neighbor rising up against neighbor, and of rifts "carved out between people who have lived in harmony for many years."[18] After the events of April, the situation was not without danger for the Catholics in the population. In particular, the radical-liberal press put the Catholics under heavy fire. This section of the press tried to ostracize, the new conservative Ultramontane Catholics, a movement within Dutch Catholicism heavily oriented toward Rome. Although most Catholics were considered to be patriots, these conservative Catholics were "internationalist by nature," and thus "very dangerous": "Patriots have nothing in common with Jesuits. Persons bound to their own country and people are of no use to this international organization."[19] These conservative Catholics were repeatedly represented as the heirs of the sixteenth-century papal Inquisition. Such criticism was not new but was a real cause of concern in Catholic circles. Catholic intellectuals did not tire of declaring their loyalty to the fatherland, but words alone were not enough. Other, more tangible evidence was needed to demonstrate this loyalty.

We could call the press campaign a form of intellectual enforcement. The behavior of Protestant revelers against Catholics in the streets and open spaces of various villages and towns was a more practical form of enforcement. Of course, these were not planned actions. The festival comprised an element of play that developed its own momentum.[20] People were infected by the festive spirit and got together in groups for all sorts of revelry. Street competed with street, neighborhood with neighborhood, and village with village, to demonstrate their support for the nation with flags, processions, and money. Noninvolvement was very difficult, if not impossible. Those who did not play by the rules were branded as outsiders. So this also forced Catholics to determine their attitude toward this sort of festivity.

The answer was found in a marked show of respect for the House of Orange. At royal jubilees and birthdays, the Catholics made a very large contribution. Catholics took part in the festival committees and joined in with the festival throng. In the Catholic churches, special prayers were said for the royal family, and the faithful were allowed to break the rules of fasting if necessary to demonstrate their patriotism in the revelry. Although the House of Orange was Protestant, the sovereign was honored as an impartial symbol. Coupled with this show of respect for the House of Orange was a notable obedience to authority. This expressed itself in, among other things, marked antisocialism. In some cases, Catholic workers were mobilized by their leaders to break a socialist strike, or to avert the danger of a red revolution. So we can see that relative newcomers on the national stage played their patriotic role with diligence and conviction.

Pluralism and Nation Building

Compared with Catholics in Germany, the Catholics in the Netherlands experienced a relatively smooth and easy process of emancipation in the second half of the nineteenth century. While, in the 1870s, the German Catholic Church fought out a very violent struggle with the government—arrests and banishment of clergy created uproar—in the Netherlands things were limited to less extreme forms of antipapism and anticlericalism.[21] Characteristic for the Netherlands was the ambivalent situation of the Catholic minority.

On one hand, the Catholics had to be satisfied with a second-class position in the political arena. For example, through the working of the system of districts (constituencies), the Catholic minority in the middle and northern Netherlands obtained disproportionately few seats in Parliament. Before World War I, a Catholic prime minister was inconceivable. Catholics were also underrepresented in the civil service. On the other hand, Catholic politicians were able to achieve notable successes. For example, the denominational schools (including the Catholic schools) were partially subsidized by the government beginning in 1889, and completely subsidized from 1921 on. The religious divisions were not only tolerated, but also financed at a national level.

To explain the relatively smooth integration of minority groups into the Dutch political system, historians often refer to a long tradition of moderation in Dutch history. The golden era of Dutch history, the seventeenth century, was characterized by the drive for regional independence. The States General was the national ruling council, made up of representatives of the largely independent, provincial governments. Each of the members acted on behalf of, and in constant contact with, his provincial government. And so the members were forced to make compromises. The political scientist Hans Daalder states: "At no time have the Dutch ruling circles been completely closed or homogeneous. Power resources have usually been spread so widely that single groups have had little chance to impose their will without serious friction. This has nurtured a feeling of mutual tolerance, strengthened a mutual willingness to seek accommodation, and made people ready to leave others alone provided they were left alone themselves."[22] According to Daalder, this tradition of moderation has continued in force into the nineteenth and twentieth centuries. Despite structural changes in the system of government, the governing elites retained their moderate political culture. They dealt with denominational contradictions as they had settled regional controversies earlier.

In accordance with this view, some Dutch historians have argued that the development toward religious and political pluralism and the process of national integration were mutually reinforcing tendencies. While it is true that the various movements that merged themselves into Dutch society in the second half of the nineteenth century emphasized their own political and cultural identities, they nevertheless did this within a national framework. It is easy to recognize this in the case of the Catholics and orthodox Protestants, but more complicated in the case of the internationally oriented socialist movement. The Catholic and orthodox Protestant leaders set up nationwide organizations to counter the dominance of the liberal elites. In this way, they brought the people in villages and towns into contact with ideas and practices from elsewhere. These people thus had their horizons expanded.[23] Furthermore, it was noticeable that in the new religious thinking propagated by these organizations, there was an important place for the fatherland. Each movement put forward its own interpretation of Dutch history in an attempt to secure its own share of the national heritage.[24] The consequent spirit of competition was an effective "promoter" of national awareness and nationalism.[25]

This view attractively analyzed both nation building and religious pluralism as modern phenomena. Religion is not simply dismissed as a product of tradition, a relic of the past, that stands in the way of a modern phenomenon such as nation building. The two processes could reinforce each other. The objection that can be raised against this view is that it is very easy to get relatively abstract categories mixed up. The question is, after all, primarily how the competition between established groups and newcomers developed on the national stage. The moderate view of Dutch history could easily lead to the misconception that the parties could operate in an atmosphere of mutual tolerance, as competitors in a free market. The example of the 1872 celebrations provides further insight into this competition.

The work of building the nation was a complicated business. Around 1870, nobody could be sure where this process would end. It called forth passionate opposing forces. Religious and political issues became interwoven in a commonplace and self-evident manner; consider, for example, the question of elementary education.

It was essential to the process of nation building that minorities were, to a certain degree, forced to adopt an appropriate role. In the Dutch example, national politics was controlled by a heterogeneous company of Protestant gentlemen of conservative and liberal tendencies. Catholic leaders and rank and file had to adapt their approach with some expediency to fit the rules established by the Protestant majority. At the commemoration of the capture of Den Briel there was no suggestion of an all-encompassing stage management. Various forces worked on each other. In particular, the actions of the revelers in the streets and squares was rather unpredictable. Nevertheless, the mechanism of "the carrot and the stick" is readily recognizable in the events.

On one hand, concessions were made in order to get Catholics involved in the festival. The festival became less Protestant in character, but Catholics still had to suppress their feelings of discontent to be able to take part.

On the other hand, there was the threat from the radical-liberal and ultra-Protestant writers who pilloried the Catholics as antinational and unpatriotic forces. The riotous antics of Protestant revelers in a large number of places also put the Catholics in a difficult position. The patriotic ritual acquired something of a forced nature. Those who did not take part found themselves shunned as unpatriotic. We can see national festivals as rituals in which these rules were inculcated into newcomers with a combination of persuasion and compulsion.

Notes

This essay was translated by Richard and Annette Morgan.

1. H. M. Enzensberger, "De grote volksverhuizing," *De Volkskrant*, 24 October 1992.

2. Constitution dated 23 April 1798, cited in Frans Grijzenhout, *Feesten voor het Vaderland: Patriotse en Bataafse feesten 1780–1806* (Zwolle, 1989) 168.

3. Jean Jacques Rousseau, *The Social Contract and Discourses*, trans. and intro. G. D. H. Cole (London, 1976), 276

4. Eric J. Hobsbawm, "Mass-Producing Traditions: Europe, 1870–1914," in Eric J. Hobsbawm and Terence Ranger, eds., *The Invention of Tradition* (Cambridge, 1989) 263–307.

5. Benedict R. Anderson, *Imagined Communities: Reflections on the Origin and Spread of Nationalism*, rev. ed. (London, 1995), 199–206. Anderson uses Ernest Renan, *Qu'est-ce qu'une nation?* (1882), as a basis.

6. Rosemonde Sanson, *Les 14 juillet (1789–1975). Fête et conscience nationale* (Paris, 1976), 51–56, 100–106; Henk te Velde, "L'origine des fêtes nationales en France et aux Pays Bas dans les années 1880," in Pim den Boer and Willem Frijhof, eds., *Lieux de mémoire et identités nationales* (Amsterdam, 1993), 105–9.

7. A Protestant pamphlet cited by J. A. Bornewasser, "Mythical aspects of Dutch Anti-Catholicism in the Nineteenth Century," in J. S. Bromley and E. H. Kossmann, eds., *Britain and the Netherlands*, vol. 5 (Den Haag, 1975), *Some Political Mythologies: Papers Delivered to the Fifth Anglo-Dutch Historical Conference*, 200.

8. More extensive empirical data on this subject may be found in my "De strijd rond Alva's bril: Papen en geuzen bij de herdenking van de inname van Den Briel, 1572–1872," *Bijdragen en mededelingen betreffende de geschiedenis der Nederlanden* 110 (1995): 161–81.

9. W. J. F. Nuyens, reader's letter in *De Tijd* dated 18 December 1871, quoted in *De Nieuwe Noord-Hollander* 31 December 1871.

10. Hobsbawm, "Mass-producing traditions," 270–72. Compare with Mary Ryan, "The American Parade: Representations of the Nineteenth Century Social Order," in Lynn Hunt, ed.,*The New Cultural History* (Berkeley, 1989), 131–53.

11. Matthias the Vries, "Nederlands bevrijding," quoted in W. J. Hofdijk, *Brielles gedenkdag. op Neêrlands derde jubilee* (Brielle, 1873), 82.

12. Ibid. 81.

13. Letter from W. J. F. Nuyens to Bishop G. P. Wilmer dated 25 December 1871 in the archive of the Diocese of Haarlem 912.01.

14. Hans Knippenberg, *De deelname aan het lager onderwijs in Nederland gedurende de negentiende eeuw: Een analyse van de landelijke ontwikkelingen en van de regionale verschillen* (Amsterdam, 1986), 230–32.

15. Hobsbawm, "Mass-Producing Traditions."

16. Bert Altena, "Continuïteit of een nieuw begin? Gilden en vakbeweging in Dordrecht, 1798–1872," in M. Bruggeman et al., eds., *Mensen van de nieuwe tijd: Een liber amicorum voor A.Th. van Deursen* (Amsterdam, 1996), 466.

17. Frans Groot, *Roomsen, rechtzinnigen en nieuwlichters: Verzuiling in een Hollandse plattelandsgemeente, 1850–1930* (Hilversum, 1992), 124–34.

18. *Nieuwe Rotterdamsche Courant (hereafter NRC)* 23 April 1872, *Dagblad van Zuid-Holland* 11 April 1872, *De Tijd* 8 April 1872.

19. "Ernstig gevaar III," *NRC* 18 April 1872. Compare with J. A. Bornewasser, "De Nederlandse katholieken en hun negentiende-eeuwse vaderland," *Tijdschrift voor geschiedenis* 95 (1982): 590.

20. J. J. MacAloon, "Sociation and Sociability in Political Celebrations," in Victor Turner, ed., *Celebration: Studies in Festivity and Ritual* (Washington, D.C., 1982), 255–71.

21. Jonathan Sperber, *Popular Catholicism in Nineteenth-Century Germany* (Princeton, N.J., 1984), 208–33.

22. Hans Daalder, "The Netherlands: Opposition in a Segmented Society," in Robert A. Dahl, ed., *Political Opposition in Western Democracies* (New Haven, Conn., 1966), 216.

23. J. van Miert, "Verdeeldheid en binding: Over lokale, verzuilde en nationale loyaliteiten," *Bijdragen en mededelingen betreffende de geschiedenis der Nederlanden* 107 (1992): 670–89.

24. N. C. F. van Sas, "*Fin de siècle* als nieuw begin: Nationalisme in Nederland rond 1900," *Bijdragen en mededelingen betreffende de geschiedenis der Nederlanden* 106 (1991): 608.

25. N. C. F. van Sas, "De mythe Nederland," *De negentiende eeuw* 16 (1992): 19.

10

Religion, Nation-State, Secularism

TALAL ASAD

Is the Idea of Secularization Worth Saving?

Religion has been central to the formation of many European national identities: Poland, Ireland, Greece, England, and others. In the New World, Protestantism played a vital part in the construction of the new American nation, and religion continues to be important despite the constitutional separation of church and state. Zionism and Arab nationalism in the Middle East have both been influenced (albeit in very different ways) by religious histories. In what follows I explore the limits of this way of understanding the public character of religion.

There is renewed interest among scholars in uncovering connections between religion and politics. This interest is linked to a widespread sense that the Enlightenment's view of the place of religion in modern life needs to be revised. The emergence of religious movements in parts of the Third World, and the phenomenon of political Islam in particular, has perplexed and alarmed many Enlightenment supporters. One consequence of this has been a more confident criticism of the predictive claim of secularization theory—that with the advance of modernity religion becomes increasingly marginalized or privatized. I approach the question of religion and nationalism indirectly, by way of an examination of this theory.

The secularization thesis in its entirety has always been at once descriptive and normative. In his impressive book on the subject, José Casanova points to three elements in that thesis, all of which have been taken—at least since Weber—to be essential to the development of modernity: (1) the increasing structural differentiation of social spaces resulting in the separation of religion from politics, economy, science, and so on; (2) the privatization of religion within its own sphere; and (3) the declining social significance of religious belief, commitment, and institutions. Casanova holds that only the first and third elements are viable.[1]

Many contemporary observers have maintained that the worldwide explosion of politicized religion in modern and modernizing societies proves that the thesis is false. Defenders have in general retorted that the phenomenon merely indicates the existence of a widespread revolt against modernity and a failure of the modernization process. This response saves the secularization thesis by making it normative: in order for a society to be modern, it has to be secular, and for it to be secular, it has to relegate religion to nonpolitical spaces because that arrangement is essential to modern society. Casanova's book attempts to break out of this tautology. It argues that the deprivatization of religion is not a refutation of the thesis if it occurs in ways that are consistent with the basic requirements of modern society, including democratic government. In other words, although the privatization of religion within its own sphere is part of what has been meant by secularization, it is not essential to modernity.

The argument is that whether religious deprivatization threatens modernity or not depends on *how* religion becomes public. If it furthers the construction of civil society (as in Poland) or promotes public debate around liberal values (as in the United States), then political religion is entirely consistent with modernity. If, on the other hand, it seeks to undermine civil society (as in Egypt) or individual liberties (as in Iran) then political religion is indeed a rebellion against modernity and the universal values of Enlightenment.

This is certainly an original position but not, I would submit, an entirely coherent one. For if the legitimate role of deprivatized religion is carried out effectively, what happens to the allegedly viable part of the secularization thesis as stated by Casanova? The answer is that the first and third elements are both undermined.

When religion becomes an integral part of modern politics, it is not indifferent to debates about how the economy should be run, which scientific projects should be publicly funded, or what the broader aims of a national education system should be. The legitimate entry of religion into these debates results in the creation of modern "hybrids": the principle of structural differentiation—according to which religion, economy, education, and science are located in autonomous social spaces—no longer holds. Hence the first element of the secularization thesis falls. Furthermore, given religion's entry into political debates issuing in effective policies, it makes no sense to measure the social significance of religion only in terms of such indices as church attendance. Hence the third element of the secularization thesis falls. Since the second element has already been abandoned, nothing retrievable remains of the secularization thesis.

This does not mean that the secularization thesis must be either accepted in its original form or dismissed as nonsense. Its numerous critics are right to attack it, but they have generally missed something vital. I try to outline what that is later on. For the moment I simply assert that neither the supporters nor the critics of the secularization thesis pay enough attention to the concept of "the secular" that emerged historically in a particular way and was assigned specific practical tasks.

I begin by examining the kind of religion that enlightened intellectuals like Casanova see as compatible with modernity. For when it is proposed that religion can play a positive political role in modern society, it is not intended that this apply to *any* religion whatever but only to those religions that are able and willing to enter the public sphere for the purpose of rational debate with opponents who are to be persuaded rather than coerced. Only religions that have accepted the assumptions of liberal moral and political discourse are being commended.

Ever since Habermas drew attention to the central importance of the public sphere for modern liberal society, critics have pointed out that it systematically excludes various kinds of people, or types of claim, from serious consideration. From the beginning the liberal public sphere excluded certain kinds of people: women, subjects without property, and members of religious minorities.[2] This point about exclusions resembles the objection made many years ago by critics of pluralist theories of liberal democracy.[3] For these critics the public domain is not simply a forum for rational debate but an exclusionary space. It is not enough for liberals to respond to this criticism, as they sometimes do, by saying that although the public sphere is less than perfect as an actual forum for rational debate, it is still an ideal worth striving for. The point here is that the public sphere is a space *necessarily* (not just contingently) articulated by power. And everyone who enters it must address power's disposition of people and things.

Another way of putting it is this. The enjoyment of free speech presupposes not merely the physical ability to speak but *to be heard*, a condition without which speaking to some effect is not possible. If one's speech has no effect whatever, it can hardly be said to be in the public sphere, no matter how loudly one shouts. *To make others listen* even if they would prefer not to hear, to speak to some consequence so that something in the political world is affected, to come to a conclusion, to have the authority to make practical decisions on the basis of that conclusion—these are all presupposed in the idea of free public debate as a liberal virtue. But these performatives are not open equally to everyone because the domain of free speech is always shaped by preestablished limits. These include formal legal limitations to free speech in liberal democracies (libel, slander, copyright, patent, and so on), as well as conventional practices of secrecy (confidentiality), without which politics, business, and morality would collapse in any society. But these examples do not exhaust the limits I have in mind. The limits to free speech are not merely those imposed by law and convention—that is, by an external power. They are also intrinsic to the time and space it takes to build and demonstrate a particular argument, to express (or understand) a particular experience—and more broadly, to become particular speaking and listening subjects. There is no public sphere of free speech *at an instant*.

Three questions follow. First, given that historical forces shape elements of "the public" differently, particular appeals can be successfully made only to some sections of the public and not to others. If the performance of free speech is dependent on free listening, its effectiveness depends on the kind of listener who can engage appropriately with what is said, as well as the time and space he or she has to live in. How have different conceptions and practices of religion helped form the ability of listeners to be publicly responsive? This question applies not only to persons who consider themselves religious but to those for whom religion is distasteful or dangerous. For the *experience* of religion in the "private" spaces of home and school is crucial to the formation of subjects who will eventually endorse a particular public culture.[4]

Second, if the adherents of a religion enter the public sphere, can their entry leave the preexisting discursive structure intact? The public sphere is not an empty space for carrying out debates. It is constituted by the sensibilities—memories and aspirations, fears and hopes—of speakers and listeners, and also by the way they exist (and are made to exist) for each other. Thus the introduction of new discourses may result in the disruption of established assumptions structuring debates in the public sphere. More strongly, they may *have* to disrupt existing assumptions in order to be heard. Far from having to prove to existing authority that it is no threat to dominant national values, a religion that enters political debate on its own terms may on the contrary inevitably threaten the authority of existing assumptions. And if that is the case, what is meant by demanding that any resulting change must be carried out by moral suasion and negotiation and never by manipulation or force?

Third, why are secularists alarmed at the thought that religion should be allowed to invade the domain of our personal choices—when the process of speaking and listening freely implies precisely that our thoughts and actions should be opened up to change by our interlocutors? Secularists accept that in modern society the political increasingly penetrates the personal. They accept that politics, through the law, has juridical consequences for life in the private sphere. This partiality can be explained by the secular doctrine that while the national law permits the essential self to make and defend itself ("our rights and duties constitute our modern liberties") religious prescriptions only confine and dominate it. Yet even if we take as unproblematic the assumption that there exists a priori a secular self to be made, the question of coercion in such a constructive task cannot easily be brushed aside. For the juridification of all interpersonal relations constrains the scope for moral suasion in public culture. In that context, far from becoming a source of moral values that can enrich public debate, deprivatized religion becomes a site of conflict over nonnegotiable rights—for example, the parent's right to determine his or her child's up-bringing, or the pregnant woman's right to dispose of her fetus.

One old argument about the need to separate religion from politics is that because the former essentially belongs to the domain of faith and passion, rational argument and interest-guided action can have no place in it. The secularist concedes that religious beliefs and sentiments might be acceptable at a personal and private level but insists that organized religion, being founded on authority and constraint, has always posed a danger to the freedom of the self as well as to the freedom of others. That may be why some enlightened intellectuals are prepared to allow depriva-tized religion entry into the public sphere for the purpose of addressing the moral conscience of its audience—but on condition that it leave its coercive powers outside the door and rely only on its powers of persuasion.

The public, however, is notoriously diverse. Modern citizens do not sub-scribe to a unitary moral system (moral heterogeneity is said to be one of modern society's defining characteristics). The puzzle here is how a deprivatized religion can appeal effectively to the consciences of those who do not accept its values. After all, the possibility of negotiation depends on the prior agreement of the parties concerned that the values to be nego-tiated are in fact negotiable. Even in a modern society such agreement does not extend to all values. The only option religious spokespersons have in that situation is to act as secular politicians do in liberal democ-racy. Where the latter cannot persuade others to negotiate, they seek to manipulate the conditions in which they act or refrain from acting. And in order to win the votes of constituents, they employ a variety of commu-nicative devices to target their desires and anxieties. I return to the idea that deprivatized religion in a secularized society cannot be any different.

My conclusion to what I have said so far is that those who advocate the view that the deprivatization of religion is compatible with modernity do not always make it clear precisely what this implies. Is the assumption that by appealing to the conscience of the nation religious spokespersons can evoke its moral sensibilities? The difficulty here is that given the moral heterogeneity of modern society referred to above, nothing can be identi-fied as a national conscience or a collective moral sensibility. So is the assumption then that religious spokespersons can at least enrich public argument by joining in political debates? But even liberal politicians do not merely engage in public talk for the sake of "enriching" it. As mem-bers of a government and as parliamentarians they possess the authority to make decisions that are implemented in national policies. What author-ity do religious spokespersons have in this matter?

Should Nationalism Be Understood as Secularized Religion?

Is nationalism, with its affirmation of collective solidarity, already a religion of the nation-state? Is that how religious spokespersons can derive their authority in the public sphere, by invoking the national community as though it were also a religious one? There is certainly a long and interesting tradition that suggests nationalism *is* a religion. Thus as far back as 1926 Carlton Hayes remarked that "Nationalism has a large number of particularly quarrelsome sects, but as a whole it is the latest and nearest approach to a world-religion."[5]

Julian Huxley, writing in 1940, maintained that "humanist religion" was destined to replace traditional theological religion, and that social movements of a religious nature like Nazism and communism were evidence of this supersession. Their cruel and repulsive character, he went on to suggest, merely reflected their youthfulness in terms of evolutionary development: "Just as many of these early manifestations of theistic religion were crude and horrible . . . so these early humanist and social religions are crude and horrible."[6] Although Huxley does not address the question of nationalism directly, the idea of nationalism as the highest stage of religion conceived within an evolutionary framework is not hard to discern in his text.

More recently, Clifford Geertz has identified the centrality of sacred symbols springing from religious impulses to all forms of political life, nationalist as well as prenationalist, in cultures both modern and premodern. The symbolic activities that take place in the center, Geertz suggests, give it "its aura of being not merely important but in some odd fashion connected with the way the world is built." This is why "the gravity of high politics and the solemnity of high worship" are akin.[7]

Margaret Jacob makes a similar point about secular rituals and the formation of modern political values. She describes how a new pattern of sentiments, beliefs, and ceremonial activities—a "new religiosity"—came to be associated with eighteenth-century Freemasonry, and how it contributed to the emergence of liberal society.[8] "Reason" and "civil society," she proposes, were thus sacralized in the life of early west European nations.

However, I am not persuaded that because national political life depends on ceremonial and symbols of the sacred, it should be represented as a kind of religion. My view is that according to the modern construction "religion" consists precisely of those representations and practices that should be distinguished by and separated from politics, and that the secular is the essential ground that enables this to be done. Notions of sanctity, spirituality, and communal solidarity are invoked in various ways to claim authority in national politics (sovereignty, the law, national glories and sufferings, the rights of the citizen, and so on). Critics often point to the words in which these notions are conveyed as signs of religion. But this evidence is not decisive. I suggest that we need to attend more closely to the historical form of concepts and not to what we take as signs of an essential phenomenon.

A writer who appears to do this is Carl Schmitt. He argues that many theological and political concepts share a common structure. "All significant concepts of the modern theory of the state are secularized theological concepts," he writes, "not only because of their historical development—in which they were transferred from theology to the theory of the state, whereby, for example, the omnipotent God became the omnipotent lawgiver—but also because of their systematic structure, the recognition of which is necessary for a sociological consideration of these concepts. The exception in jurisprudence is analogous to the miracle in theology. Only by being aware of this analogy can we appreciate the manner in which the philosophical ideas of the state developed in the last centuries."[9] Although Schmitt's thesis about the secularization of religious concepts is not about nationalism as such, it does have implications for the way we see it. For if we accept that religious ideas can be secularized, we might be induced to accept that nationalism has—in part or whole—a religious origin.

My view is that we should consider the results rather than the origins of the process referred to as secularization. For example, when it is pointed out that in the latter part of the nineteenth century Tractarianism in England and Ultramontanism in France (and in Europe generally) helped break the post-Reformation alliance between church and state,[10] and that this was done by deploying religious arguments aimed at securing the freedom of Christ's Church from the constraints of an earthly power, we should regard this development as significant not because of the essentialized ("religious") agency by which it was initiated but because of its completed outcome. That outcome not only included the development of different moral and political disciplines, such as those Foucault identified as governmentality.[11] It also involved a redefinition of the essence of religion as well as of national politics.

By way of contrast: in later eighteenth-century England, supporters of the established church regarded it as a representative institution reflecting popular sentiment and public opinion. It would not be right to say that religion was then being used for political purposes or influencing state policy. The established church, which was an integral part of the state, made the coherence and continuity of the English national community possible. We should not say that the English nation was shaped or influenced by religion: the established church (called "Anglican" only in the nineteenth century) was its necessary condition. Nor, given that it was a necessary condition of the nation-state, should we speak of the social location of religion in the eighteenth century being different from the one it came to occupy in the late nineteenth and beyond. Rather, the very essence of religion was differently defined—that is to say, in each of the two historical moments different conditions of religion's existence were in play. What we now retrospectively call "the social," that all-inclusive secular space that we distinguish conceptually from variables like "religion," "state," "national economy," and on which the latter can be constructed, re-formed, and replotted, did not exist prior to the nineteenth century.[12] Yet it was precisely the emergence of *society* as an organized secular body that made it possible for the state to oversee and facilitate an original task by redefining religion's competence: the unceasing material and moral transformation of its entire national population regardless of their diverse "religious" allegiances. It is therefore not enough to point to the structural analogies between premodern theological concepts and those deployed in secular constitutional discourse, as Schmitt does: the practices these concepts facilitate differ according to the historical formations in which they occur.[13]

I am arguing that the secular should not be thought of as the space in which real human life gradually emancipates itself from the controlling power of religion and thus achieves the latter's relocation.[14] This assumption encourages us to think of religious ideas as "infecting" the secular domain, or as replicating within it the structure of theological concepts. The concept of the secular today is part of a doctrine called secularism. Secularism does not simply valorize the human and worldly "out there" as opposed to the otherworldly; it does not simply insist that religious practice and belief be confined to a space where they cannot threaten political stability or the liberties of "free-thinking" citizens. Secularism posits a particular conception of the world ("natural" and "social") and of the problems generated by that world. In the context of early modern Europe these problems were perceived as the need to control the increasingly mobile poor in city and countryside, to govern mutually hostile Christian sects within a sovereign territory, and to regulate the commercial, military, and colonizing expansion of Europe overseas.[15]

The ideological genealogy of secularism can be traced in part to the Renaissance doctrine of humanism, in part to the Enlightenment concept of nature, and in part to Hegel's philosophy of history. Hegel—an early secularization theorist—saw the movement of world history culminating in the truth and freedom of what he called "the modern period." Like later secularists, he held that from the Reformation to Enlightenment and Revolution, there emerged at last a harmony between the objective and subjective conditions of human life resulting from "the painful struggles of History," a harmony based on "the recognition of the Secular as capable of being an embodiment of Truth; whereas it had been formerly regarded as evil only, as incapable of Good—the latter being essentially ultramundane."[16]

In fact the historical process of secularization effects a remarkable ideological inversion, though not quite the way Hegel claimed in the sentence just cited. For at one time the secular was part of a theological discourse (*saeculum*). *Secularization* (*saecularisatio*) at first denoted a legal transition from monastic life (*regularis*) to the life of canons (*saecularis*)—and then, after the Reformation, it signified the transfer of ecclesiastical real property to laypersons, that is, to the "freeing" of property from church hands into the hands of private owners, and thence into market circulation.[17] In the discourse of modernity the secular presents itself as the ground from which theological discourse was generated (as a form of false consciousness) and from which it gradually emancipated itself in its march to freedom. On that ground humans appear as the self-conscious makers of history (in which calendrical time provides a measure and direction for human events) and as the unshakable foundation of universally valid knowledge about nature and society. The human as agent is now responsible—answerable—not only for acts he or she has performed (or refrained from performing) but for events he or she was unaware of—or falsely conscious of. The domain in which acts of God (accidents) occur without human responsibility is increasingly restricted. Chance is now considered to be tamable.

The interesting thing about this view is that although religion is regarded as alien to the secular, the latter is also seen to have generated religion. Historians of progress relate that in the premodern past, secular life created superstitious and oppressive religion, and in the modern present, secularism has produced enlightened and tolerant religion. Thus the insistence on a sharp separation between the religious and the secular goes with the paradoxical claim that the latter continually produces the former.

Nationalism, with its vision of a universe of national societies, in which individual humans live their worldly existence, requires the concept of the secular to make sense. The loyalty that the individual nationalist owes is directly and exclusively to the nation. Even when the nation is said to be "under God," it has its being only in "this world"—a special kind of world. The men and women of each national society make and *own* their history. Nature and culture (that famous duality accompanying the rise of nationalism) together form the conditions in which the nation uses and enjoys the world. Mankind dominates nature and each person fashions his or her individuality in the freedom defined and protected by the nation-state.

One should not take this to mean that the worldliness of the secular members of modern nations is an expression of the truth revealed through the human senses.[18] However unworldly medieval Christian monks and nuns may have been, they too lived in the world (where else?) but they lived in it differently from laypersons. Allegiance demanded of them was solely to Christ, and through him to other Christians. Benedict Anderson quite rightly represents the worldliness of secular nationalism as a specific ideological construct (no less ideological than the one it replaces) that includes in the present an imagined realm of the nation as a community with a "worldly past." And he makes an important point when he draws our attention to the fact that nationalism employs highly abstract concepts of time and space to tell a particular story—even though that story is presented as commonsensical, that is, as accessible to all members of the nation—a story about the nation as a natural and self-evident unity whose members share a common experience. This construct is no less real for being ideological; it articulates a world of actual objects and subjects within which the secular nationalist lives. What needs to be emphasized beyond Anderson's famous thesis is that the complex medieval Christian universe, with its interlinked times (Eternity and its moving image, and the irruptions of the former into the latter: Creation, Fall, Christ's Life and Death, Judgment Day) and hierarchy of spaces (the heavens, the earth, purgatory, hell), is broken down by the modern doctrine of secularism into a duality: a world of self-authenticating things in which we *really* live as social beings and a religious world that exists only in our imagination.

To insist that nationalism should be seen as religion, or even as having been shaped by religion is, in my view, to miss the nature and consequence of the revolution brought about by the Enlightenment doctrine of secularism in the structure of modern collective representations and practices. Of course modern nationalism draws on preexisting languages and practices—including those that we call, anachronistically, "religious." How could it be otherwise? Yet it does not follow from this that religion forms nationalism.

My concern is that we should not accept the Enlightenment idea of causality always and without question. Thus if we take cause to be about the way an event is "felt" in subsequent events, we will tend to look for the continuity of religious causes in nonreligious effects. But searching in this way for the origin of elements or for the "influence" of events on one another is, I would submit, of limited value here. What requires explaining (how nationalism contains a religious influence) is being used innocently as the means of explanation (religion as at once both cause and effect). If instead we were to attend to an older sense of cause (cause answers to the question "Why?") we would ask about the reformation of historical elements in order to understand why their meaning is no longer what it was. After all, religion consists of particular ideas, sentiments, practices, institutions, traditions—as well as followers who instantiate, maintain, or alter them. To discover their meanings must surely be our first task. And so too with secularizm. We have to discover what the secular is before we can understand what is involved in the secularization of theological concepts in different times and places.

Or Should Islamism Be Regarded as Nationalism?

Let us take for granted that nationalism is essentially secular (in the sense that it is rooted in human history and society). Can we now argue that some apparently religious movements should be viewed as nationalist, and that they are therefore really secular? Many observers of political Islam have adopted this argument, although in doing so they are in effect simply reversing the terms of the secularization thesis.

To represent the contemporary Islamic revival (known by those who approve of it in the Arab world as *as-sahwa*, "the awakening") as a form of cryptonationalism,[19] to refer to it explicitly by the term *cultural nationalism*,[20] is to propose that it is best understood as a continuation of the familiar story of Third World nationalism. That proposal renders the claim by Muslim activists to be part of a historical Islamic tradition specious because, as cultural nationalists, they must be seen as part of something essentially (though distortedly) "modern." However, the fact that those active in the revival are usually highly critical of "traditional" teachers and practices does not prove that they are really rejecting tradition. Belonging to a tradition does not preclude involvement in vigorous debate over the meanings of its formative texts (even over which texts *are* formative) and over the need for radical reform of the tradition. The selectivity with which people approach their tradition does not necessarily undermine their claim to its integrity. Nor does the attempt to adapt the older concerns of a tradition's followers to their new predicament in itself dissolve the coherence of that tradition—indeed that is precisely the object of argument among those who claim to be upholding the essence of the tradition.

All of this is not to say that there is nothing in common between the motives of Islamists and of Arab nationalists. There are overlaps between the two, notably in their similar stance of opposition against "the West," which has been experienced in the Middle East in the form of predatory nationalisms of the Great Powers. Because, as individuals, Islamists and nationalists share this position, they are sometimes led to seek a common alliance—as happened at the Khartoum international conference of Islamists and Arab nationalists in the aftermath of the Gulf War.[21] However pragmatic and brittle such alliances turn out to be, they presuppose differences that the would-be allies believe should be bridged.

The differences spring from the Islamist project of regulating conduct in the world in accordance with "the principles of religion" (*usul ud-din*), and from the fact that the community to be constructed stands counter to many of the values of modern Western life that Arab nationalism endorses. Both these conditions define what one might call contemporary Islamic worldliness. The basic thrust of Arab nationalist ideology is of course supradenominational (despite its invocations of Islamic history and its concessions to Islamic popular sentiment) and it is committed to the doctrine of separating law and citizenship from religion, and of confining the latter to the private domain. In brief, religion is what secular Arabism specifies and tries to set in its proper social place.

For nationalism the history of Islam is important because it reflects the unification and triumph of the Arab nation; in that discourse the "Arabian Prophet" is regarded as its spiritual hero.[22] This is an inversion of the classical theological view according to which the Prophet is not a national inspiration for an imagined community but a model for virtuous conduct (*sunna*) that each Muslim, within a Muslim community, must seek to embody in his or her life, and the foundation, together with the Qur'an, of *din* (now translated as "religion"). Nor is Islamic history in the classical view an account of the Arab nation's rise and decline. Classical Islamic chronicles are not "history" in the sense that nationalism claims "it has a history." They grow out of *hadith* accounts (records of the sayings and doings of the Prophet) on which the *sunna* is based, and they articulate a Qur'anic worldview as expressed in the political and theological conflicts among the faithful. At any rate it is easy to see that while the Arab nation is inconceivable without its history, the Islamic *umma* presupposes only the Qur'an and *sunna*.

The Islamic *umma* in the classical theological view is thus not an imagined community on a par with the Arab nation waiting to be politically unified but a theologically defined space enabling Muslims to practice the disciplines of *din* in the world. Of course the word *umma* does also have the sense of "a people"—and "a community"—in the Qur'an. But the members of every community—or society—imagine it to have a particular character, and relate to one another by virtue of it. The crucial point therefore is not that it is imagined but that what is imagined predicates distinctive modes of being and acting. The Islamic *umma* presupposes individuals who are self-governing but not autonomous. The *shari'a*, a system of practical reason morally binding on each faithful individual, exists independently of him or her. At the same time every Muslim has the psychological ability to discover its rules and to conform to them.

The fact that the expression *alumma al'arabiyya* is used today to denote the "Arab nation" represents a major conceptual transformation by which *umma* is cut off from the theological predicates that gave it its universalizing power and made to stand for an imagined community that is equivalent to a total society, limited and sovereign like other limited and sovereign nations in a secular (social) world.[23] The *ummatu-l-muslimin* (the Islamic *umma*) is ideologically not "a society" onto which state, economy, and religion can be mapped. It is not limited nor sovereign: not limited, for unlike Arab nationalism's notion of *al-umma al-ʾarabiyya*, it can and eventually should embrace all of humanity, and not sovereign, for it is subject to God's authority. It is therefore a mistake to regard it as an "archaic" (because "religious") community that predates the modern nation.[24]

I do not mean to imply that the classical theological view is held in all its specificity by individual Islamists. All Muslims today inhabit a different world from the one their classical forebears lived in, so it cannot be said of any of them that they hold the classical theological view. Even the most conservative Muslim draws on experiences in the contemporary world to give relevance and credibility to his or her theological interpretations. As I indicated above, people who have been called Islamists are in many ways close to nationalists even though nationalism had no meaning in the doctrines of the classical theologians. Yet it is evident that Islamists, as they have been called by observers (to themselves they are simply proper Muslims), relate themselves to the classical theological tradition by translating it into their contemporary political predicament. Of course this relationship is not articulated identically in different countries, or even within the same country. But the very fact that they must interpret a millennium-old discursive tradition—and, in interpreting it, inevitably disagree with one another—marks them off from Arab nationalists with their Western-derived discourse. For example, the individual's right to the pursuit of happiness and self-creation, a doctrine easily assimilable by secular nationalist thought, is countered by Islamists (as it is in classical Islamic theology) by the duty of the Muslim to worship God as laid down in the *shariʾa*.

Both Arab nationalism (whether of the liberal or the socialist variety) and Islamism share a concern with the modernizing state that was put in place by Westernizing power—a state directed at the unceasing material and moral transformation of entire populations only recently organized as "societies."[25] In other words, Islamism takes for granted and seeks to work through the nation-state, which has become so central to the predicament of all Muslims. It is this statist project and not the fusion of religious and political ideas that gives Islamism a nationalist cast. Although Islamism has virtually always succeeded Arab nationalism in the contemporary history of the Middle East, and addressed itself directly to the nation-state, it should not be regarded as a form of nationalism.[26] The real motives of Islamists, of whether or not individuals are using religion for political ends, is not a relevant question here. (The real motives of political actors are usually plural and often fluctuating.) The important question is what circumstances oblige Islamism to emerge publicly as a political discourse, and whether, and if so in what way, it challenges the deep structures of secularism, including the assumptions of nationalist discourse.

From the point of view of secularism, religion has the option either of confining itself to private belief and worship or of engaging in public talk that makes no demands on life. In either case such religion is seen by secularism to take the form it should properly have. Each is equally the condition of its legitimacy. But this requirement is made difficult for those who wish to reform life by the ambition of the secular state itself. Given that the modern nation-state seeks to regulate all aspects of individual life—even the most intimate, such as birth and death—no one, religious or otherwise, can avoid encountering its ambitious powers. It is not only that the state intervenes directly in the social body for purposes of reform; it is that all social activity requires the consent of the law, and therefore of the nation-state. The way social spaces are defined, ordered, and regulated makes them all equally political. So the attempt by Muslim activists to ameliorate social conditions—through, say, the establishment of clinics or schools in underserviced areas—must seriously risk provoking the charge of political illegitimacy and being classified Islamist. The call by Muslim movements to reform the social body through the authority of popular majorities in the national parliament will be opposed as antidemocratic, as in Algeria in 1992 and in Turkey in 1997. Such cases of deprivatized religion are intolerable to secularists primarily because of the motives imputed to their opponents rather than to anything the latter have actually done. The motives signal the potential entry of religion into space already occupied by the secular. It is the nationalist secularists themselves, one might say, who stoutly reject the secularization of religious concepts and practices here.

The main point I underline is that Islamism's preoccupation with state power is the result not of its commitment to nationalist ideas but of the modern nation-state's enforced claim to constitute legitimate social identities and arenas. No movement that aspires to more than mere belief or inconsequential talk in public can remain indifferent to state power in a secular world. Even though Islamism is situated in a secular world—a world that is presupposed by, among other things, the universal space of the social that sustains the nation-state—Islamism cannot be reduced to nationalism. Many individuals actively involved in Islamist movements within the Arab world may regard Arab nationalism as compatible with it, and employ its discourse too. But such a stance has in fact been considered inconsistent by many Islamists—especially (but not only) outside the Arab world.[27]

Toward an Anthropology of Secularism?

In conclusion, I suggest that if the secularization thesis seems increasingly implausible to some of us, this is not simply because religion is now playing a vibrant part in the modern world of nations. In a sense what many would anachronistically call "religion" was always involved in the world of power. If the secularization thesis no longer carries the conviction it once did, this is because the categories of politics and religion turn out to implicate each other more profoundly than we thought, a discovery that has accompanied our growing understanding of the powers of the modern nation-state. The concept of the secular cannot do without the idea of religion.

True, the "proper domain of religion" is distinguished from and separated by the state in modern secular constitutions.[28] But formal constitutions never give the whole story. On one hand, objects, sites, practices, words, representations—even the minds and bodies of worshipers—cannot be confined within the exclusive space of what secularists name *religion*. They have their own ways of being. The historical elements of what come to be conceptualized as religion have disparate trajectories. On the other hand, the nation-state requires clearly demarcated spaces that it can classify and regulate: religion, education, health, leisure, work, income, justice, and war. The space that religion may properly occupy in society has to be continually redefined by the law because the reproduction of secular life within and beyond the nation-state continually affects the clarity of that space. The unceasing pursuit of the new in productive effort, aesthetic experience, and claims to knowledge, as well as the unending struggle to extend individual self-creation, undermines the stability of established boundaries. My point here is neither to discredit nor to celebrate these processes but to point to the contradictory conditions that undergird the category of the secular.

I do not deny that religion, in the vernacular sense of that word, is and historically has been important for national politics in Euro-America as well as in the rest of the world. Recognition of this fact will no doubt continue to prompt useful work. But there are questions that need to be systematically addressed beyond this obvious fact. How, when, and by whom are the categories of religion and the secular defined? What assumptions are presupposed in the acts of defining them? And finally, what conception of religion makes our secular moral and political practices possible? An anthropology of the secular as practical experience remains entirely unexplored.

Notes

Acknowledgments

My thanks to Jonathan Boyarin, Charles Hirschkind, Saba Mahmood, Macklin Trimnell, and Hent de Vries for their comments on an early draft.

1. José Casanova, *Public Religions in the Modern World* (Chicago: University of Chicago Press, 1994).

2. See, for example, Mary Ryan, "Gender and Public Access: Women's Politics in Nineteenth-Century America," and Geoff Eley, "Nations, Publics, and Political Cultures: Placing Habermas in the Nineteenth Century," both in Craig Calhoun, ed., *Habermas and the Public Sphere* (Cambridge: MIT Press, 1992), pp. 259–88, and 289–329.

3. Robert Wolff, for example, wrote in 1965: "There is a very sharp distinction in the public domain between legitimate interests and those which are absolutely beyond the pale. If a group or interest is within the framework of acceptability, then it can be sure of winning some measure of what it seeks, for the process of national politics is distributive and compromising. On the other hand, if an interest falls *outside* the circle of the acceptable, it receives no attention whatsoever and its proponents are treated as crackpots, extremists, or foreign agents." "Beyond Tolerance," in Robert P. Wolff, Barrington Moore Jr., and Herbert Marcuse, eds., *A Critique of Pure Tolerance* (Boston: Beacon Press, 1969), 52; emphasis in original. William Connolly has pushed this criticism in new and more interesting directions in *The Ethos of Pluralism* (Minneapolis: Unversity of Minnesota Press, 1995).

4. An example of this was made dramatically evident in Turkey in the summer of 1997 when the secularist army forced the resignation of the coalition government led by the pro-Islamic Welfare Party. The military-backed government that succeeded it has instituted major reforms in an effort to contain the growing resurgence of Islam in the population. A crucial part of these reforms is the formal extension of compulsory secular education for children from five to eight years, a measure designed to stop the growth of Islamic sentiment in the formation of schoolchildren.

5. C. J. H. Hayes, *Essays on Nationalism* (New York, 1926), cited in John Wolffe, *God and Greater Britain: Religion and National Life in Britain and Ireland, 1843–1945* (London: Routledge, 1994), 16.

6. Julian Huxley, *Religion without Revelation*, abridged ed. (London: Watts, 1941), viii.

7. Clifford Geertz, *Local Knowledge: Further Essays in Interpretive Anthropology* (New York: Basic Books, 1983), 124. See also Robert Bellah, "Civil Religion in America," in *Beyond Belief: Essays on Religion in a Post-Traditional World* (New York: Harper and Row, 1970).

8. See Margaret C. Jacob, *Living the Enlightenment: Freemasonry and Politics in Eighteenth-Century Europe* (New York: Oxford University Press, 1992), and especially her "Private Beliefs in Public Temples: The New Religiosity of the Eighteenth Century," *Social Research* 59 (1992): 59–84.

9. Carl Schmitt, *Political Theology* (1934; rpt., Cambridge: MIT Press, 1985), 36.

10. The constitutional privilege accorded the Church of England in the British state today is largely a formality—and to the extent that it still has material consequences, it is often cited as evidence of Britain's "incompletely modernized" state. See Tom Nairn, *The Break Up of Britain*, London: New Left Books, 1977.

11. Strictly speaking, Foucault does not think of discipline as being intrinsic to governmentality but only as something "in tension with it," That is why he speaks of "a triangle, sovereignty-discipline-government, which has as its primary target the population and as its essential mechanism the apparatus of security." See "Governmentality," in Graham Burchell, Colin Gordon, and Peter Miller, eds., *The Foucault Effect* (Chicago: University of Chicago Press, 1991), 87–104. I am not persuaded, however, that discipline can be conceptually separated from governmentality whose raison-d'être is the management of target populations within nation societies.

12. Mary Poovey notes that "By 1776, the phrase *body politic* had begun to compete with another metaphor, *the great body of the people*. . . . By the early nineteenth century, both of these phrases were joined by the image of the social body." *Making a Social Body: British Cultural Formation* (Chicago: University of Chicago Press, 1995), 7. See also the second chapter, "The Production of Abstract Space."

13. Hans Blumenberg criticizes Schmitt for not taking into account the way theological metaphors are selected and used within particular historical contexts, and therefore for mistaking analogies for transformations. See *The Legitimacy of the Modern Age* (1973–76; rpt., Cambridge: MIT Press, 1983, pt. 1, chap. 8. This point—as well as his more extensive critique of Karl Löwith's thesis about the essentially Christian character of the secular idea of progress—is well taken. But I find Blumenberg's delineation and defense of "secularism," rooted firmly as it is in a conventional history-of-ideas approach, unconvincing. His relative neglect of *practice* is remarkable given the nature of his criticism of Schmitt.

14. For an illuminating discussion of this point, see John Milbank's *Theology and Social Theory* (Oxford: Blackwell, 1990).

15. Cf. James Tully, "Governing Conduct," in Edmund Leites, ed., *Conscience and Casuistry in Early Modern Europe* (Cambridge: Cambridge University Press, 1988)—an attempt to apply a Foucauldian perspective to the intellectual history of early modern Europe.

16. G. W. F. Hegel, *The Philosophy of History*, trans. J. Sibree (Buffalo, N.Y.: Prometheus Books, 1991), 422.

17. See "Säkularisation, Säkularisierung," in Otto Brunner, Werner Conze, and Reinhart Koselleck, eds., *Geschichtliche Grundbegriffe: Historisches Lexicon zur politisch-sozialen Sprache in Deutschland*, 8 vols. (Stuttgart: Klett, 1972–97), 5: 789–830.

18. That is to say, as though there were no question about whether even the senses might in some degree be mediated. See Constance Claessen, *Worlds of Sense: Exploring the Senses in History and across Cultures* (London: Routledge, 1993). For a fascinating account of culturally different ways in which water may be sensed by the body, see G. Vigarello, *Concepts of Cleanliness: Changing Attitudes in France since the Middle Ages* (Cambridge: Cambridge University Press, 1988). See also Peter Gay, *The Education of the Senses* (New York: Oxford University Press, 1984).

19. For example A. Ayalon, "From Fitna to Thawra," *Studia Islamica* 66 (1987): 145–74; and Nikki R. Keddie, "Islamic Revival as Third Worldism," in J. P. Digard, ed., *Le cuisinier et le philosophe: Hommage à Maxime Rodinson* (Paris: Maisonneuve et Larose, 1982), 275–82.

20. Luciani, reviewing the effect of the Islamic resurgence on modern Middle Eastern politics, observes that "modern Islamic thinking, in avowedly different ways, offers radical answers to contemporary issues. These answers are, in a sense, a form of cultural nationalism, in which religion gives more substance to the rejection of Western domination." *The Arab State* (London: Routledge, 1990), xxx.

21. The delegates were mostly from countries that had opposed the U.S.-led invasion of Kuwait and Iraq, including Islamist and Marxist currents within the PLO, but oppositional elements from Muslim states that had supported the Americans—such as Egypt and Turkey—also participated. See Majdi Ahmad Husain, "al-Mu'tamar ash-sha'bi al-'arabi al-islami: al-Fikra, al-mumarasa, ath-thamara," *ash-Sha'b*, 7 May 1991, 3.

22. A Christian Arab nationalist writes with admiration of the personality of the prophet Muhammad, of his strength of conviction and firmness of belief, and concludes: "This is the spiritual message contained in the anniversary of the Arabian Prophet's birth which is addressed to our present national life. It is for this, in spite of their different tendencies and their diverse religions and sects, that the Arab nationalists must honor the memory of Muhammad b. Abdallah, the Prophet of Islam, the unifier of the Arabs, the man of principle and conviction." Qustantin Zuraiq, *al-Wa'i al-qaumi* (Beirut, 1949), cited in S. G. Haim, ed., *Arab Nationalism: An Anthology* (Berkeley: University of California Press, 1962), 171.

23. The reference here is to Benedict Anderson's definition of the nation: "It is an imagined political community—imagined as both inherently limited and sovereign." *Imagined Communities: Reflections on the Origin and Spread of Nationalism* (London: Verso, 1983), 15.

24. Cf. Anderson, *Imagined Communities*, 40.

25. It may be noted that the modern Arabic word for "society"—*mujtama'*—gained currency only in the 1930s. See Jaroslav Stetkevych, *The Modern Arabic Literary Language* Chicago: University of Chicago Press, 1970), 25. Lane's *Lexicon*, compiled in the mid-nineteenth century, gives only the classical meaning of *mujtama'*: "a meeting place."

26. The idea of an Islamic state is arguably not identifiable at the beginnings of Islamic history. See my comments on the subject in "Europa contra Islam: De Islam in Europa," *Nexus* 10 (1994): 3–17. The English version has been published in *The Muslim World* 87 (1997): 183–95.

27. Thus when a delegate from Jordan at the conference (mentioned in note 21) asserted that disagreements between the aims of the Islamic movement and those of Arab nationalism were relatively minor, and that it was certain that "any movement that is to prevail in our Arab world must be either a nationalist movement incorporating the Islamic perspective with a commitment to democracy and social justice, or an Islamic movement incorporating nationalist perspectives" (Husain, "al-Mu'tamar"), his assertion was strongly contested, especially—but not only—by delegates from non-Arab countries who insisted that the only bond between Muslims at present divided among nation-states was Islam.

28. Whether it should be so is contested even in the paradigmatic case of the United States. Thus it is pointed out that the phrase "separation of church and state" is not found in the Constitution, but represents the Supreme Court's interpretation of the Founders' intention. See David Barton, *The Myth of Separation* (Aledo, Tex.: Wallbuilder Press, 1992). But see also Winnifred F. Sullivan, *Paying the Words Extra: Religious Discourse in the Supreme Court of the United States* (Cambridge: Harvard University Press, 1994).

11

The Goodness of Nations

BENEDICT R. ANDERSON

ONE CAN SEE instantaneously where nationalism and religion part company if one tries to transpose the well-worn cliché "My Country Right or Wrong" into, say, "My Religion (Christianity or Islam or Buddhism or Hinduism) Right or Wrong." The latter are "impossible" oxymorons. How could a religion, for its adherents, conceivably be "wrong"?

Yet this contrast should not be taken wholly at face value. For if nations can, at least hypothetically, be "wrong," this wrongness is temporary, and is always set against a more permanent "good." The question then is—and one poses it in opposition to the eternal goodness of religion—what is the source of this goodness, given that the nation, no matter how grandly conceived, is intrahistorical (it has no place in heaven or in hell)? I argue that we need to think about innocence, or, more precisely, about who, in the national ambience, guarantees the nation's ultimate blamelessness.

The Unborn

The "unborn" (in the literal and metaphorical senses) are not a collectivity with which the Great Religions are much preoccupied. They are simply awaiting their turn (return) on the brief stage of life. But they figure very significantly in the national imagination, because their existence is the only sure guarantee of the nation's quasi-eternality. One can do no better, in illustrating this, than turn to the peculiar ruminations of Max Weber, in his 1895 inaugural lecture on assuming a position at the university of Freiburg.[1] The bulk of this lecture is a pitiful jeremiad about the condition of Germany. The "traditional" Prussian ruling class—the Junkers—he described as finished: "They have done their work, and today are in the throes of an economic-death struggle." From the German bourgeoisie nothing good could be expected. "One section of the haute bourgeoisie longs all too shamelessly for the coming of a new Caesar, who will protect them in two directions: from beneath against the rising masses of the people, from above against the socio-political impulses they suspect the German dynasties of harboring." Another section is "sunk in that political Philistinism from which broad strata of the lower middle classes have never awakened." The proletariat he believed to be wholly immature— "nothing [is] more destructive to a great nation than to be led by politi- cally uneducated philistinism, and the German proletariat has not yet lost this character of philistinism. That is why," he insisted, "we are politically opposed to the proletariat." One might conclude from the "analysis" that the German nation was "all wrong," with the possible exception of the learned young professor himself. But then Weber struck an altogether different, and at first very strange, note:

> If—to use a somewhat fanciful image—we could arise from the grave thousands of years hence, we would seek the distant traces of our own nature in the physi- ognomy of the race of the future. Even our highest, our ultimate, terrestrial ideals are mutable and transitory. We can not presume to impose them on the future. But we can hope that the future recognizes in our nature the nature of its own ancestors. We wish to make ourselves the forefathers of the race of the future with our labour and our mode of existence.

In this passage, with its messianic timbre, we can recognize something that mimics the religious impulse. The sober comparative sociologist of religions deliriously, longingly, imagines Germans, thousands of years into the future, imagining Weber. But what is especially striking is that these unborn Germans appear to impose obligations and responsibilities on the imaginer of 1895, who is already thinking of himself as, so to speak, dead. It is up to him and his fellow late-century Germans to fulfill the expectations of the future. Here a huge difference surfaces with the Great Religions, for which the ultimate source of judgment and obligation lies wholly outside place and history. At the same time, Weber makes a further move of the greatest significance: these thousands-of-years-ahead Germans have no social attributes beyond their Germanness: they are neither Junkers nor bourgeois nor proletarians. They long for no Caesars, and they are not even committed to "our highest, our ultimate, terrestrial ideals." The tense here is, so to speak, the future perfect. It is the remote unbornness of these Germans that proclaims their innocence—and the tense that guarantees that they can not be "wrong."

It would be imprudent to dismiss Weber's words as a moment of lunacy in an intellectual career of ordinarily sober conservatism. Less poetically and weirdly phrased, the basic rhetorical trope is every day in use in every national polity. It is, after all, in the name of the unborn that we are asked to work hard, pay taxes, and make other sacrifices—to build national parks, preserve heritages, reduce national debts, clean up environments, and de- fend national frontiers. And if we are Americans, we do not think of these unborn as continuations of the oil billionaires, welfare cheats, irresponsible absentee fathers, philistine bourgeois, racist crazies, and inner-city gangsters who currently (and variously) haunt the American nightmare. These unborn have no attributes but pure Americanness, and this means an innocence, a blamelessness, which allows them to impose obligations on us that we may find difficult to accept from living Americans.

One can observe the same logic at work among the minority of those Americans who, without being draft-age males, strenuously opposed Washington's miserable and bloody adventure in Vietnam. For many of them, when asked the reason for their active opposition, spoke in such terms as "the war makes me feel ashamed of my country." This sentiment resonates with Weber's "shame" at the Germany of 1895. Ashamed before whom? Once again, it is the unborn, perhaps future history. In other words, the shame is the obverse side of that messianic hope that the future will recognize "in our nature the nature of its own ancestors."

The Living

In an illuminating text Joseph Alter considers the recent rise of what might be called a militant Hindu "male celibacy" movement in northern India.[2] Part of the rhetoric surrounding this movement is perfectly familiar to anyone acquainted with the political culture of late-nineteenth- and early-twentieth-century Europe (indeed it also resonate with Weber's anxieties). In state after state we find vociferous complaints about moral decay and sexual profligacy among the country's youth. George Mosse's work has shown, in fine detail, the pervasive "seminal" obsession with the "national" danger represented by masturbation, nocturnal emissions, prostitution, and homosexuality—and, more generally, the threats to the nation's psychosomatic health posed by modern urban life: hedonism, materialism, and neurotic addictions of every kind.[3] There are obvious parallels between the groups Alter studied and Baden-Powell's Boy Scouts and the fin de siècle German Youth Movement—all of which spun around the axes of moral purity, sexual self-control, arduous physical regimens, male solidarity, and nationalism. In both cases, too, these movements drew heavily on local religious traditions of male asceticism. Perhaps the major difference—at least for present purposes—is that in the contemporary north Indian case a religiously derived valorization of semen is elaborately articulated in ways difficult to imagine for late-century Europe, and that "total" celibacy is given a centrality not generally found in Europe after the high medieval era.

Beyond its north Indian Hindu particularity, however, Alter's celibacy movement shows rather clearly one fundamental way in which the goodness/innocence of the nation is more generally established among the living. For the movement is both highly militant and proselytizing, and the object of the sacrifices it demands is, quite characterically, "Mother" India. She serves as the magnet around which a disorderly myriad of young Hindu males form themselves into a beautifully ordered field of force (in every sense). It is she who, metaphorically, makes them all face the same way, toward her, looking neither right nor left nor over their shoulders: close to her, but never joined or merged.

Nothing is more interesting in this regard than the way Alter's subjects remind us of the celibate vocabulary of all nationalisms and the taboos that lurk beneath it. For the mother (motherland) who makes claims on the lives of young males is the woman who gave them all birth and whom they all have in common: she is also, in a direct sense, the woman they can not/must not have, even think of having, sexually. It is her complete inaccessibility that makes any "sibling competition" unimaginable.

Furthermore, we all are aware of the pronominal predilections of nationalism, which likes to speak in a celibate language of "you, brothers and sisters," whose selfless solidarity, whose innocence, depends on a deep, unstated incest taboo. (In this language "husbands" and "wives" are strikingly absent.) And if nationalism often speaks of the nation as if it were a family writ large, it is worth remembering that it is exactly in the family that, in real life, these taboos actually function most powerfully. It is the sphere where father aside inhouse celibacy is de rigueur.[4] Here we see how nationalisms borrow from very old religiously sanctioned conceptions to achieve purposes and command commitments that are very much their modern own.

But there is another innocent site where the goodness of the nation is anchored among the living. We find it elegantly located in Lauren Berlant's brilliant essay "The Theory of Infantile Citizenship."[5] The essay begins by recounting an episode in the young life of the distinguished radical Black American writer Audré Lorde. In 1947, Lorde later recalled, her parents decided to take her and her sister on a national pilgrimage to Washington. (Lorde notes that her parents did not tell the children that the main reason for the trip was to compensate the sister for the fact that as a young Black girl she was not allowed to join the school-organized trip.) But the family found themselves treated as not-real-Americans, in the national capital. They could order an ice cream in a restaurant, but they were not allowed to eat it there. Lorde recalls that at that moment she felt physically nauseated, not least because she had recently written an innocently patriotic poem to the heroes of the Bataan Death March. But Berlant also notes that, at the very same moment, Lorde decided that she would "write to the President, to give the nation another chance not to destroy her desire for it." It is a letter written to an America that, like Weber's Germany, is still unborn. But who else but a little girl would write such a letter to the future perfect?

Berlant continues the essay by analyzing a famous episode of the hugely popular, marvelously satirical TV cartoon series *The Simpsons*, called "Mr. Lisa Goes to Washington"—an obvious parody of the absurdly all-American 1930s patriotic film *Mr. Smith Goes to Washington*. In contrast to her brutishly stupid and greedy father, Homer, and her cynical brother, Bart, little Lisa Simpson really believes in America. The story line has "Mr. Lisa" going to Washington to participate in a children's contest for the best composition on the theme "Why I Love America." Her wide-eyed belief is abruptly shaken when she happens to observe her corrupt and crooked congressman accepting a bribe from a logger with designs on a local nature preserve. But—abracadabra—the FBI appears out of the blue and arrests the congressman, who promptly becomes a born-again Christian. "Mr. Lisa" concludes that, in the end, "the system really works." The cartoon lampoons virtually every national institution and deliberately makes the happy ending completely fairy-tale. (It is as if the "real America" is the ghastly father, the dithering mother, and the bratty son—and Lisa is set quite apart.)

It is instructive that *The Simpsons* is a program viewed happily by millions of Americans, who, it would seem, situate themselves alongside Matt Groening, the satirist-creator: indeed, the American family *is* terminally dysfunctional, and Washington *is* a sink of corruption, hypocrisy, and cynicism. This is why Groening, who shows the only real patriot to be a deluded little blockhead, does not receive death threats from his viewers, but rather is immensely popular. "Mr. Lisa" ensures his ultimate good intentions, his true Americanness. But it is noticeable that it would be almost impossible—today—to substitute an adult male citizen for Mr. Lisa. (As such, "Mr. Smith" gives way, half a century later, only to Forrest Gump, who can be an innocent patriot only because he is mentally retarded.) The innocent little girl serves to guarantee the country's ultimate goodness. Until, of course, the fateful day some years ahead, when, perhaps, she will in the morning become a citizen voter for the first time and in the afternoon call on her abortionist. Till then, she is, nationally speaking, without Original Sin. "Mr. Lisa" stands in for "children" in the worldwide tropes of nationalism, those living members of the nation who are not merely sexually innocent but are also innocent of the rites of adult citizenship and political participation.

The Dead

On East Rock, a spectacular enscarpment towering behind the rundown New England town of New Haven, there is a gigantic monument to the local representatives of the national dead. The four faces of its lower pedestal are inscribed with the names of (presumably) New Haven men who died in four different wars: the emblematic War of Independence from England; the inconclusive skirmishes with the same enemy in 1812; the seedy imperialist adventure against Mexico in 1848; and the traumatic Civil War of 1861–65. The monument treats all these dead as absolutely equivalent—it makes no difference on which face any specific one of them appears. And they are also radically stripped down—one is told nothing about them in any sociological, political, or genealogical sense. No doubt some of them did their share of killing enemies, but they are there as killed, not killers. Death has paid their moral bills and cleared their books.[6] They have, by this process, become innocent, as forefathers and foremothers always end up becoming; they have moved toward an abstract Americanness that matches, in an eerie way, that of the unborn, and in "that good night" are prepared to guarantee the nation's goodness.

One might infer, reflecting on the innocence of the national dead, that they are imagined peacefully in paradise. But here nationalism again parts company with the Great Religions. Heaven harbors no nations, and the dead are no use to nationalism in so remote a sequestration. They seem, therefore, to live on animistically, in a sort of terrestrial penumbra: benign ghosts—perhaps six feet above our heads or just the other side of a neighboring hill. That is why we build monuments to them, even to the Unknown Soldier, and, having done so, do not really know how further to proceed. Unlike saints, they have no efficacy; we can not (usually) pray to them for miracles. And because they are national-collective, we are denied even the old-fashioned intimacy of familial ancestor worship.[7] Perhaps this does not really matter. For, in the end, they have their own strange modern responsibility; helping to ensure that, however momentarily wrong, Our country is really always Right.

Notes

1. This lecture, titled "The National State and Economic Policy," can be found in Keith Tribe, ed., *Reading Weber* (London: Routledge, 1989), 188–220. All the quotations given below are taken from this edition.

2. Joseph S. Alter, "Celibacy, Sexuality, and the Transformation of Gender into Nationalism in North India," paper presented to a conference on "Dimensions of Ethnic and Cultural Nationalism in Asia" held at the University of Wisconsin and Marquette University Center for International Studies, 26–27, February 1993. See also his *The Wrestler's Body: Identity and Ideology in North India* (Berkeley: University of California Press, 1992), esp. chaps. 5–6, 8, and 10.

3. See especially Mosse's *Nationalism and Sexuality: Middle-Class Morality and Sexual Norms in Modern Europe* (Madison: University of Wisconsin Press, 1985).

4. Thus it would be inconceivable for Kohl, Clinton, or Chirac to address the citizens of their countries as "my children." The "father" of a country, where he appears, is usually safely dead.

5. The essay is most easily accessed in Geoff Eley and Ronald Grigor Suny, eds., *Becoming National: A Reader* (New York: Oxford University Press, 1996), 495–508.

6. One has only to imagine the reaction of outrage that would greet the diligent scholar who, having done the necessary meticulous research, proposed to add after each name on the monument the number of enemies he killed.

7. I have dealt in more comparative detail with the question of the national dead, in "Replica, Aura, and Late Nationalist Imaginings," *Qui Parle?* 7 (1993): 1–21. The national hero is never singular; he or she can only exist as such among other national heroes, by whom he or she is always substitutable.

Bibliography

Abercrombie, Nicholas, and Bryan S. Turner. 1978. "The Dominant Ideology Thesis." *British Journal of Sociology* 29 (2): 149–70.

Abu'l-ala Maududi, Maulana. 1939 "Ihya-i din ki jidd o jahd ka sahih tariqa aur ek qabil-i taqlid namuna" [The correct means of struggle for the revival of religion and an example worth imitating]. In Muhammad Manzur Nu'mani. 1980. *Tablighi jama'at, jama'at-i islami aur barelwi hazrat* [The Tabligh Jama'at, the Jama'at-i Islami, and the Barelvi Gentlemen], 19–37. Lucknow: Al-Furqan Book Depot.

Adami, C. 1721. *Naam-lyst der predikanten in de provincie van Stadt Groningen en Ommelanden t' sedert de reductie tot aan 't jaar 1721.* . . . Groningen (3d ed., 1745).

Afigbo, A. E. 1980. "Christian Missions and Secular Authorities in South-eastern Nigeria from Colonial Times." In O. U. Kalu, ed., *The History of Christianity in West Africa*, 187–99. London: Longman.

Aggarwal, Partap C. 1971. *Caste, Religion, and Power: An Indian Case Study.* New Delhi: Shri Ram Centre for Industrial Relations.

Ahmed, Rafiuddin. 1982. *Bengal Muslims: The Quest for Identity, 1876–1906.* Delhi: Oxford University Press.

Altena, Bert. 1996. "Continuïteit of een nieuw begin? Gilden en vakbeweging in Dordrecht, 1798–1872." In M. Bruggeman et al., eds., *Mensen van de nieuwe tijd: Een liber amicorum voor A.Th. van Deursen*, 462–81. Amsterdam: Bakker.

Aldington, Richard. 1929. Death of a Hero (Rpt., London, 1965).

Alter, Joseph S. 1992. *The Wrestler's Body: Identity and Ideology in North India.* Berkeley: University of California Press.

———. 1993. "Celibacy, Sexuality, and the Transformation of Gender into Nationalism in North India." Paper presented to a conference on "Dimensions of Ethnic and Cultural Nationalism in Asia" held at the University of Wisconsin and Marquette University Center for International Studies, 26–27. February.

Ambedkar, Bhimrao Ramji. 1970. *Who Were the Shudras?: How They Came to Be the Fourth Varna in the Indo-Aryan Society.* Bombay: Thacker.

Anderson, Benedict R. 1983. *Imagined Communities: Reflections on the Origin and Spread of Nationalism.* London: Verso (2d ed., 1991; rev. ed., 1995).

———. 1993. "Replica, Aura, and Late Nationalist Imaginings." *Qui Parle?* 7 (1): 1–21.

Anderson, Olive. 1965. "The Reactions of Church and Dissent towards the Crimean War." *Journal of Ecclesiastical History* 16 (2): 209–20.

Ansari, Sarah F. D. 1992. *Sufi Saints and State Power: The "Pirs" of Sind, 1843–1947.* Cambridge: Cambridge University Press.

Arnold, Thomas. 1833. *Principles of Church Reform*, London: Fellowes.

Arnstein, Walter L. 1975. "The Murphy Riots: A Victorian Dilemma." *Victorian Studies* 19 (1): 51–72.

———. 1982. *Protestant versus Catholic in Mid-Victorian England: Mr. Newde-gate and the Nuns.* Columbia: University of Missouri Press.

Asad, Talal. 1993. *Genealogies of Religion: Discipline and Reasons of Power in Christianity and Islam.* Baltimore, Md.: Johns Hopkins University Press.

———. 1994. "Europa contra Islam: De Islam in Europa." *Nexus* 10: 3–17.

———. 1997. "Europe contra Islam: Islam in Europe." *The Muslim World* 87 (3/4): 183–95.

Augustijn, C. 1986. "Kerk en godsdienst 1870–1890." In W. Bakker et al., eds., *De Doleantie van 1886 en haar geschiedenis,* 41–75. Kampen: Kok.

Augustijn, C., J. H. Prins, and H. E. S. Woldring, eds. 1987. *Abraham Kuyper: Zijn volksdeel, zijn invloed.* Delft: Meinema.

Ayalon, A. 1987. "From Fitna to Thawra." *Studia Islamica* 66: 145–74.

Azad, Abu'l Kalam. [1940] 1993. "Presidential Address to the Indian National Congress." In Mushirul Hasan, ed., *India's Partition: Process, Strategy, and Mobilisation,* 59–68. Delhi: Oxford University Press.

Bacchetta, Paola. 1994. "Communal Property/Sexual Property: On Representations of Muslim Women in a Hindu Nationalist Discourse." In Zoya Hasan, ed., *Forging Identities: Gender, Communities, and the State in India,* 188–225. Boulder, Colo.: Westview Press.

Bakker, W., et al., eds. 1984. *De Afscheiding van 1834 en haar geschiedenis.* Kampen: Kok.

Balagangadhara, S. N. 1994. *"The Heathen in His Blindness": Asia, the West, and the Dynamic of Religion.* Leiden: Brill.

Bandyopadhyay, Saileskumar. 1988. *Jinnāh, pākistān: Natun bhābnā.* Calcutta: Mitra and Ghosh.

Banton, Michael, and Jonathan Harwood. 1975. *The Race Concept.* Newton Abbot: David and Charles.

Barkan, Elazar. 1992. *The Retreat of Scientific Racism: Changing Concepts of Race in Britain and the United States between the World Wars.* Cambridge: Cambridge University Press.

Barnett, Marguerite Ross. 1976. *The Politics of Cultural Nationalism in South India.* Princeton, N.J.: Princeton University Press.

Barton, David. 1992. *The Myth of Separation.* Aledo, Tex: Wallbuilder Press.

Bayly, C. A. 1994. "Returning the British to South Asian History: The Limits of Colonial Hegemony." *South Asia* 17 (2): 1–25.

Bayly, Susan. 1995. "Caste and Race in the Colonial Ethnography of India." In Peter Robb, ed., *The Concept of Race in South Asia,* 165–218. Delhi: Oxford University Press.

Bebbington, David W. 1982. *The Nonconformist Conscience.* London: Allen and Unwin.

Beddoe, John. 1865–66. "The Permanence of Racial Types." *Memoirs of the Anthropological Society of London* 2: 37–45.

Bellah, Robert. 1970. "Civil Religion in America." In *Beyond Belief: Essays on Religion in a Post-Traditional World.* New York: Harper and Row.

Berlant, Lauren. 1996. "The Theory of Infantile Citizenship." In Geoff Eley and Ronald Grigor Suny, eds., *Becoming National: A Reader,* 495–508. New York: Oxford University Press.

Bhattacharya, Jogendra Nath. 1896. *Hindu Castes and Sects: An Exposition of the Origin of the Hindu Caste System and the Bearing of the Sects towards Each Other and towards Other Religious Systems.* Calcutta: Thacker, Spink.

Binfield, Clyde. 1990. " 'We Claim Our Part in the Great Inheritance': The Message of Four Congregational Buildings." In Keith Robbins, ed., *Protestant Evangelicalism*, 201–24. Oxford: Blackwell.

Biswas, Kalipada. 1966. *Yukta bāṅlār śeṣ adhyāy.* Calcutta: Orient Book Company.

Blanch, Michael. 1980. "English Society and the War." In P. Warwick, ed., *The South African War: The Anglo-Boer War, 1899–1902,* 210–38. London: Longman.

Blom, J. C. H., and C. J. Misset. 1989. " 'Een onvervalschte Nederlandsche geest': Enkele historiografische kantekeningen bij het concept van een nationaal-gereformeerde richting." In: E. K. Grootes and J. den Haan, eds., *Geschiedenis, godsdienst, letterkunde: Opstellen aangeboden aan dr. S.B.J. Zilverberg ter gelegenheid van zijn afscheid van de Universiteit van Amsterdam,* 221–32. Roden: Nehalennia.

Blumenberg, Hans. [1973–76] 1983. *The Legitimacy of the Modern Age.* Cambridge: MIT Press.

Bolt, Christine. 1971. *Victorian Attitudes to Race.* London: Routledge and Kegan Paul.

Bornewasser, J. A. 1975. "Mythical Aspects of Dutch Anti-Catholicism in the Nineteenth Century." In J. S. Bromley and E. H. Kossmann, eds., *Britain and the Netherlands.* Vol. 5, *Some Political Mythologies: Papers Delivered to the Fifth Anglo-Dutch Historical Conference,* 184–206. Den Haag: Nijhoff.

———. 1982. "De Nederlandse katholieken en hun negentiende-eeuwse vaderland." *Tijdschrift voor Geschiedenis* 95 (4): 577–604.

Bose, Sugata. 1986. *Agrarian Bengal: Economy, Social Structure, and Politics, 1919–1947.* Cambridge: Cambridge University Press.

Bradley, Joseph M. 1995. *Ethnic and Religious Identity in Modern Scotland: Culture, Politics, and Football.* Aldershot: Avebury.

Brandt, Geeraert. 1671–1704. *Historie der Reformatie en andre kerkelyke geschiedenissen, in en ontrent de Nederlanden.* 4 vols. Rotterdam: Bos.

Breen, J. C. 1925. "Gereformeerde populaire historiografie in de zeventiende en achttiende eeuw." In *Christendom en Historie,* 1: 213–42. Amsterdam: Holland.

Brown, Callum G. 1996. "Religion and National Identity in Scotland since the Union of 1707." In Ingmar Brohed, ed., *Church and People in England and Scandinavia,* 287–94. Lund: Gleerup.

Brown, Stewart J. 1991. " 'Outside the Covenant': The Scottish Presbyterian Churches and Irish Immigration." *Innes Review* 42 (1): 19–45.

———. 1993. "The Campaign for the Christian Commonwealth in Scotland, 1919–1939." In W. M. Jacob and Nigel Yates, eds., *Crown and Mitre: Religion and Society in Northern Europe since the Reformation,* 203–22. Woodbridge: Boydell Press.

Brown, Stewart J., and Michael Fry, eds. 1993. *Scotland in the Age of Disruption.* Edinburgh: Edinburgh University Press.

Brunner, Otto, Werner Conze, and Reinhart Koselleck, eds. 1972–97. *Geschicht-liche Grundbegriffe: Historisches Lexicon zur politisch-sozialen Sprache in Deutschland.* 8 Vols. Stuttgart: Klett.

Campbell, George. [1865]. *Ethnology of India.* N. p.

Carey, William. 1792. *An Enquiry into the Obligations of Christians to Use Means for the Conversion of the Heathens.* Leicester: Ann Ireland.

Casanova, José. 1994. *Public Religions in the Modern World.* Chicago: University of Chicago Press.

Chakrabarty, Dipesh 1992. "Postcoloniality and the Artifice of History: Who Speaks for 'India's' Pasts." *Representations* 37: 1–26.

Chancellor, V. E. 1970. *History for Their Masters: Opinion in the English History Textbook, 1800–1914.* Bath: Adams and Dart.

Chatterjee, Partha. 1993. *The Nation and Its Fragments: Colonial and Postcolonial Histories.* Princeton, N.J.: Princeton University Press.

Chatterji, Joya. 1995. *Bengal Divided: Hindu Communalism and Partition, 1932–1947.* Cambridge: Cambridge University Press.

Chattopadhyay, Birendranath. 1947. *Ḍiliriyām (sāmpratik hāṅgāmā).* Alamba-zar: Databya Bibhag.

Claessen, Constance. 1993. *Worlds of Sense: Exploring the Senses in History and across Cultures.* London: Routledge.

Cohn, Bernard. 1987. *An Anthropologist among the Historians and Other Essays.* Delhi: Oxford University Press.

Cohn, Bernard, and Nicholas Dirks. 1988. "Beyond the Fringe: The Nation State, Colonialism, and the Technologies of Power." *Journal of Historical Sociology* 1 (2): 224–30.

Coleridge, Samuel Taylor. 1830. *On the Constitution of the Church and State.* London: Hurst, Chance.

Colley, Linda. 1992. *Britons: Forging the Nation, 1707–1837.* New Haven, Conn.: Yale University Press (2d ed., London: Pimlico, 1994).

Colls, Robert, and Philip Dodd, eds. 1986. *Englishness: Politics and Culture, 1880–1920.* London: Croom Helm.

Connerton, Paul. 1989. *How Societies Remember.* Cambridge: Cambridge University Press.

Connolly, William. 1995. *The Ethos of Pluralism.* Minneapolis: University of Minnesota Press.

Cottrell, Stella. 1989. "The Devil on Two Sticks: Franco-phobia in 1803." In Raphael Samuel, ed., *Patriotism: The Making and Unmaking of British National Identity,* London: Routledge. 1: 259–74.

Cox, Jeffrey. 1982. *The English Churches in a Secular Society: Lambeth, 1870–1930.* Oxford: Oxford University Press.

Currie, Robert, Alan Gilbert, and Lee Horsley. 1977. *Churches and Churchgoers: Patterns of Church Growth in the British Isles since 1700.* Oxford: Clarendon Press.

Curtis, L. Perry. 1971. *Apes and Angels: The Irishman in Victorian Caricature.* Newton Abbot: David and Charles.

Daalder, Hans. 1966. "The Netherlands: Opposition in a Segmented Society." In Robert A. Dahl, ed., *Political Oppositions in Western Democracies*, 188–236. New Haven, Conn.: n.p.

Das, Suranjan. 1991. *Communal Riots in Bengal, 1905–1947*. Delhi: Oxford University Press.

———. 1750. *Naam-lyst der predikanten, die in de gemeenten, gehoorende onder de IX classen van het Geldersche Synode zedert de Hervorming der kerken tot den jaare 1750 het heilig Evangelium bediend hebben*. Leiden: Van Damme.

Devji, Faisal. 1994. *Muslim Nationalism: Founding Identity in Colonial India*. Chicago: University of Chicago, Department of History.

Dikötter, Frans. 1992. *The Discourse of Race in Modern China*. London: Hurst.

Dirks, Nicholas. 1989. "The Invention of Caste." *Social Analysis* 25 (1): 42–52.

———. 1992. "Castes of Mind." *Representations* 37: 56–78.

———. 1995. "The Conversion of Caste: Location, Translation, and Appropriation." In Peter van der Veer, ed., *Conversion to Modernities: The Globalization of Christianity*, 115–37. New York: Routledge.

Duara, Prasenjit. 1995. *Rescuing History from the Nation: Questioning Narratives of Modern China*. Chicago: University of Chicago Press.

Duke, Alastair. 1990. "The Ambivalent Face of Calvinism in the Netherlands." In *Reformation and Revolt in the Low Countries*, 269–94. London: Hambledon Press.

Dumont, Louis. 1979. *Homo Hierarchicus: Essai sur le système des castes*. 3d ed. Paris: Gallimard.

Eaton, Richard M. 1994. *The Rise of Islam amd the Bengal Frontier, 1204–1760*. Delhi: Oxford University Press.

Eley, Geoff. 1992. "Nations, Publics, and Political Cultures: Placing Habermas in the Nineteenth Century." In Craig Calhoun, ed., *Habermas and the Public Sphere*, 289–339. Cambridge: MIT Press.

Ellemers, J. E. 1984. "Pillarization as a Process of Modernization." *Acta Politica* 19 (1): 129–44.

Elliot, Walter. 1868–69. "On the Characteristics of the Population of Central and Southern India." *Journal of the Ethnological Society of London* 1: 94–128.

Engineer, Asghar Ali, ed. 1987. *The Shah Bano Controversy*. London: Sangam.

Ericksen, Robert P. 1985. *Theologians under Hitler: Gerhard Kittel, Paul Althaus, and Emmanuel Hirsch*. New Haven, Conn.: Yale University Press.

Feldman, David. 1994. *Englishmen and Jews: Social Relations and Political Culture, 1840–1914*. New Haven, Conn.: Yale University Press.

Fielding, Steven. 1993. *Class and Ethnicity: Irish Catholics in England, 1880–1939*. Buckingham: Open University Press.

Fields, Karen. 1982. "Christian Missionaries as Anticolonial Militants." *Theory and Society* 11 (1): 95–108.

Firozpuri, Miyanji Muhammad 'Isa. N.d. *Tabligh ka maqami kam* [The local work of Tabligh]. Delhi: Rabbani Buk Depo.

Forbes, James. 1813. *Oriental Memoirs: Selected and Abridged from a Series of Familiar Letters Written during Seventeen Years' Residence in India, Including Observations on Parts of Africa and South America, and a Narrative of Occurrences in Four India Voyages*. 4 Vols. London.

Ford, Christopher. 1991. "Pastors and Polemicists: The Character of Popular Anglicanism in South-east Lancashire, 1847–1914." Ph.D. diss., University of Leeds.

Foucault, Michel. 1991. "Governmentality." In Graham Burchell, Colin Gordon, and Peter Miller, eds., *The Foucault Effect*, 87–104. Chicago: University of Chicago Press, 87–104.

Fris, A. 1991. *Inventaris van de archieven behorende tot het "Oud Synodaal Archief" van de Nederlandse Hervormde Kerk, 1566–1816*. The Hague: Stichting Archiefpublicaties.

Fruytier, Jacob. 1715. *Sions worstelingen, of historische samenspraken over de verscheide en zeer bittere wederwaerdigheden van Christus' kerke, met openbare en verborgen vyanden*. 3 vols. Rotterdam: Van Doesburg.

Gallagher, Tom. 1987. *Glasgow, the Uneasy Peace: Religious Tension in Modern Scotland*. Manchester: Manchester University Press.

Gangopadhyay, Chunilal. [1952?] *Bhāṅgan diner kathāmālā*. N.p.

Gay, Peter. 1984. *The Education of the Senses*. New York: Oxford University Press.

Geertz, Clifford. 1973. *The Interpretation of Cultures: Selected Essays*. New York: Basic Books.

———. 1983. *Local Knowledge: Further Essays in Interpretive Anthropology*. New York: Basic Books.

Gellner, Ernest. 1983. *Nations and Nationalism*. Oxford: Blackwell.

Gill, Robin. 1993. *The Myth of the Empty Church*. London: SPCK.

Gilley, Sheridan. 1978. "English Attitudes to the Irish in England." In Colin Holmes, ed., *Immigrants and Minorities in British Society*, 81–110. London: Allen and Unwin.

Gilley, Sheridan, and W. J. Sheils, eds. 1994. *A History of Religion in Britain: Practice and Belief from Pre-Roman Times to the Present*. Oxford: Blackwell.

Gilmartin, David. 1988. *Empire and Islam: Punjab and the Making of Pakistan*. Berkeley: University of California Press.

Gladstone, William E. 1838. *The State in Its Relations with the Church*. London: Murray.

Glasius, B. 1842–44. *Geschiedenis der Christelijke kerk en godsdienst in Nederland, na het vestigen der Hervorming tot den troonsafstand van koning Willem I*. 3 Vols. Amsterdam: Van der Hey.

Gopal, Sarvepalli, ed. 1991. *Anatomy of a Confrontation: The Babri Masjid-Ramjanmabhumi Issue*. New Delhi: Penguin Books India.

Gordon, Leonard A. 1990. *Brothers against the Raj: A Biography of Sarat and Subhas Chandra Bose*. New Delhi: Penguin Books India.

Grijzenhout, Frans. 1989. *Feesten voor het Vaderland: Patriotse en Bataafse feesten 1780–1806*. Zwolle: Waanders.

Grillo, Ralph D., ed. 1980. *"Nation" and "State" in Europe: Anthropological Perspectives*. London: Academic Press.

Groot, Frans. 1992. *Roomsen, rechtzinnigen en nieuwlichters: Verzuiling in een Hollandse plattelandsgemeente, 1850–1930*. Hilversum: Verloren.

Groot, Frans. 1995. "De strijd rond Alva's bril: Papen en geuzen bij de herdenking van de inname van Den Briel, 1572–1872." *Bijdragen en mededelingen betreffende de geschiedenis der Nederlanden* 110 (2): 161–81.

Guha, Ranajit. 1993. *A Construction of Humanism in Colonial India: The Wertheim Lecture.* Amsterdam: CASA.

Habermas, Jürgen. 1989. *The Structural Transformation of the Public Sphere: An Inquiry into a Category of Bourgeois Society.* Cambridge: MIT Press.

Haim, S. G., ed. 1962. *Arab Nationalism: An Anthology.* Berkeley: University of California Press.

Halbfass, Wilhelm. 1988. *India and Europe: An Essay in Understanding.* Albany: SUNY Press.

Halévy, Élie. 1971. *The Birth of Methodism in England.* Trans. and ed. Bernard Semmel. Chicago: University of Chicago Press.

Hall, John. 1993. "Nationalisms: Classified and Explained," *Daedalus* 122 (3): 1–29.

Hamilton, Walter. 1828. *The East-India Gazetteer.* 2d ed. 2 Vols. London.

Handelman, Don. 1990. *Models and Mirrors: Towards an Anthropology of Public Events.* Cambridge: Cambridge University Press.

Hanham, H. J. 1973. "Religion and Nationality in the Mid-Victorian Army." In M. R. D. Foot, ed., *War and Society,* 159–82. London: Paul Elek.

Haq, M. Anwarul. 1972. *The Faith Movement of Maulana Muhammad Ilyas.* London: Allen and Unwin.

Hardacre, Helen. 1991. *Shinto and the State, 1868–1988.* Princeton, N.J.: Princeton University Press.

Hardy, Peter. 1971. *Partners in Freedom—and True Muslims: The Political Thought of Some Muslim Scholars in British India, 1912–1947.* Lund: Studentlitteratur.

———. 1972. *The Muslims of British India.* Cambridge: Cambridge University Press.

Harootunian, Harry. 1990. "Disciplinizing Native Knowledge and Producing Place." In Thomas Rimer, ed., *Culture and Identity,* 111–13. Princeton, N.J.: Princeton University Press.

———. 1994. "Kindai Nihon no keikin ni okeru kokugaku to sono kioku." In Nitta Yoshiyuki et al., eds., *Datsu sei-o no shiso,* Iwanami koza *Gendai Shiso* 15, 169–90. Tokyo: Iwanami shoten.

———. 1998. "Figuring the Folk." In Stephen Vlastos, ed., *Mirrors of Modernity.* Berkeley: University of California Press.

Harrisson, Mrs. John W. 1890. *A. M. Mackay, Pioneer Missionary of the Church Missionary Society to Uganda, by His Sister.* London: Hodder and Stoughton

Hasan, Mushirul, ed. 1992. *Islam and Indian Nationalism: Reflections on Abul Kalam Azad.* Delhi: Manohar.

———. 1993. *India's Partition: Process, Strategy, and Mobilization.* Delhi: Oxford University Press.

Hashmi, Taj ul-Islam. 1992. *Pakistan as a Peasant Utopia: The Communalization of Class Politics in East Bengal, 1920–1947.* Boulder, Colo.: Westview Press.

Hastings, Adrian. 1986. *A History of English Christianity, 1920–1985.* London: Collins.

Hegel, G. W. F. 1991. *The Philosophy of History.* Trans. J. Sibree. Buffalo, N.Y.: Prometheus Books.

Helmstadter, Richard, and Paul Phillips, eds. 1985. *Religion in Victorian Society: A Sourcebook of Documents.* Lanham, Md.: University Press of America.

Hempton, David. 1996. *Religion and Political Culture in Britain and Ireland, from the Glorious Revolution to the Decline of Empire.* Cambridge: Cambridge University Press.

Hilliard, David. 1981–82. "Unenglish and Unmanly: Anglo-Catholicism and Homosexuality." *Victorian Studies* 25 (2): 181–210.

Hilton, Boyd. 1988. *The Age of Atonement: The Influence of Evangelicalism on Social and Economic Thought, 1795–1865.* Oxford: Clarendon Press.

Hiromatsu Wataru. 1980. *"Kindai no chokoku" ron.* Tokyo: Kodansha.

Hobsbawm, Eric J. 1989. "Mass-Producing Traditions: Europe, 1870–1914." In Eric J. Hobsbawm and Terence Ranger, eds., *The Invention of Tradition,* 263–307. Cambridge: Cambridge University Press.

———. 1990. *Nations and Nationalism since 1780: Programme, Myth, Reality.* Cambridge: Cambridge University Press.

Hofdijk, W. J. 1873. *Brielles gedenkdag op Neêrlands derde jubilee.* Brielle: n.p.

Holtom, D. C. 1943. *Modern Japan and Shinto Nationalism: A Study of Present-Day Trends in Japanese Religions.* Chicago: University of Chicago Press.

Honey, J. R. de S. 1977. *Tom Brown's Universe: The Development of the Victorian Public School.* London: Millington.

Hoover, A. J. 1989. *God, Germany, and Britain in the Great War: A Study in Clerical Nationalism.* New York: Praeger.

Humphries, Stephen. 1979. " 'Hurrah for England': Schooling and the Working Class in Bristol, 1870–1914." *Southern History* 1 (2): 171–207.

Hunt, James. 1863–64. "On the Negro's Place in Nature," *Memoirs of the Anthropological Society of London:* 1:1–63.

Hunter, W. W. 1876. *The Indian Musalmans.* 3d ed. London.

———. 1897. *Annals of Rural Bengal.* 7th ed. London: Smith and Elder.

Husain, Majdi Ahmad. 1991. "al-Mu'tamar ash-sha'bi al-'arabi al-islami: al-Fikra, al-mumarasa, ath-thamara." *ash-Sha'b,* 7 May 1991.

Hutchison, William R., and Hartmut Lehmann, eds. 1994. *Many Are Chosen: Divine Election and Western Nationalism.* Minneapolis, Minn.: Fortress Press.

Huxley, Julian. 1941. *Religion without Revelation.* Abridged ed. London: Watts.

Iguchi Kazuki. 1981. "Yasukuni jinjasha mondai no 'ronri.' " In Yamaguchi Keiji and Matsuo Soichi, eds., *Sengoshi to hando ideorogi,* 118–41. Tokyo: Shin Nihon suppansha.

Ihtishamu'l-Hasan Kandhalavi, Maulana. 1939. "Muslim Degeneracy and Its Only Remedy" [Musalmanon ki maujuda pasti ka wahid 'ilaj]. In Muhammad Zachariyya, ed., *Teachings of Islam: Tablighi Nisab No.1,* pt. 10. Delhi: n.p.

Inden, L. Ronald. 1990. *Imagining India.* Oxford: Blackwell.

Ivy, Marilyn. 1995. *Discourses of the Vanishing: Modernity, Phantasm, Japan.* Chicago: University of Chicago Press.

Jacob, Margaret C. 1992a. *Living the Enlightenment: Freemasonry and Politics in Eighteenth-Century Europe.* New York: Oxford University Press.

———. 1992b. "Private Beliefs in Public Temples: The New Religiosity of the Eighteenth Century." *Social Research* 59 (1): 59–84.

Jacob, Margaret C., and Wijnand W. Mijnhardt, eds. 1992. *The Dutch Republic in the Eighteenth Century: Decline, Enlightenment, and Revolution.* Ithaca, N. Y.: Cornell University Press.

Jaffrelot, Christophe. 1995. "The Ideas of the Hindu Race in the Writings of Hindu Nationalist Ideologues in the 1920s and 1930s." In Peter Robb, ed., *The Concept of Race in South Asia*, 327–54. Delhi: Oxford University Press.

Jalal, Ayesha. 1985. *The Sole Spokesman: Jinnah, the Muslim League, and the Demand for Pakistan.* Cambridge: Cambridge University Press.

Jinja Honcho, eds. 1956. *Jinja honcho junenshi.* Tokyo: Jonja Shinposha.

Jinnah, Muhammad Ali. 1968. *Speeches and Writings of Mr. Jinnah* Ed. Jamil-ud-din Ahamd. 2 vols. Lahore: Sh Mohammad Ashraf.

Jones, Kenneth W. 1976. *Arya Dharm: Hindu Consciousness in Nineteenth-Century Punjab.* Berkeley: University of California Press.

Juergensmeyer, Mark. 1982. *Religion as Social Vision: The Movement against Untouchability in Twentieth-Century Punjab.* Berkeley: University of California Press.

Kabir, Humayun. 1943. *Muslim Politics, 1909–1942.* Calcutta: Gupta, Rahman and Gupta.

Kaiser, Gerhard. 1961. *Pietismus und Patriotismus im literarischen Deutschland: Ein Beitrag zum Problem der Säkularisation.* Wiesbaden: Steiner.

Kaul, Shiv Kishan. 1937. *Wake Up Hindus: A Plea for Mass Religion, Aryanism.* Lahore: Kaul.

Keddie, Nikki R. 1982. "Islamic Revival as Third Worldism." In J. P. Digard, ed., *Le cuisinier et le philosophe: Hommage à Maxime Rodinson*, 275–82. Paris: Maisonneuve et Larose.

Kiernan, V. G. 1952. "Evangelicalism and the French Revolution." *Past & Present* 1 (1): 44–56.

Knippenberg, Hans. 1986. *De deelname aan het lager onderwijs in Nederland gedurende de negentiende eeuw: Een analyse van de landelijke ontwikkelingen en van de regionale verschillen.* Amsterdam: KNAG/ISG.

Knox, Robert. 1863. "Ethnological Inquiries and Observations." *Anthropological Review* 1: 246–63.

Kopf, David. 1979. *The Brahmo Samaj and the Shaping of the Modern Indian Mind.* Princeton, N. J.: Princeton University Press.

Koss, Stephen. 1973. *The Pro-Boers: The Anatomy of an Antiwar Movement.* Chicago: University of Chicago Press.

Kruyt, J. P., and W. Goddijn. 1962. "Verzuiling en ontzuiling als sociologisch proces." In A. N. J. den Hollander et al., eds., *Drift en Koers: Een halve eeuw sociale verandering in Nederland.* Assen: 227–63. Van Gorcum.

Kuper, Adam. 1988. *The Invention of Primitive Society: Transformations of an Illusion.* London: Routledge.

Lawrence, Bruce. 1989. *Defenders of God: The Fundamentalist Revolt against the Modern Age.* San Francisco: Harper and Row.

Lefort, Claude. 1988. "The Permanence of the Theologico-Political." In *Democracy and Political Theory.* Minneapolis: University of Minnesota Press.

Lehmann, Hartmut. 1996. *Religion und Religiosität in der Neuzeit: Historische Beiträge*. Göttingen: Vandenhoeck und Ruprecht.

Lehmann, Hartmut, and Günther Roth, eds. 1994. *Weber's "Protestant Ethic": Origins, Evidence, Contexts*. New York: Cambridge University Press.

Leopold, Joan. 1974. "British Applications of the Aryan Theory of Race to India." *English Historical Review* 89 (352): 578–603.

Lijphart, A. 1968. *Verzuiling, pacificatie en kentering in de Nederlandse politiek*. Assen: De Bussy.

Lindeboom, J. 1956. "Classicale wetboeken: Een bijdrage tot de kennis van het kerkelijke leven in de achttiende eeuw." *Nederlands Archief voor Kerkgeschiedenis* 41 (1): 65–95.

Lokhandwalla, S. T., ed. 1971. *India and Contemporary Islam: Proceedings of a Seminar*. Simla: Indian Institute of Advanced Study.

Luciani, Giacomo, ed. 1990. *The Arab State*. London: Routledge.

Ludden, David. 1994. "History outside Civilization and the Mobility of South Asia." *South Asia* 17 (1): 1–23.

MacAloon, J. J. 1982. "Sociation and Sociability in Political Celebrations." In Victor Turner, ed., *Celebration: Studies in Festivity and Ritual*, 255–71. Washington, D.C.: Smithsonian Institution Press.

MacDougall, Hugh A. 1982. *Racial Myth in English History: Trojans, Teutons, and Anglo-Saxons*. Montreal: Harvest House.

MacKenzie, John M. 1984. *Propaganda and Empire: The Manipulation of British Public Opinion, 1880–1960*. Manchester: Manchester University Press.

MacKenzie, John M., ed. 1986. *Imperialism and Popular Culture*. Manchester: Manchester University Press.

———. 1992. *Popular Imperialism and the Military, 1850–1950*. Manchester: Manchester University Press.

MacLaren, A. Allen. 1974. *Religion and Social Class: The Disruption Years in Aberdeen*. London: Routledge and Kegan Paul.

Madan, T. N. 1987. "Secularism in Its Place." *Journal of Asian Studies* 46 (4): 747–59.

Madani, Sayyid Husain Ahmad. 1990. "Maslah-yi fitna-yi qaumiyyat: 'Allama iqbal ka i'tiraz aur hazrat maulana madani rahmat allah ka jawab" [The problem of the dispute over "Qaumi yat" (nationalism): The objective of 'Allama Iqbal and the answer of the Hazrat Maulana Madani, on inborn be peace]. In Ahmad Salim, ed., *Khutbat-i madani* [Sermons of Madani], 169–77. Lahore: Nigarishat.

Mandal, Jagadischandra. 1977. *Baṅga-bhaṅga*. Calcutta: Mahapran Publishing Society.

Mangan, J. A. 1981. *Athleticism and the Victorian and Edwardian Public School*. Cambridge: Cambridge University Press.

Mani, Lata. 1990. "Contentious Traditions: The Debate on *Sati* in Colonial India." In Kumkum Sangari and Sudesh Vaid, eds., *Recasting Women: Essays in Colonial History*, 88–126. New Brunswick, N. J.: Rutgers University Press.

Marlowe, John. 1976. *Milner, Apostle of Empire: A Life of Alfred George, the Right Honourable Viscount Milner of St James's and Cape Town, KG, GCB, GCMG, 1854–1925*. London: Hamilton.

Marsden, George M. 1980. *Fundamentalism and American Culture: The Shaping of Twentieth-Century Evangelicalism, 1870–1925.* Oxford: Oxford University Press.

Marty, Martin E., and R. Scott Appleby, eds. 1991–95. *The Fundamentalism Project.* 5 vols. Chicago: University of Chicago Press.

Masselos, J. C. 1974. *Towards Nationalism: Group Affiliations and the Politics of Public Associations in Nineteenth-Century Western India.* Bombay: Popular Prakashan.

Mauss, Marcel. 1969. "La nation." In *Oeuvres*, 3: 573–639. Paris: Les Editions de Minuit.

Mayaram, Shail. 1997. *Resisting Regimes: Myth, Memory, and the Shaping of Muslim Identity.* Delhi: Oxford University Press.

McLeod, Hugh. 1974. *Class and Religion in the Late Victorian City.* London: Croom Helm.

———. 1981. *Religion and the People of Western Europe, 1789–1970.* Oxford: Oxford University Press.

———. 1986. "New Perspectives on Victorian Working Class Religion: The Oral Evidence." *Oral History Journal* 14 (1): 31–49.

Metcalf, Barbara D. 1977. "Reflections on Iqbal's Mosque." *Journal of South Asian and Middle Eastern Studies* 1 (2): 68–74.

———. 1982. *Islamic Revival in British India: Deoband, 1860–1900.* Princeton, N. J.: Princeton University Press.

———. 1993. "Living Hadith in the Tablighi Jamaʿat." *Journal of Asian Studies* 52 (3): 584–608.

———. 1994. " 'Remaking Ourselves': Islamic Self-Fashioning in a Global Movement of Spiritual Renewal." In Martin Marty and Scott Appleby, eds., *Accounting for Fundamentalisms: The Dynamic Character of Movements,* 706–25. Chicago: University of Chicago Press.

———. 1995. "Presidential Address: Too Little and Too Much: Reflections on Muslims in the History of India." *Journal of Asian Studies* 54 (4): 1–17.

Metcalf, Thomas R. 1994. *Ideologies of the Raj.* Cambridge: Cambridge University Press.

Mews, Stuart. 1983. "The Sword of the Spirit: A Catholic Cultural Crusade of 1940." In W. J. Sheils, ed., *The Church and War.* Studies in Church History, vol. 20, 409–30. Oxford: Blackwell.

Mews, Stuart, ed. 1982. *Religion and National Identity.* Studies in Church History, vol. 18. Oxford: Blackwell.

Milbank, John. 1990. *Theology and Social Theory.* Oxford: Blackwell.

Mill, James. 1858. *History of British India.* 10 vols. London 5th ed.

Minault, Gail. 1982. *The Khilafat Movement: Religious Symbolism and Political Mobilization in India.* New York: Columbia University Press.

Mines, Mattison. 1975. "Islamisation and Muslim Ethnicity in South India." In Dietmar Rothermund, ed., *Islam in Southern Asia: A Survey of Current Research,* 55–57. Wiesbaden: Steiner.

Mitchell, Timothy. 1991. "The Limits of the State: Beyond Statist Approaches and Their Critics." *American Political Science Review* 85 (1): 77–97.

Miyaji Masahito. 1981. "Handoka ni okeru Yasukuni mondai chi-i." In Yama-guchi Keiji and Matsuo Soichi, eds., *Sengoshi to hando ideorogi*. 91–117. Tokyo: Shin Nihon suppansha.

Mohammad Ali. 1930 "Speech to the Plenary Session, November 19." In *The Round Table Conference: India's Demand for Dominion Status. Speeches by the King, the Premier, the British Party Leaders and the Representatives of the Princes and People of India*, 35–50. Madras: Natesan.

Moodie, T. Dunbar. 1975. *The Rise of Afrikanerdom: Power, Apartheid, and the Afrikaner Civil Religion*. Berkeley: University of California Press.

Moonen, Arnold. 1709. *Naamketen der predikanten, die van de Hervorming tot aen 1709 in de gemeenten van het Overijss: Synode het Evangelium bedient hebben*. Deventer.

Morris, Charles. 1888. *The Aryan Race: Its Origins and Its Achievements*. Chicago: Griggs.

Morrison, C. 1984. "Three Styles of Imperial Ethnography." *Knowledge and Society* 5: 141–69.

Mosse, George L. 1985. *Nationalism and Sexuality: Middle-Class Morality and Sexual Norms in Modern Europe*. Madison: University of Wisconsin Press.

Muhammad Zakariyya Kandhalawi, Maulana. 1928–40. *Tablighi nisab* [The Tabligh Curriculum]. Lahore: Malik Brothers.

———. 1976. *Teachings of Islam* [Translation of Tablighi nisab]. New Delhi: Dini Book Dipot.

Mukarram, Ahmed. 1991. "The Tabligh Movement and Mawlana Abul Hasan Ali Nadwi: Guidance-Oriented Strand of Contemporary Islamic Thought." Typescript Oxford University.

Mukhopadhyay, Bhudeb. 1969. "Svapnalabdha bhāratbarṣer itihās.'" In Prama-thanath Bisi, ed., *Bhūdeb racanā sambhār*. 341–74, Calcutta: Mitra and Ghosh.

Murakami Shigeyoshi. 1971. *Kokka Shinto*. Tokyo: Iwanami shoten.

Murray, B. 1984. *The Old Firm: Sectarianism, Sport, and Society in Scotland*. Edinburgh: Edinburgh University Press.

Murshid, Tazeen M. 1995. *The Sacred and the Secular: Bengal Muslim Discourses, 1871–1977*. Calcutta: Oxford University Press.

Nadwi, S. Abul Hasan Ali. 1983. *Life and Mission of Maulana Mohammad Ilyas*. Lucknow: Academy of Islamic Research and Publications.

Nadwi, S. Abul Hasan Ali, ed. 1964. *Hazrat maulana muhammad ilyas aur un ki dini da'wat* [Hazrat Maulana Muhammad Ilyas and his invitation to religion]. Lucknow: Tanwir Press.

Nairn, Tom. 1977. *The Break Up of Britain*. London: New Left Books.

Nakajima Missenko. 1981. "Seiji hando ni okeru shukyo kyodan no yakuwari." In Yamaguchi Keiji and Matsuo Soichi, eds., *Sengoshi to hando ideorogi*, 142–82. Tokyo: Shin Nihon suppansha.

Nauta, C. 1757. *Compendium der kerkelijke wetten*. Leeuwarden: Van Tongerlo.

Nauta, D. 1970. "De reformatie in Nederland in de historiografie." *Serta Historica* 2 (1): 44–71.

Neal, Frank. 1987. *Sectarian Violence: The Liverpool Experience, 1819–1914*. Manchester: Manchester University Press.

Nehru, Jawaharlal. 1956. *The Discovery of India*. New York: Anchor Books.

Newman, John Henry. 1864. *Apologia Pro Vita Sua*. London: Longman.

Obeyesekere, Gananath. 1981. *Medusa's Hair: An Essay on Personal Symbols and Religious Experience*. Chicago: University of Chicago Press.

Oddie, Geoffrey A. 1991. *Hindu and Christian and South-East India*. London: Curzon Press.

Oe Shinobu. 1984. *Yasukuni Jinja*. Tokyo: Iwanami shoten.

O'Hanlon, Rosalind. 1985. *Caste, Conflict, and Ideology: Mahatma Jotirao Phule and Low Caste Protest in Nineteenth-Century Western India*. Cambridge: Cambridge University Press.

———. 1992. "Cultures of Rule, Communities of Resistance." *Social Analysis* 28: 94–114.

Ovington, J. 1696. *A Voyage to Suratt, in the Year 1689*. London.

Pandey, Gyanendra. 1990. "The Bigoted Julaha." In *The Construction of Communalism in Colonial North India*, 66–108. Delhi: Oxford University Press.

Pant, Rashmi. 1987. "The Cognitive Status of Caste in Colonial Ethnography." *Indian Economic and Social History Review* 24 (2): 145–62.

Parsons, Gerald, ed. 1988. *Religion in Victorian Britain. 4 vols. Manchester: Manchester University Press*.

Paz, D. G. 1992. *Popular Anti-Catholicism in Mid-Victorian England*. Stanford, Calif.: Stanford University Press.

Pick, Daniel. 1989. *Faces of Degeneration: A European Disorder, c.1848–c.1918*. Cambridge: Cambridge University Press.

Pike, L. Owen. 1865–66. "On the Psychical Characteristics of the English People." *Memoirs of the Anthropological Society of London* 2: 153–88.

Pinney, C. 1990. "Colonial Anthropology in the 'Laboratory of Mankind.' " In C. Bayly. ed., *The Raj: India and the British, 1600–1947*, 252–63. London: National Portrait Gallery Publications.

Pinson, Koppel S. 1934. *Pietism as a Factor in the Rise of German Nationalism*. New York: Columbia University Press.

Poliakov, Léon. 1974. *The Aryan Myth: A History of Racist and Nationalist Ideas in Europe*. New York: Basic Books.

Poovey, Mary. 1995. *Making a Social Body: British Cultural Formation*. Chicago: University of Chicago Press.

Porter, Andrew. 1992. "Religion and Empire: British Expansion in the Long Nineteenth Century." *Journal of Imperial and Commonwealth History* 20 (3): 370–93.

Prakash, Gyan. 1990. "Writing Post-Orientalist Histories of the Third World: Perspectives from Indian Historiography." *Comparative Studies in Society and History* 32 (2): 383–408.

Price Hughes, Dorothea. 1904. *The Life of Hugh Price Hughes, by His Daughter*. London: Hodder and Stoughton.

Qadiri, Muhammad Ayyub. 1971. *Tablighi Jamaʿat ka tarikhi jaʾiza* [A historical survey of the Tablighi Jamaʿat]. Karachi: Maktaba Muʿawiya.

Rae, John. 1970. *Conscience and Politics: The British Government and the Conscientious Objector to Military Service, 1916–1919*. London: Oxford University Press.

Raedts, Peter (1992). "Katholieken op zoek naar een Nederlandse identiteit, 1814–1898." *Bijdragen en Mededelingen betreffende de geschiedenis der Nederlanden* 107 (4): 713–25.

Ranade, M. G. 1900. *Rise of the Maratha Power.* Bombay: Pubalekar.

Rashid, Harun-Or. 1987. *The Foreshadowing of Bangladesh: Bengal Muslim League and Muslim Politics, 1936–1947.* Dacca: Asiatic Society of Bangladesh.

Raychaudhuri, Tapan. 1988. *Europe Reconsidered.* Delhi: Oxford University Press.

Renan, Ernest. 1882. *Qu'est-ce qu'une nation?: Conférence.* Paris.

Robbins, Keith. 1982. "Religion and Identity in Modern British History." In Stuart Mews, ed., *Religion and National Identity.* Studies in Church History, vol. 18, 465–89. Oxford: Blackwell.

———. 1988. *Nineteenth-Century Britain: Integration and Diversity.* Oxford: Clarendon Press.

———. 1993. *History, Religion, and Identity in Modern Britain.* London: Hambledon Press.

Ronaldshay, Earl of. 1925. *The Heart of Aryavarta: A Study of the Psychology of Indian Unrest.* London: Constable.

Rousseau, Jean Jacques. 1976. *The Social Contract and Discourses.* Trans. and intro. G. D. H. Cole. London: Dent.

Roy, Asim. 1990. "The High Politics of India's Partition: The Revisionist Perspective." *Modern Asian Studies* 24 (2): 385–415.

Roy, Parama. 1995. "The Spectral Nargis." Typescript. University of California.

Ryan, Mary. 1989. "The American Parade: Representations of the Nineteenth-Century Social Order." In Lynn Hunt, ed., *The New Cultural History,* 131–53. Berkeley: University of California Press.

———. 1992. "Gender and Public Access: Women's Politics in Nineteenth-Century America." In Craig Calhoun, ed., *Habermas and the Public Sphere,* 259–88. Cambridge: MIT Press.

Ryoen, Minamoto. 1994. "The Symposium on Overcoming Modernity." In James W. Heisig and John C. Maraldo, eds., *Rude Awakenings: Zen, the Kyoto School, and the Question of Nationalism,* 197–229. Honolulu: University of Hawaii Press.

Sadiq, Muhammad. 1984. *A History of Urdu Literature.* 2d ed. Delhi: Oxford University Press.

Samuel, Raphael, ed. 1989. *Patriotism: The Making and Unmaking of British National Identity.* 3 vols. London: Routledge.

Sanson, Rosemonde. 1976. *Les 14 juillet (1789–1975): Fête et conscience nationale.* Paris: Flammarion.

Sarkar, Kamala. 1990. *Bengal Politics, 1937–1947.* Calcutta: Mukherjee.

Sarkar, Sumit. 1973. *The Swadeshi Movement in Bengal, 1903–1908.* New Delhi: People's Publishing House.

Schmitt, Carl. [1934] 1985. *Political Theology.* Cambridge: MIT Press.

Schöffer, Ivo. 1987 "Abraham Kuyper and the Jews." In *Veelvormig verleden: Zeventien studies in de vaderlandse geschiedenis,* 159–70. Amsterdam: De Bataafsche Leeuw.

Sen, Amiya P. 1993. *Hindu Revivalism in Bengal, 1872–1905: Some Essays in Interpretation*. Delhi: Oxford University Press.

Sen, Satyen. 1947. *Paneroi āgaṣṭ*. Calcutta: City Book Company.

Sen, Shila. 1976. *Muslim Politics in Bengal, 1937–1947*. New Delhi: Impex India.

Sengupta, Amalendu. 1989. *Uttāl calliś: Asamāpta biplab*. Calcutta: Pearl Publishers.

Sengupta, Nareschandra. 1961. *Yugaparikramā*. Vol. 2. Calcutta: Firma K. L. Mukhopadhyay.

Sepp, Christiaan. 1886. *Bibliotheek van Nederlandsche Kerkgeschiedschrijvers: Opgave van hetgeen Nederlanders over de geschiedenis der Christelijke kerk geschreven hebben*. Leiden: Brill.

Shell, Marc. 1993. *Children of the Earth: Literature, Politics, and Nationhood*. New York: Oxford University Press.

Siddiqi, Majid Hayat. 1986. "History and Society in a Popular Rebellion: Mewat, 1920–33." *Comparative Studies in Society and History* 28 (3): 442–67.

Smetius, Johannes. 1698. *Ordre of reglement voor de classis in Gelderland*. Nijmegen: Van Wesel.

———. 1699. *Synodale ordonnantien ende resolutien tot nut, dienst en gerief der kercken, onder de Chr. Synodus van 't hertogdom Gelre en graef-schap Zutphen gehoorende*. Nijmegen: Van Wesel.

Smith, A. D. 1986. *The Ethnic Origins of Nations*. Oxford: Blackwell.

Smytegelt, Bernardus. 1765. *Keurstoffen of verzameling van vyftig uitmuntende predicatien*. Middelburg: Van Thol.

Soermans, Martinus. 1695. *Kerkelyk register van de plaatsen en namen der predikanten van alle de classes, gehorende onder de Synodus van Zuyd-Holland, van 't begin der Reformatie, tot nu toe*. Dordrecht (2d ed., Haarlem: Van Kessel, 1702).

Sperber, Jonathan. 1984. *Popular Catholicism in Nineteenth-Century Germany*. Princeton, N. J.: Princeton University Press.

Spivak, Gayatri. 1988. "Can the Subaltern Speak." In Cary Nelson and Lawrence Grossberg, eds., *Marxism and the Interpretation of Culture*, 271–313. Urbana: University of Illinois Press.

Stanley, Brian. 1983. "Christian Responses to the Indian Mutiny of 1857." In W. J. Sheils, ed., *The Church and War*. Studies in Church History, vol. 20, 277–91. Oxford: Blackwell.

———. 1990. *The Bible and the Flag: Protestant Missions and British Imperialism in the Nineteenth and Twentieth Centuries*. Leicester: Apollos.

Stetkevych, Jaroslav. 1970. *The Modern Arabic Literary Language*. Chicago: University of Chicago Press.

Stocking, George W. 1968. *Race, Culture, and Evolution*. New York: Free Press.

Stoler, Ann. 1989. "Rethinking Colonial Categories: European Communities and the Boundaries of Rule." *Comparative Studies in Society and History* 31 (1): 134–61.

Storch, Robert D. 1982. " 'Please to Remember the Fifth of November': Conflict, Solidarity, and Public Order in Southern England, 1815–1900." In Robert D. Storch, ed., *Popular Culture and Custom in Nineteenth-Century England*, 71–99. London: Croom Helm.

Sullivan, Winnifred F. 1994. *Paying the Words Extra: Religious Discourse in the Supreme Court of the United States*. Cambridge: Harvard University Press.

Taylor, Charles. 1989. *Sources of the Self: The Making of the Modern Identity*. Cambridge: Harvard University Press.

ter Haar, B. et al., eds. 1864–69. *Geschiedenis der Christelijke kerk in Nederland in tafereelen*. 2 vols. Amsterdam: Bolle.

te Velde, Henk. 1993. "L'origine des fêtes nationales en France et aux Pays Bas dans les années 1880." In Pim den Boer and Willem Frijhof, eds., *Lieux de mémoire et identités nationales*, 105–19. Amsterdam: Amsterdam University Press.

Thapar, Romila. 1989. "Imagined Religious Communities? Ancient History and the Modern Search for a Hindu Identity." *Modern Asian Studies* 23 (2): 209–31.

Thompson, Edward P. 1977. *The Making of the English Working Class*. Harmondsworth: Penguin.

Thorne, Susan. 1990. "Protestant Ethics and the Spirit of Imperialism: British Congregationalists and the London Missionary Society, 1795–1925." Ph.D. diss., University of Michigan.

Thurlings, J. M. G. 1978. *De wankele zuil: Nederlandse katholieken tussen assimilatie en pluralisme*. 2d rev. ed. Deventer: Van Loghum Slaterus.

Tinker, Hugh. 1979. *The Ordeal of Love: C. F. Andrews and India*. Delhi: Oxford University Press.

Tribe, Keith, ed. 1989. *Reading Weber*. London: Routledge.

Troll, Christian W. 1985. "Five Letters of Maulana Ilyas (1885–1944), the Founder of the Tablighi Jama'at, Translated, Annotated, and Introduced." In Christian W. Troll, ed., *Islam in India: Studies and Commentaries*. Vol. 2, *Religion and Religious Education*, 138–76. Delhi: Vikas.

Tully, James. 1988. "Governing Conduct." In Edmund Leites, ed., *Conscience and Casuistry in Early Modern Europe*, 12–71. Cambridge: Cambridge University Press.

Umar, Badruddin. 1987. *Baṅgabhaṅga o sāmpradāyik rājnīti*. Calcutta: Chirayata.

van der Veer, Peter. 1994. *Religious Nationalism: Hindus and Muslims in India*. Berkeley: University of California Press.

———. 1996a. "Gender and Nation in Hindu Nationalism." In Hans Antlov and Stein Tonneson, eds., *Asian Forms of the Nation*, 188–213. Richmond: Curzon Press.

———. 1996b. "Writing Violence." In David Ludden, ed., *Contesting the Nation*, 250–70. Philadelphia: University of Pennsylvania Press.

van Miert, J. 1992. "Verdeeldheid en binding: Over lokale, verzuilde en nationale loyaliteiten." *Bijdragen en mededelingen betreffende de geschiedenis der Nederlanden* 107 (4): 670–89.

van Rhenen, Henricus. 1705. *Lyste van de namen der predikanten, die zedert de reformatie de kerken behoorende onder de provintie van Utrecht, zo by leeninge als anderzints, bedient hebben*. Utrecht: Visch (2d ed., 1724).

van Rooden, Peter. 1991 "Van geestelijke stand naar beroepsgroep: De professionalisering van de Nederlandse predikant, 1625–1874." *Tijdschrift voor Sociale Geschiedenis* 17 (4): 361–93.

———. 1993. "Studies naar lokale verzuiling als toegang tot de geschiedenis van de constructie van religieuze verschillen in Nederland." *Theoretische Geschiedenis* 20 (4): 439–54.

———. 1996. *Religieuze regimes: Over godsdienst en maatschappij in Nederland, 1570–1990.* Amsterdam: Bakker.

van Sas, N. C. F. 1991. *"Fin de siècle* als nieuw begin: Nationalisme in Nederland rond 1900." *Bijdragen en mededelingen betreffende de geschiedenis der Nederlanden* 106 (4): 595–609.

———. 1992. "De mythe Nederland." *De negentiende eeuw* 16 (1): 4–22.

van Swigchem, C. A., T. Brouwer, and W. van Os. 1984 *Een huis voor het Woord: Het protestantse kerkinterieur in Nederland tot 1900.* The Hague: Staatsuitgeverij.

van Tijn, Theo. 1975. "The Party Structure of Holland and the Outer Provinces in the Nineteenth Century." In G. A. M. Beekelaar et al., eds., *Vaderlands Verleden in Veelvoud: 31 opstellen over de Nederlandse geschiedenis na 1500,* 560–89. Den Haag: Nijhoff.

Veeris, Melchior. 1697. *Chronologia ecclesiastica, dat is Kerkelyk Tyd-register.* Amsterdam: Boom (2d ed., 1705).

Verburgt, J. W. 1938. "De totstandkoming van den Staten-Bijbel en de bewaring zijner oorspronkelijke stukken." *Leids Jaarboekje* 30: 138–63.

Vigarello, G. 1988. *Concepts of Cleanliness: Changing Attitudes in France since the Middle Ages.* Cambridge: Cambridge University Press.

Viswanathan, Gauri. 1989. *Masks of Conquest: Literary Study and British Rule in India.* New York: Columbia University Press.

Vos Azn, G. J. 1888. *Geschiedenis der Vaderlandsche Kerk: Van 630 tot 1842.* 2d ed. Dordrecht: Revers.

Wake, C. Staniland. 1870. "The Aim and Scope of Anthropology." *Journal of Anthropology* 1 (1): 1–18.

Waliullah, Mohammad. 1978. *Āmāder mukti-saṃgrām.* Dacca: Bangla Academy.

Waller, P. J. 1981. *Democracy and Sectarianism: A Social and Political History of Liverpool, 1868–1939.* Liverpool: Liverpool University Press.

Ward, W. 1817–20. *A View of the History and Religion of the Hindoos, Including a Minute Description of Their Manners and Customs, and Translations from Their Principal Works.* 3d ed. 4 vols. London: Black, Parbury and Allen.

Weber, Max. 1920–21. *Gesammelte Aufsätze zur Religionssoziologie.* 3 vols. Tübingen: Mohr.

West, Shearer, ed. 1996. *The Victorians and Race.* Aldershot: Scolar Press.

White, Gavin. 1983. "The Fall of France." In W. J. Sheils, ed., *The Church and War.* Studies in Church History, vol. 20. Oxford: Blackwell.

Wilkinson, Alan. 1978. *The Church of England and the First World War.* London: SPCK.

———. 1986. *Dissent or Conform?: War, Peace, and the English Churches, 1900–1945.* London: SCM Press.

Williams, Sarah. 1993. "Religious Belief and Popular Culture: A Study of the South London Borough of Southwark, c. 1880–1939." Ph.D. diss., University of Oxford.

Wiltens, Nikolaas. 1722–1807. *Kerkelyk plakaat-boek, behelzende de plakaaten, ordonnantien, ende resolutien, over de kerkelyke zaken.* 5 vols. The Hague: Scheltus.

Wolff, Robert P. 1969. "Beyond Tolerance." In Robert P. Wolff, Barrington Moore Jr., and Herbert Marcuse, eds., *A Critique of Pure Tolerance*, 3–52. Boston: Beacon Press.

Wolffe, John. 1991. *The Protestant Crusade in Great Britain, 1829–1860.* Oxford: Clarendon Press.

———. 1994. *God and Greater Britain: Religion and National Life in Britain and Ireland, 1843–1945.* London: Routledge.

Woltjer, J. J. 1992. *Recent verleden: De geschiedenis van Nederland in de twintigste eeuw.* Amsterdam: Balans.

Wtenbogaert, Johannes. 1646. *De kerckelicke historie, vervattende verscheyden gedenckwaerdige saecken, inde Christenheyt voorgevallen, van het jaer vierhondert af, tot in het jaer sesthienhondert ende negenthien.* N.p.

Young, Hugo. 1993. *One of Us: A Biography of Margaret Thatcher.* Red. ed. London: Macmillan.

Young, Robert J. C. 1995. *Colonial Desire: Hybridity in Theory, Culture, and Race.* New York: Routledge.

Ypey, A., and I. J. Dermout. 1819–27. *Geschiedenis der Nederlandsche Hervormde Kerk.* 4 vols. Breda: Van Bergen.

Zaret, David. 1992. "Religion, Science, and Printing in the Public Spheres in Seventeenth-Century England." In Craig Calhoun, ed., *Habermas and the Public Sphere*, 212–36. Cambridge: MIT Press.

Zastoupil, Lynn. 1994. *John Stuart Mill and India.* Stanford, Calif.: Stanford University Press.

Notes on Contributors

Benedict R. Anderson is Professor of Government at Cornell University. He is the author of *Imagined Communities: Reflections on the Origin and Spread of Nationalism* and, most recently, *The Spectre of Comparison: Politics, Culture, and the Nation.*

Talal Asad is Professor of Anthropology at the City University of New York, Graduate Center. His most recent book is *Genealogies of Religion: Discipline and Reasons of Power in Christianity and Islam.*

Susan Bayly is Fellow at Christ's College, Cambridge University. She is the author of *Saints, Goddesses, and Kings: Muslims and Christians in South Indian Society, 1700–1900.*

Partha Chatterjee is Director of the Center for Studies in Social Sciences in Calcutta. He is the author of *The Nation and Its Fragments: Colonial and Postcolonial Histories* and, most recently, *A Possible India: Essays in Political Criticism.*

Frans Groot teaches history and is the author of *Roomsen, Rechtzinnigen en Nieuwlichters.*

Harry Harootunian is Professor and Director of East Asian Studies at New York University. He is the author of *Things Seen and Unseen: Discourse and Ideology in Tokugawa Nativism; Undercurrents in the Floating World: Censorship and Japanese Prints; Toward Restoration: The Growth of Political Consciousness in Tokugawa Japan;* and editor of *Questions of Evidence: Proof, Practice, and Persuasion across the Disciplines.*

Hartmut Lehmann is Professor and Director of the Max-Planck-Institute in Gottingen, Germany. One of his recent publications in German is *Max Weber's Protestantische Ethik.* He has also edited several books in English, including *In and Out of the Ghetto: Jewish-Gentile Relations in Late Medieval and Early Modern Germany; Many Are Chosen: Divine Election and Western Nationalism;* and *Weber's Protestant Ethic: Origins, Evidence, Contexts.*

Hugh McLeod is Professor of Church History at the University of Birmingham. He is the author of *Religion and the People of Western Europe, 1789–1990; Piety and Poverty: Working-Class Religion in Berlin, London, and New York, 1870–1914; Religion and Society in England: 1850–1914;* and *European Religion in the Age of the Great Cities, 1830–1930.*

Barbara D. Metcalf is Dean of Social Sciences and Professor of History at the University of California, Davis. She is the author of *Islamic Revival in British India: Deoband, 1860–1900* and the translator of *Perfecting Women: Maulana Ashraf 'Ali Thanawi's Bihishti Zewar.*

Peter van der Veer is Dean of the Amsterdam School for Social Science Research and Professor at the Research Centre for Religion and Society at the University of Amsterdam. He is the author of *Religious Nationalism: Hindus and Muslims in India* and the editor of *Conversion to Modernities: The Globalization of Christianity.*

Peter van Rooden is Lecturer at the Research Centre for Religion and Society at the University of Amsterdam. He is author of *Religieuze Regimes.*

Index

CPSIA information can be obtained at www.ICGtesting.com
Printed in the USA
BVOW07s1142090714

358582BV00002B/117/P